Table of Contents

A Key to the Symbols

 Designates a dish that can be
prepared quickly and easily

 Designates a dish which has a
reduced fat content

Homecoming

Special Foods, Special Memories

BAYLOR UNIVERSITY ALUMNI ASSOCIATION
WACO, TEXAS

Baylor University, chartered in 1845 by the Republic of Texas, is the oldest university in Texas and the largest Baptist university in the world. More than 85,000 alumni in all 50 states and in 136 countries are making contributions through their professional, community, and humanitarian roles.

The Baylor University Alumni Association represents alumni interests in dealings with the university administration, faculty, student body, and other university constituencies. Programs of the association are designed to promote Baylor interests, foster friendships, and enhance the benefits of a Baylor education.

Proceeds realized from the sale of *Homecoming* will support special projects of the Baylor University Alumni Association.

Additional copies may be obtained from the Baylor University Alumni Association, P. O. Box 97116, Waco, TX 76798-7116.

First Printing   8,000   October, 1994
Second Printing   10,000   June, 1995

ISBN: 0-9640969-0-0
LCCN: 94-071086

Printed in the USA by

WIMMER
The Wimmer Companies, Inc.
Memphis • Dallas

Foreword

What is it about food that draws people together? It seems natural, this breaking of bread. It is not something we wish to do alone: it is a shared experience, a gathering of like minds, a circle of friends enclosed in the warmth of an evening. The coming together is as essential as the food. Nothing less than a kind of communion.

Of course we come to eat, to taste, but food satisfies other senses: the crusty loaf of bread, warm in our hands as we break it. Steam rising from tea in a blue porcelain cup. The colors and shapes astonish us: rounded plums from the market, misty purples, smooth in our palms; apricots, deep yellows flecked with reds; globed pears in their green shadings. Tough, pocked avocados, the rich gold of cheddar. The crunch of winesap apples, tart on the tongue. Strawberries heaped in a basket.

This sharing of food, this celebration of the senses is a part of what this book is about. But you will find also an added dimension that makes it distinctively Baylor. A something that takes place here, that seems to hold past the years.

On a campus, you move from one world to another, "from gym to Greek to chlorophyll." You remember the people, the place, the times hung in memory. The friends, in all their unity and diversity. You studied, you played, you cooked, you confided in and blessed each other. You remember the professor whose *B* was precious as some *A*'s were not. The Byron scholar who made you look until you saw, who demanded until you gave more than you knew you had. All those who made you know the importance of language, of philosophy, of economics—and of caring.

Here you will find the names of men and women who are a part of this university. All have felt the Baylor influence. We hope this book is a legacy, making you feel the presence of the past. If it reminds you that you have a place to come to, if it captures some of what one student calls "the spirit of the place," then it has fed not only the body, but also, and perhaps more, the soul.

Ann Vardaman Miller '50, MA '51
Baylor Professor of English and Master Teacher

Editor
Mona Rogers Burchette

| **Design Coordinator** | **Production Coordinator** | **Cookbook Advisor** |
| Paula Price Tanner | Judy Henderson Prather | Sherry Boyd Castello |

Recipe Coordinators	**Editor's Assistants**	**Marketing Coordinators**
Catherine Osborne	Sally Mebane Dickenson	Bob Anne McMullan
Davenport	Denna Johnson	Senter
Carolyn Logsdon Wilkes		Judy McConathy Graves

| **Editorial Coordinator** | **Financial Coordinator** | **Student Coordinator** |
| Judith Witt Francis | David Coker | Michele Royal |

Advisory Board

Bill Cooper	Maxine Barton Hart	Joy Copeland Reynolds
Orlin Corey	Marilyn Wyrick Ingram	Donell Teaff
Wilma Griffin	Nick Klaras	Janelle Walters

Publishing Consultant
Sheryn Jones

Executive Vice President
Baylor University Alumni Association
Ray Burchette, Jr.

No project of this kind could ever be successful without the willingness and help of countless people. Baylor alumni and friends were asked to submit their favorite recipes, and hundreds of recipes were submitted. Each was tested twice for accuracy and quality. While we do not claim originality of recipes, we do present this collection as some of the best from Baylor kitchens.

Cover and interior art: David Kacmarynski, Saint Paul, Minnesota
Design: Pam Watson Allen '76, Waco, Texas

Coming Home to Baylor

I'll never forget the day I came home from World War II—to Baylor. I hitch-hiked all the way from Sacramento to Dallas. When I got to "Big D," I remembered how, before the war, I'd ridden the Texas Interurban between central and north Texas; so I decided to abandon the asphalt roads and take what the Baylor kids at that time dubbed "The Leaping Lena."

After buying a ticket at the barn-like terminal in downtown Dallas, I found a seat aboard the roughly rocking old trolley which jerked like an electric dragon, nose pointing south. The thing jostled along at a blazing thirty-miles-an-hour average, stopping at every rural and rustic town in the direction of Waco—not just Waxahachie and Hillsboro, mind you, but Lancaster, Italy, Abbott, West . . .

As I went home that day aboard the Texas Interurban to Waco, I dozed in my heavy OD army suit and looked out the window at skirring hills, low wooded places and farm lands, turning from parched summer browns to the ochres and reds of a late Texas autumn, splashing and painting its way across the distant rims in Indian Summer fashions, as scrub oaks and mesquites spotted the countryside in roughly-textured western designs.

This was the land I knew—not the South Pacific where I'd been, not New Guinea where I'd almost died. This was the ground of my being, this space with its stretching clear-blue sky over acres and acres of wild, black soil.

Below my window, rolling mounds of earth brushed by where bluebonnets would grow next spring. They were not there on my returning day, but I could wait for them; and in the waiting, I would witness pecan trees shedding, hear leaves fall with an ancient, crackling sound, and catch a scent of dust. I could see and smell and taste those nuts, sweet and firm and golden brown. The changes I would come to know in the earth and sky and river runs would be the same as always, changes that were changeless and, therefore, comforting and secure.

Riding over bridges and under trees, through the junction stations, beside stores and age-stained houses beyond the line of evergreen and pine, with the brilliance of sun dancing through the car window, the three hours of swaying, rocking motion ended with a hurried swoosh-swoosh across that single-span cabled bridge which straddled the dark brown river called *Los Brazos de Dios*—The Arms of God. How suitable, how welcoming!

Leaping Lena passed Second Street, where farmers were selling tomatoes and corn and okra in papersack baskets, crawled around the square and down four slow streets, coming to a squeaking, sighing stop inside an oil-stained terminal just off Fourth and Austin.

The doors flapped back with a rubbery smash. A woman and her children got off, chattering in Spanish. I stepped down and looked around. I had thought, overseas, when this moment came, I'd throw myself flat on my face and kiss the pavement, but I knew in an instant that coming back to that particular spot was no big thing. My real home town was inside me; I had merely brought the inside back to where it all had started.

I saw the Baylor campus that late afternoon as if for the first time: Old Main, Pat Neff Hall, the Baylor Theater—all those symbols I had said goodbye to when I joined the army three years earlier and thought perhaps I'd never see again.

When I got off the bus, I walked joyfully around that beautiful old green and touched the greeting hands of Baylor people—ah, those special people—those kind, exciting, genuine people—Dr. "A." who taught me Shakespeare—Dr. Courtney, for whom my son is named—Mr. Capp, who was the best of all debate teachers—Mr. Baker, who was the most exciting drama teacher this side of . . . anywhere.

I knew then that I had, indeed, at last and in fullness, come home!

Dr. Porter J. Crow '47

Appetizers & Beverages

Now that I think of it, food may have been my major at Baylor, for I certainly spent more time in the old Alexander Dining Hall than in any classroom.

For four years—in return for all my meals—I served food to the freshmen (freshwomen?) who dined in genteel splendor at tables of eight. Food was served family style, and my job was to bring out the trays laden with the serving bowls, individual salads, desserts, and drinks from the combined Memorial-Alexander kitchen.

None of us were actually trained for our jobs, and on more than one occasion, I managed to throw a tray loaded with sixteen shimmering jello salads against the wall after colliding with some other "bus boy" racing through the swinging doors from the kitchen. It's a good thing the young women of Baylor didn't see all that was going on behind those doors.

One day, we locked a particularly hot-tempered kitchen employee into a walk-in refrigerator until we thought she had "cooled down" enough. Another time we stashed some grape juice in jars hidden in the uniform closet—in hopes of creating a little home brew. Months later, it had a disgusting head on it which we scraped off and proceeded to drink like a bunch of refugees from a Speakeasy.

My greatest "show trick" in the dining hall—often to the accompaniment of applause—was carrying sixteen drinking glasses at one time. Thanks to long, bony fingers I could get a grip on ten glasses (one finger in each glass) and have another eight perched inside the rim of eight of those.

In fact, it was while working on this little gimmick that I met my wife. In my haste one evening to clear my section of tables, I was picking up glasses of iced tea (what else?) and stuck my finger into a glass in front of a pretty young coed who screamed, "Stop that! I'm still drinking that tea!"

It wasn't exactly a moonlight and violins moment, but forty years later, we're still dining—and drinking tea—together. And that's a food memory worth keeping.

Hal Wingo '57, Baylor Regent

SOUTH-OF-THE-BORDER LAYERED DIP

"Always an old favorite, but this one is particularly flavorful."

2 (9-ounce) cans bean dip
3 avocados, mashed
2 tablespoons lemon juice
1 teaspoon garlic salt
¼ teaspoon pepper
1 (8-ounce) jar of picante
    sauce
1 cup sour cream
½ cup mayonnaise
1 (1¼-ounce) package taco
    seasoning mix

1 bunch green onions,
    chopped
3 tomatoes, chopped
2 (3½-ounce) cans chopped
    ripe olives
8 ounces Cheddar cheese,
    grated
8 ounces Monterey Jack
    cheese, grated

Spread bean dip in a 7x11-inch dish or 14-inch platter. Mix mashed avocados, lemon juice, garlic salt, pepper, and picante sauce; spread over bean dip. Mix sour cream, mayonnaise, and taco seasoning; pour over avocado layer. Top with remaining 5 ingredients in order given. Serve with tortilla chips. **Yield**: 12 to 15 servings

Note: *Frozen avocado dip may be substituted for the avocados, garlic salt and pepper. Especially pretty served in a deep clear glass dish so that all of the layers show.*

Sandra Fleming Ferguson '71

MEXICAN PIE

1 (8-ounce) package cream
   cheese, softened
1 (19-ounce) can hot chili,
   without beans
1 bunch green onions,
   chopped

1 green pepper, chopped
6 jalapeño peppers, finely
   chopped, optional
2½ cups grated Cheddar
   cheese
Corn chips

Layer softened cream cheese, chili, green onions, peppers and
Cheddar cheese in a 10-inch pie plate. Bake at 350° for 30 to 45
minutes or until cheese is bubbly. Serve with dip-size corn chips.
Yield: About 4 cups

Hint: *Serve this as an easy supper dish with warm tortillas and a
green salad with mandarin oranges, strips of jicama, red onion
rings, and a honey-mustard dressing.*

Cindy Waltman Schuhmann '84

GREAT GUACAMOLE
"Try it! You won't believe it!"

1 (10-ounce) package frozen
   asparagus spears, cooked
   and drained
¾ cup non-chunky picante
   sauce
½ cup diced fresh tomatoes
1 teaspoon oregano
1½ teaspoons cumin

2 tablespoons fat-free cream
   cheese
1¼ teaspoon chopped
   cilantro
⅛ teaspoon garlic powder
Dash of garlic salt and chili
   powder, or to taste
1 package dry butter
   substitute

Blend all ingredients in blender or food processor until smooth.
Chill and serve. **Yield**: 8 servings

June McLean Jeter '80
Author of *The Lite Switch: Low Fat Cookbook*
and Health Guide

FRIED CRAB-STUFFED JALAPEÑOS

1 (27-ounce) can whole
   jalapeño peppers, drained
1 pound flaked crabmeat
2¼ cups cracker meal
1¼ cups milk
2 tablespoons finely-
   chopped green pepper
2 tablespoons finely-
   chopped onion

2 tablespoons finely-
   chopped dill pickle
3 eggs
1 clove garlic, minced
1 teaspoon black pepper,
   divided
¾ teaspoon salt
⅛ teaspoon cayenne pepper

Wearing rubber gloves, cut peppers in half lengthwise. Discard veins and seeds. Rinse carefully and drain.

Combine crab, ¼ cup cracker meal, ¼ cup milk, green pepper, onion, pickle, 1 beaten egg, garlic, ½ teaspoon pepper, ¼ teaspoon salt, and cayenne in a large bowl; mix well. Spoon filling into pepper halves; set aside.

Combine remaining milk, eggs, pepper, and salt in a small but deep dish. Place remaining cracker meal in a shallow dish. Dip stuffed peppers in egg mixture, then coat with cracker meal. Repeat procedure. Deep fry at 365° until golden. Drain well. Serve warm. **Yield**: 30 appetizers

Hint: *Peppers may be prepared and frozen uncooked. To serve, cook as directed.*

Carol Watson Barclay '60

De gustibus non disputandum.

Often quoted by Baylor English Professor, Dr. Charles G. Smith (translation: *There's no accounting for taste.*)

STUFFED JALAPEÑOS

2 (12-ounce) cans mild
  pickled jalapeño peppers,
  cut in half
1 (8-ounce) package cream
  cheese, softened
4½ tablespoons mayonnaise

4 tablespoons dried onion
  flakes
4 tablespoons dill pickle
  relish
Seasoned salt to taste

Rinse peppers and drain well. Dry on paper towels. Combine cheese, mayonnaise, onion, and pickle relish until mixed. Stuff peppers and sprinkle with seasoned salt. Serve the day they are made. **Yield**: 6 to 10 servings

Hint: *A pastry bag makes stuffing the peppers a breeze.*

Martha Newton Garber '71

GREEN CHILE-AND-CHEESE BAKE

1 (8- to 10-ounce) can whole
  green chiles
16 ounces Cheddar cheese,
  grated
16 ounces Monterey Jack
  cheese, grated

3 eggs
3 tablespoons flour
1 (5-ounce) can evaporated
  milk
1 (8-ounce) can tomato sauce

Wash chiles, and remove seeds. Drain well. Cover bottom of 9x13-inch buttered casserole. Mix the 2 kinds of grated cheese, and sprinkle on top of chiles. Mix eggs, flour, and milk in blender and pour over top of cheese. Bake for 30 minutes at 300°. Remove from oven, and spread tomato sauce over the top. Return to oven and continue baking for 15 more minutes. Chill; cut into small squares, and serve with party picks. **Yield**: About 8 to 9 dozen small appetizers

Note: *Use the best quality tomato sauce. Good served hot as a brunch item.*

Marjory Cretien
Wife of Dr. Paul Cretien,
Baylor Professor of Banking and Finance

GREEN AND GOLD MEXICAN CORN DIP

2 (12-ounce) cans Mexican corn
1 cup sour cream
1 cup mayonnaise
⅛ teaspoon sugar
2 small green onions, chopped, including tops

1 (4-ounce) can chopped green chiles
10 ounces Cheddar cheese, grated
5 fresh jalapeño peppers, chopped

Mix all ingredients together. Serve in a bowl surrounded by corn chips or tortilla chips. **Yield**: About 20 servings

Hint: *Most of the heat of jalapeños is in the seeds. Leave some seeds if you want the dip hot. Otherwise rinse out seeds and remove veins. Use gloves if possible when handling fresh jalapeños, and do not rub your eyes!*

Debra Bradley Mann '80

TEXAS CAVIAR
"Provide a fork and this could be a great salad."

2 (14-ounce) cans black-eyed peas, drained
1 (15½-ounce) can white hominy, drained
2 medium tomatoes, chopped
4 green onions, chopped
2 cloves garlic, minced

1 medium green pepper, chopped
1 jalapeño pepper, seeded and chopped
½ cup chopped onion
1 (8-ounce) bottle Italian dressing
Tortilla chips

Combine first 8 ingredients; mixing well. Pour salad dressing over mixture. Marinate, covered, in refrigerator for at least 2 hours or overnight. Drain. Serve with tortilla chips. **Yield**: 15 to 20 servings

Diane Sanderson '87

PERDERNALES DIP

1 pound lean ground beef
1 cup chopped onion,
    divided
½ cup hot ketchup
1 (15-ounce) can red kidney
    beans, undrained and
    mashed
1 teaspoon salt
1 tablespoon chili powder
1 cup cubed sharp Cheddar
    cheese
½ cup sliced stuffed green
    olives
Broken tortillas or corn chips

Brown beef and ½ cup onion. Add ketchup, beans, salt, chili powder, and cheese; pour into hot chafing dish. When cheese is melted,
add olives and remaining onion. Serve with chips. **Yield**: About
4 to 6 cups

Becky Dyer '69

TORTILLA ROLL-UPS

"My mother and I serve these at all our parties."

3 (8-ounce) packages cream
    cheese, softened
2 cups sour cream
1 small onion, grated
3 to 5 jalapeño peppers,
    seeded and finely
    chopped
Juice of ½ lime
2 to 3 tablespoons picante
    sauce
30 flour tortillas
Picante sauce

Mix first 6 ingredients. Steam tortillas a few at a time to soften.
(Or place 3 or 4 in microwave on high for 20 to 30 seconds.) Spread
cheese mixture on tortillas. Roll tightly. With seam-side down,
place on cookie sheet; cover with plastic wrap and chill. Slice into
bite-size pieces. Serve with party picks for dipping in picante
sauce. **Yield**: 20 to 30 servings

Diane Sanderson '87

GREEN CHILE DIP

1 (4-ounce) can chopped
  green chiles
1 (3½-ounce) can chopped
  ripe olives
2 large tomatoes, chopped
  fine

3 to 4 green onions, chopped
  fine
2 tablespoons oil
2 tablespoons vinegar
Salt and pepper to taste
1 to 2 cloves garlic, crushed

Mix ingredients well. Chill before serving. Serve with corn chips or tortilla chips. **Yield:** Approximately 1½ cups

Hint: *Add chopped cilantro as an option.*

Ethel Ann de Cordova Porter '58

PHOENIX DIP

1 (8-ounce) package cream
  cheese, softened
1 (½-ounce) package Italian
  dressing mix
1 tablespoon mayonnaise

Juice of ½ lemon
1 medium avocado, chopped
1 medium tomato, chopped
Dash of hot pepper sauce

Mix all ingredients; refrigerate overnight to allow flavors to blend. Serve with assorted crackers or raw fresh vegetables. **Yield:** Approximately 4 cups

Kathleen Day Oates '76

SPINACH TORTILLA BITES

2 (10-ounce) packages frozen
    chopped spinach, thawed
    and well-drained
6 green onions, chopped
1 (½-ounce) package ranch-
    style salad dressing mix
1 cup mayonnaise
1 (3-ounce) jar bacon bits,
    not imitation
1 cup sour cream
10 large flour tortillas

Mix together first 6 ingredients. Spread on tortillas; roll tightly to enclose filling. Place on cookie sheet, seam-side down; wrap in plastic wrap and chill overnight. Slice into bite-size piece s, about ½ inch thick. Let stand at room temperature for 15 minutes before serving. **Yield**: About 100 pieces

Hint: *For a Bear crowd, garnish each with a bit of yellow bell pepper. Or use chopped tomato, pimiento, or red bell pepper.*

The Cookbook Committee

GOOD LUCK PICANTE SAUCE

1 (8-ounce) can tomato sauce
    with tomato bits
1 (10-ounce) can tomatoes
    with green chiles
1 medium onion, quartered
1 to 2 jalapeño peppers, or to
    taste
1 tablespoon flavor enhancer
1 teaspoon cumin
Dash of salt
1 (15-ounce) can black-eyed
    peas, drained

Put all ingredients except peas in blender. Process for a few seconds, just long enough to chop onions. Stir peas into sauce. **Yield**: 5 to 6 cups

One of our favorite times to entertain is on New Year's Day, and this is a welcome change from all the holiday sweets. It's also an easy way to get in your black-eyed peas for good luck.

Judy Henderson Prather '73

EAT YOUR VEGETABLES PICANTE SAUCE

2 large garlic cloves, minced
1 tablespoon mustard seed
1 large onion, chopped
1 large green pepper, chopped
2 large jalapeño peppers with seeds, chopped
3 quarts tomatoes, peeled and diced
¾ cup sugar
1 cup white vinegar
5 teaspoons salt

Tie minced garlic and mustard seed in small piece of cloth. Combine all ingredients. Simmer until thick, about 1 hour and 15 minutes, stirring occasionally. Remove bag of garlic and mustard seed. Vary amount of jalapeño peppers according to taste. **Yield:** 1½ quarts

One of my roommates, Lisa Christmas '91, gave me this recipe. During Baylor, her grandmother kept us well supplied with picante. Along with our friends, we went through enormous quantities of it. When our parents told us to eat our vegetables, this was definitely our first choice!

Kelly Soter '89

THE "REAL THING" HOT SAUCE
"It's smoking!"

8 medium ripe tomatoes
1 medium onion
6 medium serrano peppers

2 cloves garlic, finely
  chopped
½ cup chopped cilantro
Salt and pepper

Using a blender set at coarse grind, blend tomatoes, onion, peppers, chopped garlic, and cilantro until mixed. Be careful not to overgrind. (All ingredients can be chopped by hand instead of blended.) Add salt and pepper to taste. Place in refrigerator to "brew" for 1 hour. **Yield**: About 1 quart.

Hint: *Good on chips, tortillas, tamales, enchiladas, turkey, ham, and eggs.*

David Cochran '79

SESAME CHICKEN BITES

1 (8-ounce) package cream
  cheese, softened
½ teaspoon lemon juice
¼ teaspoon onion powder
¼ teaspoon basil
⅛ teaspoon thyme
⅛ teaspoon oregano
1 cup finely-chopped cooked
  chicken

⅓ cup finely-chopped celery
1 (2-ounce) jar diced
  pimientos, drained
2 (8-ounce) cans refrigerated
  crescent dinner rolls
1 large egg, beaten
1½ teaspoons sesame seeds

Mix first 6 ingredients together in large bowl. Stir in chicken, celery and pimientos. Divide rolls into 8 rectangles, sealing perforations. Spread ¼ cup chicken mixture onto each rectangle. Working from long side of each rectangle, roll dough as for a jelly roll, overlapping long sides to seal. Brush with egg and sprinkle with sesame seeds. Cut each roll into 5 pieces. Place seam-side down on a lightly-greased baking sheet. Bake at 375° for 12 to 15 minutes. **Yield**: 40 snacks

Hint: *Great for tailgating at Baylor football games. Easy to double.*
Michelle Bodine Stevenson '87

SMOKED SALMON AND ONION CHEESECAKE

5 tablespoons freshly-grated Parmesan cheese, divided
2 tablespoons fine dry breadcrumbs
3 tablespoons butter, melted
1 cup chopped onion
1 cup chopped red bell pepper
3½ (8-ounce) packages cream cheese, softened
4 eggs
⅓ cup heavy cream
½ pound smoked salmon trimmings, chopped
½ cup freshly-grated Gruyere cheese (about 2 ounces)
Salt and freshly-ground pepper to taste
1 tablespoon fresh lemon juice
Dash of hot pepper sauce

Butter bottom and sides of an 8- or 9-inch springform pan. Mix 2 tablespoons of Parmesan cheese with breadcrumbs and sprinkle into prepared pan, coating all sides with crumb mixture. Wrap foil around the bottom and 2 inches up outside of pan. In a skillet over medium heat, sauté onion and red bell pepper in melted butter until tender, about 5 minutes. Cool.

Using an electric mixer, beat cream cheese, eggs, and cream until well blended. Fold salmon, Gruyere, and remaining Parmesan cheese into onion mixture. Stir in salt and pepper, lemon juice, and hot pepper sauce. Fold into cream cheese mixture. Pour mixture into springform pan. Place cheesecake pan inside a larger pan. Add boiling water to larger pan. (Water level should be 2 inches up the sides of springform pan.) Bake at 300° for 1 hour and 40 minutes or until firm to touch. Cool cheesecake on a wire rack for at least 2 hours. Garnish with fresh herbs or red pepper rings. Serve with crackers and fruit. **Yield**: 30 servings

Hint: *Can be made ahead and served at room temperature.*

Karen McNeely Zecy '79

SMOKY SALMON BALL

1 (14¾-ounce) can salmon, drained, with skin and bones removed
1 (8-ounce) package cream cheese, softened
1 teaspoon minced onion
1 tablespoon lemon juice

1 teaspoon horseradish
½ teaspoon salt
¼ teaspoon liquid smoke
½ cup chopped pecans
3 tablespoons chopped parsley

Combine first 7 ingredients with a fork until well mixed. Chill if necessary to shape. Form a ball. Roll in pecans and parsley; chill. Serve with crackers or chips. **Yield**: About 2 cups

Hint: *This is best when made a day before.*

Mollie Carpenter Bedwell '65

LAYERED CRAB SPREAD

"It's beautiful and it's delicious."

1 (8-ounce) package cream cheese, softened
3 teaspoons horseradish
¾ pound imitation crab, chopped in food processor

1 to 2 tablespoons lemon juice
1 (12-ounce) bottle chili sauce
Chopped fresh parsley
8 green onions, finely chopped

On a round 12-inch platter spread cream cheese which has been mixed with horseradish. Mix crab with lemon juice, and spoon over cream cheese. Spread chili sauce over top. Sprinkle with parsley and green onions. Serve with crackers. **Yield**: 10 to 15 servings

Madelyn Jones, Baylor Registrar

POLISH MISTAKES
"A winner!"

2 pounds hot sausage
2 pounds lean ground beef
2 (16-ounce) boxes
　pasteurized process
　cheese, cubed

2 teaspoons garlic powder
4 teaspoons Worcestershire
　sauce
2 teaspoons oregano
4 packages party rye bread

Brown sausage and beef. Drain in a colander, and blot with paper towels. Combine with next 4 ingredients, and stir over low heat until cheese is melted. Spread on rye bread slices. Place on cookie sheets or wax paper, and freeze. When frozen, store in zip-lock bags in freezer. When ready to eat, remove from freezer, and bake at 325° for 10 to 15 minutes. Garnish with a bit of pimiento or a slice of olive. **Yield**: About 12 dozen

Note: *Easily halved.*

Amy Duncan '93

BACON ROLL-UPS

1 large loaf thinly-sliced
　sandwich bread, crusts
　removed

1 (8-ounce) container
　whipped cream cheese
　with chives
1 pound bacon, cut in half
　cross-wise

Cut each bread slice in half. Spread with cream cheese. Roll bread up like a jelly roll. Wrap each with a half slice of bacon, securing with a wooden pick. Bake on a pan with a rack so bacon will drain. Bake at 350° for 45 minutes or until brown and bacon is cooked. **Yield**: About 4 dozen rolls

Hint: *Make ahead, and freeze on a cookie sheet. Transfer frozen roll-ups to a freezer bag. Keeps well for 3 months.*

Mary Leigh Cook '88

SHRIMP PATE

1½ pounds shrimp, cooked,
   peeled and deveined
1 small onion, minced
½ cup butter, melted

⅓ cup mayonnaise
1 tablespoon fresh lemon
   juice
Cucumber Dill Sauce

Chop shrimp coarsely; combine with onion, butter, mayonnaise and lemon juice. Press firmly into 4-cup mold. Refrigerate several hours or overnight. Unmold on serving platter. Serve with Cucumber Dill Sauce and assorted crackers. **Yield**: 1 large mold

Cucumber Dill Sauce:

1 large cucumber, peeled,
   seeded and chopped
1⅓ cup sour cream
⅔ cup mayonnaise
2 tablespoons lemon juice

Salt and pepper to taste
Dash of cayenne pepper
¼ cup chopped fresh dill
Fresh chives and dill for
   garnish

Place cucumber in a colander; salt lightly and drain 20 to 30 minutes. Blot cucumbers between layers of paper towels. Combine sour cream, mayonnaise, lemon juice, and seasonings. Add cucumber; pour into small serving bowl and chill. Garnish with fresh chives and dill when ready to serve.

Lisa Abercrombie Beach '82

SHRIMP MOLD

2 pounds shrimp, boiled,
  peeled, and deveined
1½ envelopes unflavored
  gelatin
½ cup boiling water
1 (3-ounce) package cream
  cheese, softened
½ teaspoon salt
½ teaspoon black pepper
½ teaspoon red pepper

1 cup mayonnaise or salad
  dressing
1 (10-ounce) can cream of
  mushroom soup with ½
  soup can of water
Worcestershire sauce,
  optional
Garlic powder, optional
Hot pepper sauce, optional
1 cup finely-chopped celery
½ cup chopped green onion

Chop shrimp with a knife into very small pieces, about the size of a pea. Set aside. Add gelatin to boiling water, and stir until dissolved. Add cream cheese, and beat until smooth. Add seasonings, mayonnaise, soup, and optional flavorings. Stir in shrimp, celery, and green onion. Lightly grease a large mold, and pour mixture into mold. Refrigerate until set, preferably overnight. Unmold, and serve chilled with a choice of crackers. **Yield**: About 20 servings

Note: *Success depends on quality of shrimp used — don't take short cuts.*

Sarah Jane Harris Prewett '88

 ## DIPPY SHRIMP
"Great!"

1 (8-ounce) package cream
  cheese, softened
1 (8-ounce) carton sour cream
½ cup chopped onion
Juice of 1 lemon

Salt and pepper to taste
Red pepper to taste
2 (4½-ounce) cans shrimp,
  drained and rinsed,
  drained again

Combine cream cheese and sour cream. Add onion, lemon juice, and seasonings. Mash shrimp and mix in. Best if made a few hours ahead and kept in refrigerator, tightly covered. Serve with crackers or chips. **Yield**: About 3 cups

Note: *Must be refrigerated.*

Denna Johnson
Wife of Darrel Johnson, Baylor head basketball coach

CLAM PUFFS

1 (6½-ounce) can clams   2 eggs
¼ cup margarine or butter   Filling
½ cup flour

Drain clams into measuring cup; add enough water to clam juice
to make ½ cup. Set clams aside for filling. In small saucepan, heat
clam juice and margarine until boiling. Remove from heat, and
stir in flour all at one time. Stir with wooden spoon until mixture
forms a ball and leaves the sides of pan. With spoon, beat in eggs,
1 at a time, until well mixed. Drop by teaspoonfuls onto a greased
cookie sheet, 2 inches apart. Bake at 375° for 25 to 30 minutes.
Cool. When completely cool, cut open and spoon Filling into each
puff. May be heated in oven for 5 minutes before serving. **Yield**:
40 puffs

Filling:
1 (8-ounce) package cream   1 teaspoon lemon juice
   cheese, softened   ⅛ teaspoon Worcestershire
Dash of hot pepper sauce   Dash of cayenne
⅛ teaspoon garlic powder

Combine cream cheese and seasonings; blend well. Stir in drained
clams that have been set aside.

Note: *After filling, can be frozen for up to 4 months. To serve,
place frozen puffs on cookie sheet, and heat at 350° for 15 to 20
minutes.*

Celeste Sauls '90

ITALIAN ARTICHOKE BALLS

"Excellent"

2 cloves garlic, pressed
2 tablespoons olive oil
1 (14-ounce) can artichoke
   hearts, drained and
   mashed

2 eggs, slightly beaten
¾ cup grated Parmesan
   cheese, divided
¾ cup Italian-seasoned
   breadcrumbs, divided

Sauté garlic in oil about 2 minutes. Add artichokes and eggs; cook, stirring constantly, over low heat 5 minutes. Remove from heat; stir in ½ cup cheese and ½ cup breadcrumbs. Roll into 1-inch balls. Combine remaining cheese and breadcrumbs. Roll balls in crumbs. Bake at 350° for 5 to 10 minutes. Cool. **Yield**: 3 to 3½ dozen

The Cookbook Committee

TINY BROCCOLI QUICHE

Prepared pastry for 2 (9-inch)
   pie crusts
2 tablespoons margarine,
   melted
½ (10-ounce) package
   chopped frozen broccoli,
   thawed

1 cup grated Swiss cheese
3 eggs
1 cup half-and-half
1 teaspoon salt

Prepare 36 greased and floured 1¾ inch muffin tins Roll out pie crust dough ⅛-inch thick. Using a 3-inch round cutter, cut 36 "pie crusts." Place crusts in muffin tins. Brush each with melted butter. Refrigerate until well chilled.

Drain broccoli well. Place 1 teaspoon of broccoli in each cup. Top with grated cheese. Beat eggs with half-and-half and salt. Pour 1 tablespoon egg mixture over cheese. Bake at 400° for 25 minutes. **Yield**: 36 appetizers

Lois Bowes Shumate '70

SWEET AND SOUR WATER CHESTNUTS

1 (8-ounce) can whole water chestnuts, drained	1 cup ketchup
½ pound bacon, cut in thirds	¾ cup brown sugar
	1 tablespoon lemon juice

Slice each water chestnut in half horizontally. Wrap ⅓ slice of bacon around each chestnut and secure with a wooden pick. Place in casserole dish and bake at 450° for 15 minutes. Mix ketchup, brown sugar, and lemon juice; pour over water chestnuts. Return to oven for 15 to 20 minutes. Let sit 3 to 5 minutes before serving. **Yield**: 8 servings

Hint: *Baking for the first 15 minutes on a rack in a shallow baking dish will allow bacon to drain. Remove rack before sauce is added.*

Nancy McKinney
Wife of Dr. Joseph McKinney, Baylor Professor of Economics

MARINATED MUSHROOMS
"Great teamed with various cheeses and finger sandwiches on a buffet table"

3 pounds mushrooms, washed and drained	2 cloves garlic, crushed
1 tablespoon salt	1 cup olive oil
¼ teaspoon black pepper	¼ cup sugar
⅛ teaspoon oregano	2 tablespoons seasoned salt flavor enhancer
1 tablespoon finely-chopped red onion	2 cups red wine vinegar

Place mushrooms in large bowl. Mix remaining ingredients, and pour over mushrooms. Marinate, covered, in refrigerator for 3 days. Stir gently every day. One hour before serving, remove mushrooms from marinade with slotted spoon and drain. **Yield**: 15 to 20 servings

Hint: *Leftover marinade makes a very nice salad dressing.*

Fran Booth Porter '54

PETER RABBIT'S PIZZA
"Turn your food processor loose on this one"

2 (8-ounce) cans refrigerated crescent dinner rolls
2 (8-ounce) packages cream cheese, softened
1 (1-ounce) package ranch-style dressing mix
¾ cup salad dressing
¾ cup finely-chopped broccoli
¾ cup finely-chopped cauliflower
¾ cup finely-chopped celery
¾ cup finely-chopped onions
¾ cup finely-chopped radishes
¾ cup finely-chopped carrots
¾ cup finely-chopped green pepper
¾ cup grated Cheddar cheese

Grease 11x15-inch cookie sheet with sides or a jelly roll pan. Unroll crescent rolls into 8 rectangles. Line bottom of cookie sheet with rectangles of dough, pinching perforations together to make a seal. Bake according to directions; cool. Combine cream cheese, dressing mix, and salad dressing. Spread over the crust. Mix chopped vegetables, and layer over cream cheese mixture. Top with cheese. Cover with plastic wrap and refrigerate overnight. Cut into 1x3-inch slices. **Yield**: 5 dozen pieces

Note: *Make the day before and refrigerate. For best results, chop green pepper by hand.*

Joan Parsons
Wife of Dr. James Parsons, Baylor Professor of Accounting and Master Teacher

NEW ORLEANS BAKED WHOLE GARLIC

"Try this and see how sweet and nutty garlic can be."

1 bulb garlic
3 tablespoons olive oil
½ tablespoon Greek
  seasoning

½ tablespoon Italian
  seasoning
Salt and pepper

Remove loose outer leaves from bulb, but do not peel. Cut off top of bulb so that each clove is open at the top. Place bulb in a small dish, right-side up. Drizzle with olive oil and sprinkle with seasonings. Salt and pepper to taste. (Work seasonings into the bulb by turning it upside down and pressing it against the bottom and sides of the dish.) Bake at 350° for 45 minutes to 1 hour, until garlic is tender and husks are golden. Baste occasionally with olive oil. **Yield**: 2 servings

Note: *May be served whole. Each clove can be broken off and easily squeezed out to be eaten as a side dish or as a delicious spread on bread. Serve with a dip of olive oil seasoned with Italian spices. Add baked garlic to any sauce or salad.*

D'Anne Powell Hobbs '87

"Garlic is the catsup of intellectuals." Anonymous

TOUCHDOWN SAUSAGE CHEESE DIP

"No football game is complete without this dip"

1 pound hot sausage
1 pound ground beef
1 onion, minced
2 pounds pasteurized
  process cheese, cubed

1 (10-ounce) can tomatoes
  with green chiles
1 (10¾-ounce) can mushroom
  soup
1 teaspoon garlic powder

Brown sausage, ground meat, and onion. Drain off fat. Add cheese and melt over low heat. Stir in remaining ingredients. Serve with corn chips or tortilla chips. **Yield**: 20 to 25 servings

I have not been an alumnus very long, so the memories are still very real of my parents coming to visit on Parents' Weekend and on Home-coming and bringing my favorite foods, or cooking the entire week-end and leaving the refrigerator full for me, my brother, my roomies, and everyone else who lived near.

Clint Showalter '93

ITZA CHEESE BALL

4 (8-ounce) packages cream
  cheese, softened
4 cups shredded Cheddar
  Colby cheese
1 cup chopped green onions

2 tablespoons
  Worcestershire sauce
2 teaspoons lemon juice
1 teaspoon garlic powder
Dash of salt and pepper
Chopped parsley

Mix ingredients well, and form into a ball. Refrigerate. Before serving, roll ball in chopped parsley. Serve with an assortment of crackers. **Yield**: 1 large ball or 2 smaller ones

Hint: *Make 2 balls, one to serve and one to freeze.*

Betty Skinner Dison '46

STRAWBERRY CHEESE RING

"Wonderful combination of flavors."

1 (16-ounce) package extra
    sharp Cheddar cheese,
    grated
1 (16-ounce) package
    medium Cheddar cheese,
    grated
1 small onion, grated

1 cup mayonnaise
1 teaspoon red pepper
1 cup chopped pecans,
    divided
1 (18-ounce) jar strawberry
    preserves
Parsley

Combine first 5 ingredients. Sprinkle ¼ cup pecans in an oiled 7-cup ring mold. Press cheese mixture into mold. Chill until firm. Unmold onto platter, and pat remaining pecans into cheese ring. Spoon strawberry preserves into center of ring. Garnish with parsley. Provide spreaders, and serve with crackers. **Yield**: 25 to 30 servings

Kay Washington Moore '71

THE BEST CHEESE STRAWS

1 (16-ounce) package extra-
    sharp Cheddar cheese,
    grated
½ cup butter (not margarine),
    softened

½ teaspoon salt
½ teaspoon red pepper
1¾ cups flour

In a large mixer bowl, beat cheese with butter, salt, and red pepper. Add flour, a small amount at a time. Mix well. Put dough in a cookie press, using the star disc or ribbon disc. Make long strips on a cookie sheet. Bake at 350° for 12 to 15 minutes or until lightly browned. Cut strips in desired lengths while still warm. **Yield**: Approximately 2 to 3 dozen straws

Hint: Dough can be formed into 2 rolls. Chill, slice into thin wafers, and bake as above.

Ruth Collins Wilkerson '57

HONEY MUSTARD BRIE

1 (15-ounce) round Brie
　cheese
¼ cup honey mustard
½ cup sliced almonds or
　chopped pecans, toasted

Apple wedges
1 (6-ounce) can pineapple
　juice

Remove rind from top of cheese, cutting to within ½ inch of outside edges. Place Brie on a large serving plate, and spread mustard over top. Sprinkle with almonds. Cover and let stand at room temperature at least 1 hour. Toss apple wedges in pineapple juice, and drain. Arrange fruit around Brie; serve immediately. **Yield**: 10 to 14 servings.

The Cookbook Committee

STUFFED OLIVE BALLS

2 cups grated Cheddar
　cheese
½ cup margarine, softened
1¼ cups flour
½ teaspoon salt

1 teaspoon paprika
Medium or large pimiento-
　stuffed olives, about 30
　to 40

Mix cheese and margarine. Add dry ingredients. Mix by hand until smooth. Pinch off a small piece of dough and roll around an olive. (Expose the red pimiento for a touch of color.) Chill until firm. Bake at 400° for 15 minutes on an ungreased cookie sheet. **Yield**: 40 balls

Pat McCarty Marshall '52

I have always loved olives. Even as a child, I never had my fill. For several Christmases, Santa left a big bottle of pimiento-stuffed green olives in the toe of my Christmas stocking in place of candy. Later I would learn it was not Santa Claus, of course, but my wonderful, reserved father who truly wanted to please his daughter. Even today, olives make me smile and feel loved.

Mona Rogers Burchette '58

GREEN AND GOLD SPREAD

"Have your colors and eat them too!"

2 (8-ounce) packages cream
   cheese
1 (10-ounce) jar green jam
   (mint or jalapeño)

1 (10-ounce) jar gold jam
   (apricot, peach, or orange)
Crackers

Place cream cheese blocks on separate serving dishes. Generously spoon green jam over 1 block and gold jam over the other. Provide spreaders and serve with crackers. **Yield**: 20 to 30 servings

Hint: *Other toppers for cream cheese blocks could be picante sauce. Or chutney. Or soy sauce with a heavy sprinkling of toasted sesame seeds.*

Vivian Ruth Saxon Cochran '55

DIP IN DOUGH

1 (16-ounce) carton sour
   cream
2 cups mayonnaise
2 tablespoons parsley flakes
2 tablespoons dill weed

1 tablespoon seasoned salt
1 tablespoon instant onion
   flakes
1 loaf Pumpernickel bread,
   unsliced

Combine first 6 ingredients, and mix well. Refrigerate about 4 hours. Immediately before serving, slice top off of bread loaf. Hollow out bread loaf, reserving the bread pieces. Pour dip mixture into hollow loaf. Use bread pieces for dipping. **Yield**: 4 cups

Hint: *Vary by using different herbs and spices in different types of bread.*

Darlene Griffin Blair '69

BUTTERSCOTCH APPLE DIP

Fruit dips are a favorite of the Baylor family, and these next three were highly rated by our testers.

1 (14-ounce) can sweetened
  condensed milk
1 cup butterscotch-flavored
  chips
¼ teaspoon salt

2 teaspoons white vinegar
¼ to ½ teaspoon ground
  cinnamon
Apple wedges

In heavy saucepan over low heat, combine sweetened condensed milk, chips, and salt. Cook and stir until chips melt. Remove from heat. Stir in vinegar and cinnamon. Serve warm as a dip for apple wedges. **Yield**: About 1¾ cup

Hint: *Can be made several weeks ahead. Store tightly covered in refrigerator. To reheat, mix with a small amount of water over low heat, stirring constantly. Also good served warm over ice cream.*

Phyllis Wyrick Patterson '74

CINNAMON APPLE DIP

"Tastes like fresh apple pie"

1 (8-ounce) package cream
  cheese, softened
½ teaspoon cinnamon

6 tablespoons brown sugar
1 tablespoon milk
Apple wedges

Combine all ingredients except apple wedges. Add a little more milk if needed for dipping consistency. (Dip should be light and fluffy, but not thin, and should hold its shape on apple wedge.) Serve with fresh apple wedges for dipping. **Yield**: 1 cup

Hint: *A platter of red and green apples are especially pretty during the holidays.*

Leslie Peebles Jones '76

CREAMY FRUIT DIP

Our testers agree this is delicious.

1 cup powdered sugar
1 (12-ounce) package cream
   cheese, softened
1 (7-ounce) jar marshmallow
   cream

1 (8-ounce) carton sour cream
2 teaspoons vanilla
2 teaspoons almond extract
2 teaspoons cinnamon
Toasted pecans

Mix all ingredients, except toasted pecans. Refrigerate. When ready to serve, sprinkle pecans on top of dip. Serve with fresh fruit. **Yield**: About 30 servings

Hint: *It is better if made a day ahead.*

The Cookbook Committee

 # PADRE ISLAND CRAB DIP

½ cup mayonnaise
1 (8-ounce) package cream
   cheese, softened

1 (6½-ounce) can crab meat,
   drained
½ teaspoon dill seed
½ teaspoon paprika

Cream mayonnaise and cream cheese, and mix in crab meat. Place in 9-inch glass pie plate. Sprinkle with dill seed and paprika. Bake at 300° for 20 minutes. Serve with crackers. **Yield**: About 8 servings

Hint: *Tastes best when served 30 minutes or so after baking.*

Kathy Casner Goodrich '80

HOT ARTICHOKE DIP
"Easy—and oh, so good."

1 (14-ounce) can artichoke
  hearts, drained
1 cup mayonnaise, not salad
  dressing
¾ cup grated Parmesan
  cheese

Dash of hot pepper sauce
Dash of Worcestershire
  sauce
Dash of garlic salt
Dry breadcrumbs

Chop artichoke hearts finely. Mix with next 5 ingredients. Pour into a 1-quart casserole dish. Top with breadcrumbs. Bake at 350° about 25 minutes or until bubbly and brown. (If divided into smaller dishes, shorten baking time.) Serve with whole wheat crackers or melba rounds. **Yield**: 8 to 10 servings

Beverly Barron Smith '57

GOLDEN EGG DIP
"Very nice for a brunch"

12 hard-cooked eggs, sieved
2 teaspoons prepared
  mustard
2 drops hot pepper sauce
½ to ¾ teaspoon salt
¾ cup mayonnaise

2 tablespoons butter,
  softened
1 tablespoon lemon juice
2 teaspoons Worcestershire
  sauce
1½ teaspoons liquid smoke
½ teaspoon pepper

Combine all ingredients. If mixture is too stiff, gradually add small amount of milk or cream until proper consistency for dip. Put into chilled bowl and sprinkle with paprika. Serve with crackers or chips. **Yield**: About 2 cups

The Cookbook Committee

THREE'S A CROWD

2 cups butterscotch morsel chips	2 cups salted peanuts
	2 cups raisins

Mix all together. Store in airtight container. Travels well. **Yield**: 1½ quarts

Deanna Ruth Cochran Laird '89

CARAMEL CORN FOR A CROWD

"This is as good as I've ever eaten."

¾ cup unpopped popcorn kernels	2 cups firmly-packed brown sugar
2 cups pecans, roasted	1 cup butter or margarine
2 cups cocktail peanuts or Spanish peanuts, roasted	½ cup light corn syrup
	1 teaspoon salt
	½ teaspoon baking soda

Pop popcorn kernels using an air popper. Pour popped popcorn into 2 or 3 9x13-inch baking pans. Sprinkle pecans and peanuts evenly over popcorn.

Combine sugar, butter, corn syrup, and salt in a large 3-quart saucepan. Bring mixture to a boil. Boil for 5 minutes, stirring constantly to prevent sticking. Remove from heat, add baking soda and stir well; it will be foamy. Pour over popcorn and nuts. Toss with spoons to coat pieces well. Bake at 250° for 1 hour, stirring every 20 minutes. Pour out onto wax paper to cool. Store in tightly sealed container. Keeps for about 2 or 3 days. **Yield**: About 7 quarts

Hint: *Popcorn will stay fresh and you will eliminate unpopped "duds" if you will store it in the freezer.*

Sarah Jane Harris Prewett '88

CHILLED CROSS STITCH TEA

5 tablespoons + 1 teaspoon
   instant tea
2 to 2½ cups sugar

Boiling water
¾ cup white grape juice
1 cup apple juice

Mix tea and sugar with just enough boiling water to make a liquid. Stir until sugar is dissolved. Add juices, and mix well. Add water to make 1 gallon. Serve cold. **Yield**: 1 gallon

Patricia G. Pennington '92

APRICOT PUNCH

1 (46-ounce) can pineapple
   juice
1 (46-ounce) can apricot
   nectar

3 (6-ounce) cans frozen
   limeade, thawed
3 (1-quart) bottles ginger ale

Mix 3 juices and refrigerate. When ready to serve, add ginger ale.
Yield: 35 to 40 servings

Carolyn Griffin Keathley '65

SUMMERTIME ALMOND TEA

1½ cups sugar
3 tablespoons unsweetened
   lemon tea mix
2 cups boiling water

2 (6-ounce) cans frozen
   lemonade, thawed
1 tablespoon almond extract
1 tablespoon vanilla

Dissolve sugar and tea mix in boiling water in a 2½-quart saucepan. Cool; pour into a 1-gallon container. Add remaining ingredients and stir. Add enough water to make 1 gallon. Serve over crushed ice. **Yield**: 10 to 12 servings

Royce Goforth
Wife of Dr. Thomas Goforth, Baylor Professor of Geophysics

FROZEN BANANA PUNCH

A great favorite of our testers

4 cups sugar
6 cups water
6 bananas, not overly ripe
1 (46-ounce) can pineapple
   juice
2 (12-ounce) cans frozen
   orange juice, thawed

1 (12-ounce) can frozen
   lemonade (not pink),
   thawed
6 (1-quart) bottles lemon-
   lime drink

Mix sugar and water in medium saucepan. Heat, stirring frequently, until sugar dissolves. Cool. Puree 2 or 3 bananas in
blender with enough pineapple juice to fill container ¾ full. Repeat until all bananas are pureed. Mix together sugar syrup, bananas, and 3 juices. Freeze in a large-mouth container to make it
easier to remove. Two hours before serving, remove from freezer
to soften. When ready to serve, spoon into punch bowl, and add
lemon-lime drink. **Yield**: 50 to 60 punch cup servings

Priscilla Richman Owen '77

BESSIE MAE LYNN'S SPICED TEA

*Served at the Ralph Lynns' traditional Homecoming Open
House for former students.*

1 stick of cinnamon, broken
2 tablespoons whole cloves
1½ gallons water
6 regular-size tea bags
3 cups sugar

1 (12-ounce) can frozen
   orange juice, thawed
1 (6-ounce) can frozen
   lemonade, thawed

Drop cinnamon and cloves into water, and bring to a boil. (A
metal tea ball works well to hold the spices.) Remove from heat;
add tea bags and steep for 10 minutes. Discard tea bags and spices.
Add sugar, orange juice, and lemonade; stir. Allow to stand for 3
or 4 hours. Reheat to serve. **Yield**: 50 servings

*Hint: Keeps for 3 or 4 weeks in refrigerator. Inexpensive and
quickly made.*

Submitted by Edna Holcomb SoRelle White '55, MS '61

BAYLOR FLING SLUSH

Editor's note: This was served at Baylor Fling, a special spring weekend for alumnae.

1 (12-ounce) can frozen
    orange juice, thawed and
    diluted
1 (12-ounce) can frozen
    lemonade, thawed and
    diluted

1 (46-ounce) can pineapple
    juice
5 cups milk
Crushed ice

Combine orange juice, lemonade, and pineapple juice. Stir in milk. Place 4 cups liquid in blender with 1 cup crushed ice; process until slushy. Repeat with remaining liquid, processing 4 cups at a time. Serve from a pitcher or small punch bowl. **Yield**: About 30 cups

Kay Nethery Elliott '64

PINEAPPLE PERCOLATED PUNCH

"A welcoming aroma for the family to come home to—good for a crowd, too."

1 tablespoon whole cloves
½ tablespoon whole allspice
3 sticks cinnamon
½ cup firmly-packed brown
    sugar

¼ teaspoon salt
3 cups water
3 cups pineapple juice

Combine first 5 ingredients in basket of electric percolator. Pour water and pineapple juice into percolator. Percolate for full cycle. **Yield**: 6 cups

Note: *For 30 cups, use a party-size coffee maker and increase each ingredient by 5 times.*

Debra Dobbins Burleson '79

MAMA'S GREEN PARTY PUNCH

3 cups water
3 cups sugar
4 teaspoons vanilla
4 teaspoons almond

1 (3-ounce) package lime-
   flavored gelatin
1 quart pineapple juice
1 (8-ounce) bottle lemon
   juice

Bring water and sugar to a boil, stirring until sugar dissolves. Pour into a 1-gallon jar or container, and add remaining ingredients. Finish filling gallon jar with water. Chill and serve. **Yield**: 50 servings

Note: *Use a sun tea jar for an easy 1-gallon container.*

Martha Lou Chadwick Scott '71
Baylor Dean for Student Life

GALVESTON ARTILLERY CLUB PUNCH
"For a crowd"

3 cups sugar
12 cups water, divided
12 cups pineapple juice
3 cups cranberry juice

3 cups orange juice
2 cups lemon juice
½ cups lime juice.
3 quarts ginger ale

Boil sugar and 3 cups of water for 5 minutes. Add remaining 9 cups of water and juices; mix well. Freeze in coffee cans lined with plastic bags. Remove from freezer 30 to 40 minutes before serving. Add ginger ale; stir. **Yield**: About 4 gallons or 100 punch cup servings

Beth Warren Harris '68

🕐 PAPA GILLEN'S NUTRITIOUS ORANGE DRINK

"A granddad's treat made for all his Baylor grandchildren"

1 (6-ounce) frozen orange
   juice, thawed
1 cup milk
1 cup water

¼ cup sugar, optional
1 teaspoon vanilla
10 to 12 large ice cubes

Place all ingredients in blender. Blend at high speed. Serve promptly. **Yield**: 4 servings

Wynell Gillen Patterson '50

MY FAMILY'S SUMMERTIME TEA

2 quarts water
2 family-size tea bags
12 to 15 large sprigs mint
1 (6-ounce) can frozen
   limeade, thawed

1 (46-ounce) can pineapple
   juice
1½ cups sugar

Bring water to a boil in a saucepan. Add tea bags and mint; steep 8 to 10 minutes. Add sugar, stirring to dissolve, and pour into a gallon container. Add pineapple juice and limeade to tea. Chill. Serve over ice in glasses for family meals or in punch cups at a summer party. **Yield**: 12 to 15 glasses

Julia Nell McConathy Graves '60

GOLDEN BEAR FRUIT PUNCH

1 orange, sliced
1 lemon, sliced
1 (6-ounce) jar green
   maraschino cherries
1 (6-ounce) can frozen
   orange juice, thawed
1 (6-ounce) can frozen
   limeade, thawed

1 (6-ounce) can frozen
   lemonade, thawed
8 (6-ounce) cans of water
1 (48-ounce) can pineapple
   juice
1 (l-liter) bottle ginger ale

Arrange orange and lemon slices in bottom of a ring mold that has been coated with non-stick vegetable spray. Top with cherries; add enough water or orange juice to cover fruit but not cause it to float. Freeze until firm. Fill remainder of mold with water or juice. Freeze again.

Combine next 5 ingredients in a 1-gallon jar. (A sun tea jar works well.) Chill until serving time. When ready to serve, pour into punch bowl. Add cold ginger ale. Unmold ice ring and float in punch. Yield: 25 to 30 punch cups

Hint: *Great for large receptions where there is no kitchen. May need crushed ice for larger groups.*

Mary Chambers Hull '67

MINT LEMONADE

1½ cups water
2 cups sugar
Juice of 6 lemons

Juice of 2 oranges
Grated rind of 1 orange
1 cup fresh mint leaves

Mix water and sugar in saucepan. Bring to boil and cook 5 minutes. Combine juices, rind, and mint leaves in a large bowl. Pour hot liquid over juice mixture. Cover; let stand 2 to 3 hours and strain. Dilute before serving, approximately 1 part syrup with 2 parts water. The syrup may be kept up to 2 weeks in refrigerator. **Yield**: 1 quart syrup

Hint: *For a really refreshing cooler, use 1 part syrup, 1 part water, and 1 part club soda.*

Linda Corbin '69

HOUSTON COFFEE PUNCH
"Popular with the Baylor Women's Association of Houston"

4 cups cold strong coffee
2 teaspoons vanilla
1 teaspoon cinnamon

½ gallon vanilla ice cream
1 cup whipping cream,
  whipped

Combine coffee, vanilla, and cinnamon; chill well. When ready to serve, put ice cream in punch bowl and cut into large chunks. Pour cold coffee mixture over ice cream. Do not blend; leave chunky. Fold in whipped cream, being careful not to overmix. **Yield**: Approximately 1 gallon or 25 punch cups

Note: *One (8-ounce) carton of frozen whipped topping may be used instead of whipped cream. Also chocolate ice cream in place of vanilla makes this a mocha punch.*

Princess Mike Cameron '60

HOT SPICED TEA

7 cups water, divided	1 stick cinnamon
6 teaspoons tea	Juice of 1 orange
1 teaspoon whole allspice	Juice of 1 lemon
1 teaspoon whole cloves	1 cup sugar

Bring 6 cups of water to boil. Remove from heat; add tea and spices, and steep for 10 minutes. Strain; add fruit juices. Make a sugar syrup by boiling remaining 1 cup of water and sugar together in a small saucepan for 5 minutes. Add to tea. Serve hot. **Yield**: 12 to 15 servings

When my son left home for college and was asked what favorite home memory would be missed, he responded with "the aroma of Mom's hot spiced tea," frequently found simmering on the stove on cold winter days.

Carrie Millard Pearce, MSEd '70

Soups & Salads

*W*hen I think of food and my student days at Baylor, I think of Martha and Esther Leuschner's home on South Seventh, across from Pat Neff Hall. For many years, there was a note beside the Leuschners' front door which said, "If no answer at this door, try the back door please!" And they meant it. Any student who went around the house to the back door, whether Martha and Esther knew the person or not, was probably invited in, offered a drink, and treated to some fun conversation.

Back when I was a student, after church at Seventh and James Baptist, a bunch of Baylor kids would often sit around their kitchen table and feast on fried donuts, hot chocolate, homemade ice cream, cheese dip, and wonderful chocolate chip cookies.

Then World War II interrupted my studies, and I went to war. When I ended up in a prisoner of war camp, thoughts of food were always on my mind, and I would dream of all the good food at the Leuschner home. When the war ended, I returned to Baylor, treasuring in a new way the wonderful food, fellowship, and hospitality of the Leuschners.

Judge Bill Logue '47, JD '49

CHILLED GAZPACHO

1 clove garlic, minced
½ cup chopped onion
½ cup chopped green pepper
2 medium cucumbers,
    peeled and chopped
1 (14½-ounce) can canned
    tomatoes with basil
1 (46-ounce) can tomato juice
2 tablespoons olive oil
3 tablespoons vinegar
½ teaspoon salt

⅛ teaspoon pepper
⅛ teaspoon hot pepper sauce
Chopped onion
Chopped hard-cooked eggs
Chopped celery
Chopped green pepper
Chopped cucumber
Chopped avocado
Croutons
Lime slices

Process first 5 ingredients in a blender until almost smooth. Pour into a large container, and add next 6 ingredients. Stir to blend well. Chill thoroughly. Serve cold in individual mugs with choice of garnishes. Guests may add to suit their taste. **Yield:** About 2 quarts

Diane Wimberly Danner '64

SPICY BUTTERNUT SQUASH SOUP

"First served to us in a 250-year old adobe hacienda in New Mexico"

1 large butternut squash
3 cloves roasted garlic, chopped
1 small red onion, chopped
1 tablespoons olive oil
3 large tomatoes, diced

2 tablespoons ground red chile
4 cups chicken stock
Salt and pepper to taste
Sour cream and cilantro for garnish

Cut butternut squash in ½ lengthwise. Place in shallow baking pan, cut-side down in ¼ inch of water. Bake at 350° for 1 hour or until squash is very soft. Cool until squash can be handled. Scoop squash out of skins, and set aside.

To roast garlic, place cloves with skin in hot, greaseless sauté pan or skillet. Heat until skin is blackened. Peel and discard skin.

In a large saucepan, sauté red onion in olive oil for 2 minutes. Add garlic and sauté for another minute. Add tomatoes and simmer for 5 minutes. Add red chile, stirring for 1 minute being careful not to burn chile. Add squash and chicken stock, and simmer for 30 minutes. Pour mixture into blender, and whip until smooth. Return to low heat. Do not let soup boil. Season with salt and pepper. Serve with a dollop of sour cream and chopped cilantro.
Yield: 6 to 8 small servings

Note: *A wonderful first-course soup. Use New Mexico ground red chile if you have access to it. Otherwise use commercial chili powder.*

Dixie Cavitt Soong '82

HARD ROCK CAFE BAKED POTATO SOUP

**6 to 8 slices bacon, fried
crisp, drippings reserved
1 cup diced yellow onions
⅔ cup flour
6 cups hot chicken stock
4 cups, diced, peeled baked
potatoes
2 cups heavy cream
½ cup chopped parsley**

**1½ teaspoons granulated
garlic
1½ teaspoons dried basil
1½ teaspoons salt
1 teaspoon hot pepper sauce
1½ teaspoons coarse black
pepper
1 cup grated Cheddar cheese
½ cup diced green onions**

Crumble bacon and set aside. Cook onions in remaining drippings until transparent, about 3 minutes. Add flour, stirring to prevent lumps; cook for 3 to 5 minutes, until mixture just begins to turn golden. Add chicken stock gradually, whisking to prevent lumps, until liquid thickens. Reduce heat to simmer; add bacon and all ingredients except grated cheese and green onions. Simmer for 10 minutes; do not allow to boil. Add grated cheese and green onions; heat until cheese melts smoothly. May garnish each serving with bacon, grated cheese, and/or chopped parsley.
Yield: 6 to 8 servings

Catherine Osborne Davenport '53

CHEESY VEGETABLE SOUP

½ cup margarine
3 cups sliced carrots
2 cups chopped celery
1 cup chopped white onion
1 (10-ounce) package frozen
   broccoli cuts
2 (10½-ounce) cans cream of
   chicken soup
3 cups chicken broth

2 soup cans water
1 (10-ounce) can tomatoes
   and green chiles
½ cup flour
½ cup milk
8 ounces American cheese,
   grated
8 ounces pasteurized process
   cheese, cubed

Microwave first 4 vegetables in margarine for 10 minutes on medium. Stir, and microwave for 10 minutes longer at medium high; stir again. Microwave for 10 minutes on high.

In a Dutch oven, combine soup, broth, water, and tomatoes; bring to a boil. Add vegetables, and stir. Whisk flour and milk with ¼ cup of hot soup mixture. Add to soup and vegetables. Stir until soup thickens. Add cheese and stir until melted. **Yield**: 12 servings

Susan Reed Fletcher '85

TIFFANY'S BEAN POT SOUP

2 cups pinto beans
1 pound ham, cubed
1 quart water
1 (22-ounce) can tomato juice
2 cups chicken stock
3 onions, chopped
3 cloves garlic, minced or
    pressed
3 tablespoons chopped
    parsley
¼ cup chopped green pepper
2 tablespoons brown sugar
1 tablespoon chili powder
1 teaspoon salt

1 teaspoon crushed bay leaf
1 teaspoon oregano
½ teaspoon cumin
½ teaspoon rosemary leaves,
    crushed
½ teaspoon ground thyme
½ teaspoon ground
    marjoram
½ teaspoon basil
½ teaspoon celery seed,
    crushed
1 cup cream sherry
Green onions, finely
    chopped, optional

Soak beans overnight; drain. Add rest of ingredients, except sherry and green onions. Bring to a boil, and cook slowly for three hours, or until tender. Add sherry. Top with green onions, if desired. **Yield:** 8 to 10 servings

The Cookbook Committee

TAILGATE MINESTRONE

Great on crisp autumn days at the stadium

2 pounds soup bones with
    meat
3 quarts cold water
1 tablespoon salt
1 cup diced celery
1 cup diced carrots
1 cup cut green beans
1 cup diced, pared potatoes
1 cup sliced zucchini
2 cups shredded cabbage
1 (16-ounce) can red kidney
    beans, drained

1 (16-ounce) can tomatoes
3 tablespoons instant
    minced onion
½ teaspoon garlic powder
2 tablespoons minced fresh
    or dried parsley flakes
¼ teaspoon pepper
3 tablespoons olive or salad
    oil
1 cup elbow macaroni
Grated Parmesan cheese to
    garnish

Put bones, water and salt in a 5-quart kettle. Cover and simmer from 2 to 3 hours or until meat falls off bones. Remove bones and meat from stock. Skim stock of any fat. (If time allows, chill stock in refrigerator for 1 hour to facilitate skimming.) Discard bones; cut meat into bite-size pieces, and return to stock. Add all other ingredients except cheese, and simmer 30 minutes. Sprinkle grated Parmesan cheese on each serving. **Yield**: 16 servings

Anne Rike Winstead '52

TEXAS GULF COAST GUMBO

"The best gumbo I've ever cooked"

1 pound bacon, diced
1 cup chopped green onion
6 cloves garlic, finely
   chopped, or 1 tablespoon
   garlic powder
8 to 10 tablespoons flour
12 drops hot pepper sauce, or
   to taste
3 teaspoons salt
4 teaspoons black pepper
1 teaspoon dried thyme

4 bay leaves
4 (14½-ounce) cans chicken
   broth
3 (14½-ounce) cans stewed
   tomatoes
1 (10-ounce) package frozen
   okra
3 cups seafood (crab, shrimp,
   fish chunks, king fish)
Hot cooked rice

In Dutch oven fry bacon until crisp; drain and set aside. Sauté onions and garlic in bacon drippings until tender. Add flour to thicken; stir until smooth. Add seasonings, chicken broth and stewed tomatoes. Simmer, stirring occasionally to prevent sticking, for 30 minutes. Add okra and cook for 15 minutes or longer. When almost ready to serve, add seafood and cook until done. Remove bay leaves. Serve in bowls over a mound of rice. Sprinkle bacon bits over top. **Yield:** 6 to 8 servings

Hint: *Freezes well with or without seafood.*

Virgina Hollifield Stegall '54

CLAM CHOWDER

2 (6½-ounce) cans minced
  clams, drained, juice
  reserved
1 (10-ounce) package frozen
  cauliflower
1 large carrot, grated
½ cup margarine
¾ cup flour

1 (13-ounce) can evaporated
  milk
1½ cup milk
1 cup cubed ham
Salt and pepper, to taste
½ teaspoon sugar
Few drops hot pepper sauce
3 tablespoons white wine

Pour juice from clams over frozen cauliflower and carrots in 3-quart saucepan. Add just enough water to cover, and cook until tender. Do not drain. Cut cauliflower into bite-size pieces, if necessary.

In separate dish, microwave margarine to melt; add flour and stir. Whisk in milks; microwave on high until smooth and thick, about 5 minutes, whisking each minute. Combine with cauliflower mixture. Stir in clams, ham, and remaining ingredients. Add additional milk if soup is too thick. Garnish with parsley or crisp bacon bits. Serve steaming hot. **Yield**: 6 servings

Note: *Lower the fat content by using skim milks and omitting ham.*

Kathryn White Devine '69

CHICKEN GUMBO

1 large chicken, cut into
   serving-size pieces
3 quarts water
Salt, pepper, cajun
   seasonings to taste
2 cups chopped celery
2 cups chopped onion

1 large chopped bell pepper
2 cloves garlic, minced
1½ cups flour
1½ cups oil
Hot cooked rice
File powder, optional

Place chicken pieces in large Dutch oven with the water. Cook until tender. Flavor broth with seasonings to taste. Remove chicken from pot, and bone. Set aside chicken and broth.

Make a roux, using a seasoned cast-iron skillet. Brown flour in oil until very dark, being careful not to scorch or burn. (If this happens, start again. Making the roux takes time and patience.) When roux is very dark, add chopped vegetables and stir to coat. Sauté vegetables in roux until tender. Stir vegetables and roux into broth and chicken. Simmer for 2 hours. Serve over rice with file powder. **Yield**: 16 servings

Hint: *Adding cajun sausage to this soup gives even more good flavor.*

Sharon Harper Cushman '69

At one of her dinners when she was Newcomer's sponsor, Mrs. Eulalie Carroll Wilbanks served a delicious French jambalaya. I wanted the recipe, but I had heard that although she would gladly share the recipe, she would leave out one ingredient so that her dish could not be duplicated. Finally, gathering my courage, I bravely asked her for the complete recipe. She laughed at my honesty and gave it to me.

Dorcas Beaver
Wife of Dr. Harold Beaver, Professor and Chair,
Department of Geology

CREAM OF CRAB SOUP
"For that special meal"

3 tablespoons margarine or
    butter
1 medium onion, minced
2 tablespoons flour
2 cups clam juice
1 pound lump crabmeat
2 cups half-and-half
¼ cup dry white wine

¼ teaspoon pepper
Dash cayenne
¼ teaspoon salt
Dash hot pepper sauce
1 teaspoon Old Bay
    seasoning
¼ teaspoon garlic powder
1 teaspoon minced parsley
    for garnish

In margarine, sauté onion until tender but not brown. Add flour and stir for 2 or 3 minutes. Whisk in clam juice. Bring to a boil, stirring constantly. Reduce heat and simmer 10 minutes. Add crab, saving some lumps for garnish. Add half-and-half, wine, and remaining seasonings, except parsley. Simmer 3 minutes. Melt 1 teaspoon margarine in small saucepan, add reserved crab and minced parsley. Ladle soup into individual bowls, and top with a spoon of parsley and crabmeat. **Yield:** 6 to 8 servings

Celeste Sauls '90

MOM'S HAM CHOWDER

2 cups diced potatoes
2 cups water
½ cup sliced carrots
½ cup sliced celery
¼ cup chopped onion
1½ teaspoons salt
¼ teaspoon pepper

¼ cup margarine
¼ cup flour
2 cups milk
8 ounces American cheese, grated
1 cup cubed ham

In a Dutch oven, bring first 7 ingredients to a boil, and boil for 10 minutes. Do not drain. In a separate saucepan, melt margarine; add flour and stir until smooth. Gradually add milk, and heat through. Combine milk mixture with cooked vegetables in Dutch oven. Add cheese and ham, and stir until cheese melts. **Yield:** About 6 cups

Hint: *A delicious use for leftover ham. Try Swiss cheese in place of American for a change of flavor.*

Susan Reed Fletcher '86

SAN ANTONIO CHEESE SOUP

½ cup margarine
½ cup chopped onion
3 green onions, chopped
3 ribs celery, chopped
2 carrots, grated
2 (10¾-ounce) cans chicken broth
3 (10¾-ounce) cans cream of potato soup

8 ounces American or Cheddar cheese, grated
1 (8-ounce) carton sour cream
3 tablespoons cooking sherry
3 tablespoons parsley
⅛ teaspoon pepper

Melt margarine in a large pot. Add onions, celery and carrots; sauté on medium heat 5 minutes. Stir in chicken broth. Cover and simmer 20 minutes. Add potato soup and cheese, and mix well. Stir in last 4 ingredients and simmer until well blended. **Yield:** 4 to 6 servings

Hint: *To reduce fat, use low-fat cheese and light sour cream.*

Lisa Mullins Vines '83

CHILE CHEESE SOUP

2 cups canned chicken broth
1 medium tomato, chopped
1 medium onion, chopped
1 (4-ounce) can chopped
  green chiles
2 tablespoons margarine

2 tablespoons flour
2 cups milk
½ teaspoon salt
Pepper to taste
2 cups grated Monterey Jack
  cheese

In a large saucepan simmer first 4 ingredients together until on-ion and tomato are clear. In a 1-quart saucepan melt margarine, stir in flour, and cook for 1 minute. Stir in milk, and cook until thickened, stirring often. Add salt and pepper. Pour into chicken broth. Stir in cheese. **Yield:** 6 to 8 servings

Hint: *Make this soup using a combination of Monterey Jack cheese and American cheese.*

Dorothy Swift Newsom '46

GREEN CHILE SOUP
"Make this in your microwave"

1 (10-ounce) can cream of
  mushroom soup
1 (4-ounce) can mild green
  chiles
1 cup cooked white chicken,
  shredded

2½ to 3 cups chicken broth
¼ to ½ teaspoon cumin
  powder
¼ to ½ teaspoon oregano
¼ teaspoon garlic powder

Combine ingredients and heat thoroughly. Garnish servings with a dollop of sour cream, plain yogurt, or toasted sunflower seeds. **Yield**: 3 to 4 servings

Hint: *Use 1 (4-ounce) can white chicken chunks or leftover holiday turkey in place of chicken.*

Betty Sewell Peebles '46

SANTA FE TACO SOUP

"A great soup—serve with hot cornbread or warm corn tortillas"

2 pounds lean ground beef
  or turkey
1 large onion, chopped
2 (14½-ounce) cans stewed
  tomatoes
1 (14½-ounce) can stewed
  tomatoes, Mexican style
1 (4-ounce) can chopped
  green chiles
1 (15-ounce) can pinto beans
1 (15-ounce) can kidney
  beans
1 (15-ounce) can black-eyed
  peas
1 (15-ounce) can hominy
1 (14½-ounce) can whole
  kernel corn
1½ cans of water
1 (1¼-ounce) package taco
  seasoning mix
1 (½-ounce) package ranch-
  style dressing mix

In large Dutch oven, brown meat and onion together. Drain off fat. Add canned vegetables with their liquid; do not drain. Stir in water and seasoning mixes. Bring to a boil. Reduce heat; cover and simmer for 30 to 45 minutes. **Yield:** 16 to 20 servings

Andrea Wilkes Willson '91

"We may live without friends; we may live without books, but civilized man cannot live without cooks."

Bulwer-Lytton

TORTILLA SOUP

The Baylor family across the country is fond of Tortilla Soup.

2 large chicken breasts,
skinned and boned,
(about 2 pounds)
2 cups water
1 (14½-ounce) can beef broth
1 (14½-ounce) can chicken
broth
1 (14½-ounce) can tomatoes
with green chiles,
undrained
1 (6-ounce) can tomato sauce
½ cup chopped onion
¼ cup chopped green pepper

1 (8¾-ounce) can whole
kernel corn, drained
1 teaspoon chili powder
½ teaspoon ground cumin
⅛ teaspoon black pepper
3 cups tortilla chips, coarsely
crushed
1 cup grated Monterey Jack
cheese
1 avocado, peeled and sliced,
optional
Snipped cilantro, optional
Lime wedges, optional

Cut chicken into 1-inch cubes; set aside. In large saucepan combine water, beef broth, chicken broth, tomatoes, tomato sauce, onion, and green pepper. Bring to boiling. Add chicken; reduce heat. Cover and simmer for 10 minutes. Add corn, chili powder, cumin, and pepper. Simmer, covered for 10 minutes more. To serve place crushed tortilla chips into each bowl. Ladle soup over chips. Sprinkle with cheese, avocado, and cilantro, if desired. Serve with lime wedges. **Yield:** 6 servings

Ernie Boyd '84

CHICKEN TORTILLA SOUP WITH RICE

6 corn tortillas
⅓ cup vegetable oil
⅓ cup sliced green onions,
including tops
1½ cups cooked rice
½ (10-ounce) can tomatoes
with green chiles,
undrained
1 cup cooked and cubed
chicken breasts
1 (4-ounce) can chopped
green chiles, undrained

4 cups chicken broth
2 tablespoons chopped
cilantro
1 teaspoon salt
1 tablespoon lime juice
1½ cups grated Cheddar
cheese
½ cup chopped tomato
1 small avocado, cut in small
cubes
1 lime, sliced, optional

Cut fresh tortillas in ½-inch wide strips. Heat vegetable oil to 350°. Fry tortilla strips until golden. Drain on paper towels. Sauté green onions in 2 teaspoons oil in Dutch oven until tender. Add next 6 ingredients. Cover and simmer for 20 minutes. Stir in salt and lime juice.

To serve place tortilla strips and 3 tablespoons grated cheese in bottom of each bowl. Ladle in soup; top with more tortilla strips, tomato and avocado. Garnish with lime slice and cilantro sprigs. **Yield**: 4 to 6 servings

Janet McMurtry McConnell '61

HUNTER'S VENISON CHILI

2 pounds ground venison, including small amount of fat
2 tablespoons minced onion
1 (15-ounce) can ranch-style beans
1 (15-ounce) can kidney beans
2 (15-ounce) cans tomato sauce
1 (2½-ounce) can sliced ripe olives, drained
1 tablespoon garlic salt
¼ teaspoon black pepper
2 tablespoons chili powder
½ teaspoon cumin
½ teaspoon oregano

In a Dutch oven, brown ground venison with onion, and drain. Stir in remaining ingredients. Bring to slow boil over medium heat. Reduce to low heat, and simmer covered for 15 to 30 minutes. **Yield:** 8 to 10 servings

Dan Joseph Proctor '83

"Wish I had time for just one more bowl of chili."
Alleged to be the dying words of Kit Carson

HOT CHICKEN SALAD AUSTIN

2 cups chopped cooked
chicken
1 cup diced celery
3 hard-cooked eggs, diced
½ cup mayonnaise
1 tablespoon lemon juice
1 (10¾-ounce) can cream of
chicken soup

1 (5-ounce) can water
chestnuts, sliced
⅓ cup slivered almonds,
optional
½ teaspoon salt
½ teaspoon pepper
½ cup chopped pimiento
Potato chips or chow mein
noodles

Combine all ingredients, mixing well. Add more mayonnaise if needed to make salad moist and creamy. Spoon into 7x11-inch baking dish. Cover with crushed potato chips or chow mein noodles. Bake at 400° for 20 minutes. **Yield:** 8 to 10 servings

June Page Johnson '45

FRUIT AND NUTS CHICKEN SALAD

Highly rated by our testers

4 cups cooked chicken, cut
into bite-size pieces
1 cup sliced celery
1 (2-ounce) package slivered
almonds, lightly toasted
1 (11-ounce) can mandarin
oranges, drained

1½ cups green grapes,
halved
1 cup mayonnaise (not salad
dressing)
¼ cup sour cream
½ teaspoon salt
Dash of black pepper
Dash of garlic powder.

Combine first 5 ingredients in large bowl. Mix mayonnaise, sour cream and seasonings. Pour over chicken, and mix carefully. Serve on lettuce. **Yield:** Approximately 8 servings

Celeste Sauls '90

SOUTH-BY-SOUTHWEST CHICKEN SALAD

"What is more Southern than chicken salad? Yet this has a Southwestern zing!"

1 carrot, coarsely sliced
1 rib celery
1 pound chicken tenders or
   boneless breasts
4 canned jalapeños, seeded
   and diced

⅓ cup mayonnaise
4 green onions, thinly sliced
½ cup sour cream
1 teaspoon ground cumin

Bring 4 cups water to a rolling boil. Add carrot, celery, and chicken; cook for approximately 10 minutes or until done. Remove from heat and let stand for 10 minutes. Drain liquid, and discard vegetables. Cool chicken; shred into bite-size pieces, discarding tendons. Combine with remaining ingredients, and adjust seasonings to taste. **Yield:** 2 cups

The Cookbook Committee

LIGHTLY-ITALIAN CHICKEN SALAD

1 chicken or 6 chicken
   breast halves, cooked and
   cut in bite-size pieces
1 to 2 cups Italian dressing
1 cup chopped celery
½ tablespoon minced onion
1 cup mayonnaise

2 dashes cayenne pepper or
   to taste
3 avocados, sliced and
   soaked in lime juice
Almonds, browned in 1
   tablespoon butter, to
   garnish

Marinate chicken overnight in Italian dressing. Drain and add remaining ingredients. Stir carefully. Serve on lettuce leaves or in avocado shells. Sprinkle almonds on top. **Yield:** 6 to 8 servings

Note: *Allow time to marinate chicken.*

Ethel Ann de Cordova Porter '58

CHICKEN FAJITA SALAD

2 tablespoons cooking oil,
  divided
¼ cup lime juice
1 garlic clove, minced
½ teaspoon ground cumin
½ teaspoon salt
½ teaspoon oregano
1 pound boneless, skinless
  chicken breasts, cut into
  thin strips

1 onion, cut into thin
  wedges
1 sweet red pepper, cut into
  thin strips
1 (7-ounce) can chopped
  green chiles, drained
Shredded lettuce
3 tomatoes, cut in wedges
1 cup slivered almonds,
  toasted

Combine 1 tablespoon oil, lime juice, garlic, cumin, salt, and oregano. Toss with chicken; marinate at least 30 minutes.

Heat remaining oil in skillet on medium-high. Sauté onion 2 minutes. Drain chicken, reserving marinade. Add chicken to skillet. Stir-fry until it begins to brown. Add red pepper, chiles, and reserved marinade. Cook 2 minutes. Serve over shredded lettuce. Garnish with tomatoes and almonds. Serve with salsa if desired. **Yield**: 4 to 6 servings

Sandra Bobo Karnes '60

MANGO CHUTNEY CHICKEN SALAD

½ cup mayonnaise
1 (9-ounce) jar mango
  chutney
½ teaspoon curry
½ teaspoon salt

2 cups grated Cheddar
  cheese
3 cups diced cooked chicken
2 cups chopped apple
1 cup dry roasted peanuts

In small bowl, mix together first 4 ingredients. In a larger bowl, mix remaining ingredients. Combine both mixtures just before serving. **Yield:** 4 to 6 servings.

Dot C. Martin
Mother of Vicki Martin Shellenberger '74

ORIENTAL CHICKEN SALAD WITH CHUTNEY

5 cups diced cooked chicken breasts
1 cup pineapple tidbits, drained
1 cup sliced celery
1 cup water chestnuts, sliced
½ cup slivered almonds
1 to 2 (10-ounce) cans mandarin oranges, drained
Dash of ginger
4 tablespoons Major Grey chutney
1 cup mayonnaise
1 cup sour cream
1 teaspoon curry powder
Chinese noodles
Paprika
Parsley

Mix chicken with pineapple, celery, water chestnuts, almonds, oranges, and ginger. Combine chutney, mayonnaise, sour cream, and curry powder; stir into chicken mixture. Refrigerate for at least 1 hour before serving. Just before serving, sprinkle each portion with warmed Chinese noodles, paprika and parsley. **Yield**: 6 to 8 servings

Jeanne Wood Nowlin '42

The table's set, the food is hot;
With all God's bounty, we want for not.
Should a guest approach our door,
There's always room to feed one more.

Anonymous

CHICKEN CREOLE SALAD WITH MUSHROOMS

1 pound mushrooms, thinly sliced
2 cup cherry tomatoes, halved
2 cups chopped, cooked chicken breasts
½ pound zucchini, thinly sliced

1 green pepper, seeded and diced
3 green onions, thinly sliced
½ cup salad oil
2 tablespoons wine vinegar
2 tablespoons lemon juice
1 teaspoon salt
¼ teaspoon pepper
½ teaspoon sugar

Mix first 6 salad ingredients together, and chill for 30 minutes. Combine oil, vinegar, lemon juice, and seasonings; mix well. Before serving, pour dressing over salad ingredients and toss. **Yield:** 8 to 10 servings

Hint: *Delicious with shrimp, too.*

Dorothy Swift Newsom '46

Few Baylor students before World War II had cars. So on Sunday mornings most of them walked to Seventh and James or to First Baptist. At First, my mother, Mrs. J.M. Dawson, taught the girls. About 200 were usually enrolled. Dr. A. J. Armstrong taught the boys— not quite so many as the girls, but equally loyal.

Every Monday afternoon Mother invited twenty or so to our house adjacent to the campus. I would hurry home from school to help pass the Madeira napkins and then the plates of "refreshments." Often there was chicken salad, tiny hot biscuits, potato chips, mince meat tarts topped with whipped cream, or chocolate fudge cake squares, and iced tea.

Alice Dawson Cheavens '29

BEIJING TUNA SALAD

2 (6-ounce) cans tuna, not water packed, drained
1 cup diced celery
1 (5-ounce) can water chestnuts, sliced
1 to 2 garlic cloves, crushed
⅓ cup diced onion
¼ cup pimiento, chopped, optional

½ cup ripe olives, pitted and diced
½ cup salad dressing
2 tablespoons white vinegar
2 tablespoons light cream or whole milk
1 (3-ounce) can chow mein noodles

Mix first 7 ingredients in large bowl. Combine salad dressing, vinegar and cream. Pour over tuna mixture and combine well. Refrigerate at least 2 hours to blend flavors. Just before serving, add chow mein noodles. Stir carefully. Spoon on lettuce leaf, and serve immediately. **Yield:** 6 to 8 servings

Doris Hollingsworth Gage '47

 ## PICNIC PASTA
"Need to take something to feed a crowd? This is the dish."

1 pound macaroni, cooked and drained
¾ cup Italian salad dressing
¾ cup chopped celery
¾ cup chopped green pepper
8 green onions, chopped, including tops
1 (2-ounce) jar pimientos
4 dashes hot pepper sauce
2 tablespoons chopped green chiles
1 teaspoon salt

1½ teaspoon seasoned pepper
½ teaspoon seasoned salt
1 (16-ounce) can green peas, drained
1 (16-ounce) can corn, drained
1 (4-ounce) can chopped ripe olives, drained
1½ cups mayonnaise
3 tablespoons picante sauce
1 avocado, sliced

Combine all ingredients except avocado. Refrigerate at least 24 hours. Garnish with avocado slices. **Yield:** 20 servings

 Note: *For low-fat version, use low-fat Italian dressing, reduced-fat mayonnaise, and omit ripe olives and avocado.*

Carol Watson Barclay '60

BASIL FETTUCCINE SALAD
"Five star rating"

2 cups fresh basil leaves
8 ounces fettuccine
1½ cups Red Wine Basil
  Vinaigrette, divided
1 pound tender green beans,
  stem ends snapped off
6 ripe plum tomatoes, each
  cut into 8 wedges

2 cups pitted, whole black
  olives
2 tablespoons chopped fresh
  parsley
4 ounces Parmesan or
  Romano cheese

Slice bunches of fresh basil into slivers, cutting diagonally. Set aside ½ cup for the vinaigrette.

Cook fettuccine according to package directions. Drain, place in a bowl and coat with ½ cup vinaigrette. Set aside. Steam green beans just until tender. Drain and rinse under cold water. Drain again and set aside.

Place fettuccine in a large (preferably tall) clear glass bowl. Cover with green beans. Top with tomatoes, then whole olives and slivered basil. Sprinkle with parsley, and pour remaining cup of vinaigrette over salad. Shave cheese with a cheese server to get thin, wide slices; place on top of salad. Toss well before serving. **Yield**: 8 servings

Red Wine Basil Vinaigrette:

2 cloves garlic, peeled and
  crushed
2 tablespoons Dijon-style
  mustard
½ cup red wine vinegar

1 teaspoon freshly-ground
  black pepper
1 cup light olive oil
½ cup reserved slivered
  basil leaves
½ cup chopped fresh parsley

Whisk garlic, mustard, vinegar, and pepper together in a small bowl. Pour oil into bowl in a slow steam, whisking constantly until vinaigrette has thickened slightly. Fold in basil and parsley. **Yield**: 1½ cups.

Hint: *A complete meal for lunch, a picnic, or as a simple supper. Can be served hot or cold, and is very good leftover.*

Lois Wroten Boatwright '59

CHILLED PASTA MEDLEY

2 packages oriental-flavor
   ramen noodles
6 cups water
1 teaspoon olive oil
4 green onions, chopped
3 ribs celery, chopped
1 red bell pepper, seeded
   and chopped

1 (2¼-ounce) can sliced ripe
   olives, drained
1 (6½-ounce) jar marinated
   artichoke hearts, drained
   and marinade reserved
Dressing

Slightly break ramen noodles. Set aside seasoning packets from packages of noodles to be used in Dressing. In a large saucepan, cook noodles in 6 cups boiling water, to which olive oil has been added, for 3 minutes, stirring occasionally. Drain and rinse in cold water. Place in large bowl, and add remaining ingredients. Pour Dressing over salad, and mix gently. Chill in refrigerator until ready to serve. **Yield:** 6 to 8 servings

Dressing:
Reserved marinade from
   artichoke hearts
1 seasoning packet from
   noodles
1 tablespoon lemon juice

1 tablespoon rice vinegar
1 tablespoon olive oil
¼ cup grated Parmesan
   cheese
Black pepper to taste

In small bowl, combine all ingredients. Whisk until well blended.

Kathy Justman '85

GREEK TORTELLINI SALAD

2 (9-ounce) packages of cheese tortellini, cooked and drained	1 small red onion, thinly sliced
2 red or green bell peppers, cut in thin strips	¼ cup sliced ripe olives
	Lemon-Mint Dressing
	½ cup crumbled Feta cheese

In a large bowl combine pasta, peppers, onion, and olives. Toss Lemon-Mint Dressing with pasta. Chill 4 to 24 hours. Just before serving, toss with Feta cheese. **Yield:** 6 to 8 servings

Lemon-Mint Dressing:

½ cup white wine vinegar	2 tablespoons dry sherry
½ cup olive oil	1½ teaspoons seasoned salt
3 tablespoons snipped fresh mint, or 1 tablespoon dried mint	1 teaspoon garlic powder
	¼ teaspoon crushed red pepper
3 tablespoons lemon juice	1 teaspoon black pepper

Combine all dressing ingredients, and blend well.

Karen McNeely Zecy '79

ATOMIC SALAD

3 cloves garlic, crushed	¼ cup salad oil (or less if desired)
¼ teaspoon dry mustard	Fresh spinach, leaves torn
1 teaspoon salt	2 kinds of lettuce, leaves torn
½ teaspoon pepper	Cherry tomatoes
2 tablespoons lemon juice	Croutons, optional
2 tablespoons Parmesan cheese	

Combine first 7 ingredients in a large salad bowl or 3-quart plastic container. Place lettuce and spinach on top. Do not toss. Cover and refrigerate. When ready to serve, add tomatoes and croutons and toss. **Yield:** 6 to 8 servings.

Hint: *Salad is best if prepared a day ahead of time. Use whatever ratio of spinach to lettuce you like or whatever you have on hand.*

Deanna Stephens Payne '60

STRAWBERRY SPINACH SALAD

"An excellent combination of textures and tastes"

10 ounces fresh spinach,
washed and stemmed
1 small jicama, peeled and
cut in julienne strips

1 pint fresh strawberries,
stemmed and halved
2 to 3 cups fresh bean
sprouts
Strawberry Dressing

Combine spinach, jicama, strawberries and bean sprouts in a large bowl. Toss with Strawberry Dressing just before serving. **Yield:** 6 servings

Strawberry Dressing:
1 cup strawberries, halved
2 tablespoons red wine
vinegar or raspberry
vinegar

2 tablespoons sugar
¼ cup vegetable oil
Few drops sesame oil
Salt and pepper to taste

Puree dressing ingredients in food processor, using steel blade.

Hint: *Garnish with edible flowers for a very contemporary presentation.*

Lisa Abercrombie Beach '82

"Doubtless God could have made a better berry, but doubtless God never did."

Dr. William Butler, 1535-1618

BARB'S GREEN SALAD

2 tablespoons salad oil
1 clove garlic, crushed
2 tomatoes, cut in chunks
1 large head romaine
  lettuce, torn into bite-size
  pieces

4 green onions, chopped
¼ cup grated Parmesan or
  Romano cheese
½ pound bacon, fried and
  crumbled
Dressing

Pour salad oil in a large bowl. Add crushed garlic and tomatoes; stir just to coat. Add lettuce, green onions, cheese, and bacon. Do not stir until ready to finish salad. Toss with well-blended Dressing just before serving.

Dressing:
⅓ cup salad oil
¼ cup lemon juice or juice
  from 1 lemon

Pepper and salt to taste
½ teaspoon oregano

Mix ingredients in a jar with a tight sealing lid. Shake vigorously until well blended. **Yield:** 4 to 6 servings

Hint: *To keep bacon slices from sticking together in the package, roll the package up like a tube and secure with a rubber band.*

When my family was living in Oregon, a neighbor gave my mother this recipe. The neighbor didn't know who "Barb" was. In fact, no one I know knows who Barb is, but anyone who has eaten this salad loves her. God bless Barb!

Amy Fitzpatrick Hinrichs '87

SPINACH SALAD WITH A SURPRISE

1 (10-ounce) bag fresh
    spinach, torn
1 pint fresh strawberries,
    hulled and halved

1 to 2 bananas, sliced
½ cup chopped walnuts
Poppy Seed Dressing

Place salad ingredients in a large bowl. Toss with Poppy Seed Dressing. **Yield:** 6 to 8 servings

Poppy Seed Dressing:
1½ cups sugar
1½ teaspoons paprika
¾ teaspoon dry mustard
1½ teaspoons
    Worcestershire sauce

1½ cups oil
1½ teaspoons minced dried
    onion flakes
¾ cup vinegar
⅓ cup poppy seed

Combine ingredients, except poppy seed, and mix in a blender until thoroughly combined. Stir poppy seed in by hand. Refrigerate dressing. Dressing will keep up to 6 weeks. Makes 2½ cups.

Hint: *Dressing is easy to divide by ⅓, adjusting the poppy seed as desired.*

Donell Teaff
Wife of Grant Teaff, former Baylor head football coach
and athletic director

SUPER SPINACH SALAD

1 (10-ounce) bag fresh
   spinach, torn
1 head iceburg lettuce, torn
4 ounces Swiss cheese,
   grated or torn into bite-
   size pieces

¼ cup cottage cheese
4 pieces bacon, fried crisp
   and drained
1 or 2 hard-cooked eggs,
   chopped

Gently toss all ingredients in a large bowl. Shake Dressing well, and pour over salad just before serving. **Yield:** 10 to 12 servings

Dressing:
½ cup oil
½ cup white vinegar
¼ cup sugar
1 teaspoon poppy seed

½ teaspoon salt
½ teaspoon dry mustard
1 small purple onion, finely
   chopped

Mix all dressing ingredients in glass container. Chill at least 3 hours or overnight.

Hint: *Always tear fresh greens for salads because cutting or slicing will give the greens a bitter taste.*

Ann Bailey Brothers '80

Baylor Homecoming (and the morning after) provide many memories. For two years in a row, we awoke the Sunday morning following Homecoming to discover rows upon rows of white plastic forks carefully planted with tines down on our front lawn. A note attached to the front door informed us that "The Club" had enjoyed a wonderful Homecoming and wanted to share a part of their Saturday picnic with us.

Joy Copeland Reynolds '74
Wife of Baylor President, Dr. Herbert H.Reynolds

⊙ MANDARIN ORANGE SALAD WITH ALMONDS

1 tablespoon + 1 teaspoon
  sugar
½ cup slivered almonds
1 head romaine lettuce,
  shredded

1 (10-ounce) can mandarin
  oranges, drained
1 red onion, cut into rings

Cook sugar and almonds over medium heat, stirring constantly, until sugar is dissolved. Remove from heat, and set aside. Mix lettuce, oranges, and onion in a large bowl. When ready to serve, pour Dressing over lettuce and toss well. Sprinkle almonds over top. **Yield**: 6 to 8 servings

Dressing:
½ cup oil
2 tablespoons sugar
2 tablespoons red wine
  vinegar

¼ teaspoon salt
¼ teaspoon pepper

Shake oil, sugar, vinegar, and seasonings together in a jar with a tight lid.

Lisa Davis Miller '86

BROCCOLI AND SUNFLOWER SEED SALAD

Editor's note: This broccoli salad was a favorite of alumni across the country. Here are two versions.

Flowerets from two bunches
   of broccoli
6 green onions, sliced
12 slices bacon, fried crisp
   and crumbled
½ cup raisins

1 cup mayonnaise
⅓ cup sugar
2 tablespoons white vinegar
1 cup sunflower seed,
   roasted and salted

Cut flowerets into bite-size pieces. Toss broccoli, onion, bacon and raisins in a large bowl. Add dressing. Mix mayonnaise, sugar, and vinegar in a small bowl. Add to broccoli mixture. Chill. Add seeds just before serving. **Yield:** 6 to 8 servings

Eva Dudley DenBesten '77

BROCCOLI AND GRAPE SALAD

"The dressing ties the unusual combination of ingredients together."

4 cups raw chopped broccoli
   flowerets
1 cup chopped celery
¼ cup chopped green onion
2 cups seedless red grapes,
   halved
⅓ cup sugar

1 cup mayonnaise
1 tablespoon red wine
   vinegar
⅔ cup sliced almonds
½ pound bacon, fried crisp
   and crumbled

Mix broccoli, celery, onion, and grapes together in a large bowl. In a small bowl mix sugar, mayonnaise, and vinegar. Pour over broccoli mixture and toss. Refrigerate overnight. Before serving, add almonds and bacon. **Yield:** 8 to 12 servings

Carol Ohlenbusch Chappell '79

"Sure, women love a crazy salad with their meat."

William Butler Yeats

CREAMY ASPARAGUS SALAD

2 envelopes unflavored
  gelatin
1 (10½-ounce) can asparagus
  pieces, drained, and juice
  reserved
1 (10¾-ounce) can cream of
  asparagus soup
1 (8-ounce) package cream
  cheese, softened

¼ cup mayonnaise
½ cup chopped pecans
1 cup chopped celery
½ cup chopped stuffed
  green olives
1 tablespoon grated onion
Stuffed olive slices for
  garnish

Soak gelatin in asparagus juice. Bring undiluted soup to a boil, and add gelatin mixture. Mix and set aside to cool to lukewarm.

Whip cream cheese and mayonnaise; add lukewarm soup. Fold in pecans, celery, olives, grated onion, and asparagus pieces. Pour in 7x11-inch dish and chill. Cut in squares, and place a slice of stuffed olive on each square before serving. **Yield:** About 10 servings

Marilyn Sebesta '71

CORN CONFETTI
"A do-ahead salad"

1 (16-ounce) can whole
  kernel corn, drained
1 (16-ounce) can shoe peg
  corn, drained
1 onion, chopped
3 ribs celery, chopped

1 (2-ounce) jar diced
  pimientos, drained
½ green pepper, chopped
½ cup sugar
½ cup oil
¼ cup vinegar
1 teaspoon salt

Toss vegetables together in a large container. Whisk together sugar, oil, vinegar, and salt. Pour over vegetables. Refrigerate overnight. **Yield:** 8 to 10 servings

Note: *May also be served as a relish to accompany meat.*

Sharon Elaine Howard '73

CAULIFLOWER GARDEN SALAD
"An overnight salad"

4 green onions, chopped
1 medium tomato, diced
3 ounces Colby cheese,
   diced
1 rib celery, chopped
4 radishes, sliced

1 head cauliflower flowerets
1 cup mayonnaise
3 teaspoons horseradish
Garlic powder to taste
10 drops hot pepper sauce

Combine first 6 ingredients in large bowl. Combine remaining ingredients for dressing. Blend well and pour over vegetables. Mix carefully. Refrigerate overnight so flavors can blend. **Yield:** 8 to 10 servings

Note: *Both fat-reduced cheese and mayonnaise may be used successfully.*

Kyrene Sims '35

"Cauliflower is nothing but cabbage with a college education."

Mark Twain

⏰ LA MARTINIQUE GREEN BEAN SALAD

3 (16-ounce) cans whole
   green beans, well drained
1 (14-ounce) can artichoke
   hearts, drained and cut
   into bite-size pieces
1 small purple onion, cut in
   rings

1 (4¼-ounce) can sliced ripe
   olives, drained
1 (14-ounce) can hearts of
   palm, drained and cut
   into bite-size pieces
1 (8-ounce) bottle La
   Martinique salad dressing

Combine first 5 ingredients in large bowl. Pour salad dressing over all. Marinate overnight, or for several days. **Yield:** 8 servings

Patricia Erwin Bielamowicz '59

GRANDMOTHER'S FRIED OKRA AND TOMATO SALAD

"A nice, light, summer dish."

1 (16-ounce) bag frozen
  breaded okra, or fresh
  okra, cut and rolled in
  cornmeal
Oil for frying

2 large tomatoes, chopped
½ medium white onion,
  chopped
Garlic salt to taste

Fry okra in oil until golden and crisp. Drain on paper towels. Toss tomatoes with okra in a large bowl. Sprinkle with garlic salt. Serve immediately. **Yield:** 4 to 6 servings

Note: *Homegrown tomatoes are best, of course.*

Karen Gibson Hunter '86

GRILL-SIDE GARDEN SALAD

2 medium tomatoes, seeded
  and chopped (about 2
  cups)
1 medium zucchini, diced
1 cup frozen whole kernel
  corn, thawed
⅓ cup thinly-sliced green
  onions, with tops
1 small avocado, chopped

⅓ cup picante sauce
2 tablespoons vegetable oil
2 tablespoons chopped fresh
  cilantro
1 tablespoon lime or lemon
  juice
¾ teaspoon garlic salt
¼ teaspoon ground cumin

Combine first 5 ingredients in large bowl. Combine remaining ingredients; mix well. Pour over vegetables, and mix. Chill 3 to 4 hours. **Yield:** 8 servings

Hint: *One cup cooked fresh corn or one (8¾-ounce) can whole kernel corn, drained, may be substituted.*

Kay Deaton Gentsch '78

FAR EAST SALAD DELIGHT

"Noodles add a nice little crunch"

½ head cabbage, chopped
2 tablespoons sesame seeds
½ cup slivered almonds,
  toasted
4 green onions, chopped,
  including tops
1 (3-ounce) package ramen
  noodles, broken

3 tablespoons rice vinegar
½ cup oil
2 teaspoons sugar
¼ teaspoon salt
¼ teaspoon pepper
½ of ramen seasoning
  package

Combine first 4 ingredients. Break ramen noodles into bite-size pieces, and set aside. Mix rice vinegar, oil and seasonings until well blended. Just before serving, add ramen noodles and dressing, and toss. **Yield:** 4 to 5 servings

Note: *Add chopped chicken, ham or shrimp to make a complete meal.*

Donell Teaff
Wife of Grant Teaff, former Baylor head football coach
and athletic director

BACON CURRY COLESLAW

½ cup mayonnaise
1 tablespoon white vinegar
1 teaspoon sugar
½ teaspoon curry
3 cups shredded cabbage
½ cup white raisins

3 tablespoon diced green
  onions
6 slices bacon, fried and
  crumbled
½ cup salted peanuts

Combine mayonnaise, vinegar, sugar, and curry; chill at least 1 hour or overnight. Combine next 4 ingredients, and chill several hours. Just before serving, add peanuts. Toss with chilled dressing. **Yield:** 10 servings

Sue Dickson Davis '52

KANSAS COLESLAW
"Very easy—very good."

1½ pounds cabbage,
  shredded
1 teaspoon salt
⅔ cup sugar

⅓ cup cider vinegar
1 cup whipping cream,
  unwhipped

Shred cabbage; cover, and refrigerate. Thirty minutes before time to serve, mix ingredients in order given. Return coleslaw to refrigerator until ready to serve. **Yield:** 6 to 8 servings

Note: *Small amounts of shredded red cabbage and grated carrots may be added for color.*

Karen McNeely Zecy '79

EXOTIC GINGER-LIME FRUIT SALAD
"A beautiful salad—light and tangy"

2 pints strawberries, hulled
  and halved
2 cups fresh pineapple
  chunks
4 kiwifruit, peeled and
  sliced

4 seedless oranges, peeled
  and sliced
1 starfruit, sliced, optional
⅓ cup fresh lime juice
2 tablespoons honey
1 tablespoon crystallized
  ginger, minced

In large glass bowl, combine 5 fruits. In a small bowl, combine lime juice, honey and ginger; pour over fruit. Toss gently. Cover with plastic wrap, and refrigerate until chilled, 2 hours or overnight. **Yield:** 10 to 12 servings

Note: *1 (20-ounce) can pineapple chunks, drained, can be substituted for the fresh pineapple.*

Katherine Ann Ragan '65

DONALITA'S OVERNIGHT SALAD

4 egg yolks
¼ teaspoon prepared
  mustard
Juice of 2 lemons
2 cups whipping cream,
  whipped

1 cup chopped nuts
1 (20-ounce) can pineapple
  chunks, drained
30 cubed marshmallows or 1
  (10½-ounce) package
  miniature marshmallows

Cook egg yolks, mustard, and lemon juice in top of double boiler over hot water until thick. Cool. Add remaining ingredients, mixing carefully. Refrigerate overnight. **Yield:** 10 to 12 servings

Donalita Grantham Adkins '41

TWICE-AS-PEACHY SALAD MOLD

1 (29-ounce) jar spiced
  peaches
1 (16-ounce) can sliced
  peaches

1 (3-ounce) package lemon-
  flavored gelatin
½ package unflavored
  gelatin

Drain juice from both containers of peaches into a 2-cup measure. Add water to make 2 cups. Pour into a medium saucepan, and heat over medium heat. Dissolve lemon-flavored gelatin in hot juice, stirring well. Soften unflavored gelatin in ¼ cup cold water. Stir into lemon gelatin. Chill until it begins to thicken. Cut spiced peaches into chunks, and cut sliced peaches in half. Stir peaches into gelatin, and pour into mold. Chill overnight. **Yield:** 8 to 10 servings

Note: *Works equally well as a warm weather salad or with Thanksgiving turkey and dressing.*

Celeste Sauls '90

⏱ LIME-APPLESAUCE SALAD

"Very easy, quick, and good"

1 (3-ounce) package lime-
    flavored gelatin
1 cup applesauce

1 (8-ounce) bottle lemon-
    lime carbonated drink

Heat applesauce in medium saucepan. Add gelatin to hot applesauce; stir until dissolved. Add lemon-lime drink. Chill until thickened slightly. Pour into an 8-inch square glass dish or into small
molds. Chill until set. Cut into squares or unmold. Serve on lettuce leaves with a favorite salad dressing. **Yield:** 6 servings

Debbie Russell Hembree '74

RETHA'S UNDER-THE-SEA SALAD

From the personal files of the late Miss Retha Sanders, Baylor
Home Economics professor

8 ounces marshmallows
2 (3-ounce) packages cream
    cheese
1 (3-ounce) package orange-
    flavored gelatin
2 to 3 tablespoons
    mayonnaise

1 (8-ounce) can crushed
    pineapple, undrained
1 cup whipping cream,
    whipped
1 (3-ounce) package lime-
    flavored gelatin

Melt marshmallows, cream cheese, and dry orange-flavored gelatin in top of a double boiler. Let cool. Add mayonnaise, pineapple, and whipped cream. Pour into 9x13-inch pan, and refrigerate until set.

Prepare lime-flavored gelatin as directed on package. Cool
completely; pour over congealed orange gelatin mixture. **Yield:**
12 to 15 servings

Hint: *Substitute strawberry-flavored gelatin for the orange at*
Christmas for a holiday touch.

Joyce Hornaday Packard '52

RED AND GREEN CHRISTMAS SALAD

1 (3-ounce) package
   raspberry-gelatin
1 (10-ounce) package frozen
   raspberries, thawed
1 cup half-and-half
½ cup sugar
1 envelope unflavored
   gelatin

1 cup sour cream
1 teaspoon vanilla
1 (3-ounce) package lime-
   flavored gelatin
1 (8-ounce) can crushed
   pineapple
2 tablespoons sour cream
1 banana, sliced

Dissolve raspberry-flavored gelatin in 1 cup boiling water. Drain juice from raspberries into a measuring cup. Add enough water to make ¾ cup. Add to gelatin. Stir in raspberries. Pour into a deep mold, and refrigerate until congealed.

Heat half-and-half and sugar, but do not boil. Dissolve unflavored gelatin in ¼ cup cold water. Stir into warm cream. When cool, add 1 cup sour cream and vanilla; beat well. Pour over congealed raspberry layer, and refrigerate until set.

Dissolve lime-flavored gelatin in 1 cup boiling water. Drain pineapple well into a measuring cup. Add this scant ¾ cup juice to gelatin. Beat in 2 tablespoons sour cream. Add pineapple and sliced banana. Pour into mold and refrigerate. Unmold just before serving. **Yield**: 12 to 15 servings

Mary Elizabeth Plummer Wimpee '75

RAZZ-A-MA-TAZZ JELLED SALAD
"Our holiday classic"

1 (6-ounce) package
   raspberry-flavored gelatin
2 cups hot water
1 (15-ounce) can crushed
   pineapple

1 (14-ounce) container cran-
   orange relish
1 cup chopped pecans

Mix gelatin with hot water in a large mixing bowl, stirring until dissolved. Drain juice from pineapple into a large measuring cup; add enough water to make 2 cups. Add juice, pineapple, and relish to gelatin. Refrigerate until mixture has thickened to a syrupy consistency. Add nuts, and pour into a mold or individual molds. Chill until set. **Yield:** 12 servings

Note: *Cran-orange relish may be a seasonal item in your store and not available all year.*

Dixie Cavitt Soong '82

CRANBERRY SUPREME SALAD
"Use a clear glass or crystal bowl for a lovely presentation."

4 cups fresh cranberries
1½ cups sugar
2 cups seedless red grapes,
   halved

½ cup chopped pecans
1 cup whipping cream

Finely chop cranberries in blender or food processor. Combine cranberries and sugar. Place in a colander over a bowl; refrigerate overnight to drain. Combine grapes, nuts and well-drained cranberry mixture. Whip cream until very stiff; fold into cranberry mixture. Refrigerate until ready to serve. **Yield:** 8 to 10 servings

Note: *Save cranberry juice, and mix with ginger ale for a festive holiday drink.*

Karen Kernodle Martin '82

BESSIE MAE'S FRESH CRANBERRY SALAD

Editor's note: The late Bessie Mae Lynn was the wife of Dr. Ralph Lynn, retired Baylor history professor.

1 (3-ounce) package
  strawberry-flavored
  gelatin
1 cup boiling water
1 cup sugar
1½ cup coarsely chopped
  cranberries

1 (8-ounce) can crushed
  pineapple, drained
1 (10-ounce) package frozen
  strawberries, thawed and
  drained
¾ cup nuts, chopped

Mix gelatin in boiling water. Add sugar, and stir until dissolved. Cool, and add chopped cranberries. Set aside for 15 to 20 minutes. Add remaining ingredients. Pour into ring mold. **Yield:** 1 ring mold

Note: *May double recipe and mold in a bundt pan.*

Submitted by Edna SoRelle White "at the request of Ann Miller and other friends"

LORRAINE'S FESTIVE CRANBERRY SALAD
"A beautiful salad, and full of goodies"

1 (6-ounce) package cherry-flavored gelatin	1 large orange, peeled
2 cups boiling water	½ cup chopped celery
1 (10-ounce) package fresh cranberries	1 cup chopped apples, unpeeled
2 to 4 tablespoons sugar	1 cup chopped pecans
	1 cup white grapes, halved

Dissolve gelatin in boiling water in a large mixing bowl, stirring thoroughly. Refrigerate until gelatin has cooled and begun to thicken.

In a food processor, chop cranberries coarsely. Sprinkle cranberries with sugar, 2 tablespoons for tart salad, 4 tablespoons if a sweeter salad is preferred. Stir into gelatin. Slice orange crosswise into ½-inch thick slices; chop slices coarsely. Add orange and any juice to gelatin. Stir in celery, apples, pecans, and grapes. Combine thoroughly. Pour into 9x13-inch dish or a glass or crystal bowl. Chill until set. **Yield**: 12 servings

Hint: *Use kitchen shears or scissors to cut grapes in half.*

Judy Taylor '68

SURPRISE PRETZEL SALAD

From our testers: "This is a winner! Could easily be a light dessert."

2 cups pretzels, coarsely
  crushed
3 tablespoons sugar
¾ cup margarine, melted
1 (8-ounce) package cream
  cheese, softened
1 cup sugar

2 cups frozen whipped
  topping, thawed
2 (3-ounce) packages
  strawberry-flavored
  gelatin
2 cups boiling water
2 (10-ounce) packages
  frozen strawberries

Combine pretzels, sugar, and margarine. Pat into 9x13-inch pan. Bake at 400° for 8 to 10 minutes. Do not overbake. Cool. Combine cream cheese and sugar. Fold in whipped topping. Spread over cooled crust. Dissolve gelatin in boiling water. Stir in frozen strawberries. Refrigerate for 10 minutes. Pour over cream cheese mixture. Keep refrigerated. **Yield:** 12 servings

Darlene Winkelmann Gorham '72

Did you know Baylor women made AP national coverage in the 1950s with a dining hall food strike? Seems we were tired of being served the "same old thing," and the brave seniors orchestrated a plan. Everyone on campus vacated the dining halls for one meal in protest. All that food, and no one showed up to eat it! Little did we realize that years later we strikers would be on the side of the "establishment" while our own children complained of the "same old thing" for dinner!

Anonymous member of the Class of 1958

FROZEN BUTTERMILK SALAD

"No one will ever guess that it's made with buttermilk! Tastes like dessert!"

1 cup buttermilk	1 (8-ounce) carton frozen
1 cup sugar	whipped topping, thawed
½ teaspoon vanilla	1 cup chopped pecans
1 (8-ounce) can crushed	5 maraschino cherries,
pineapple	halved
4 medium bananas, sliced	

Combine buttermilk, sugar and vanilla in large mixing bowl; stir until sugar is dissolved. Drain pineapple, saving juice in a small bowl. Carefully stir sliced bananas into juice, coating thoroughly. Using a slotted spoon, drain banana slices. Add to buttermilk mixture. Add pineapple, whipped topping and pecans. Mix well. Pour into a 9-inch square pan. Freeze overnight. Thaw about 15 to 20 minutes before slicing. Serve on lettuce leaf and garnish with a cherry half. **Yield:** 9 servings.

Note: *Must be made ahead.*

Ginny Sims Griffith '65

FROZEN CHRISTMAS SALAD

"Distinct flavor of each fruit"

1 (8-ounce) package cream	2 large bananas, diced
cheese, softened	1 (10-ounce) package frozen
¾ cup sugar	strawberries, thawed
1 (15½-ounce) can pineapple	1 (12-ounce) carton frozen
tidbits, drained	whipped topping, thawed

Blend cream cheese and sugar. Add remaining ingredients. Spoon into a 9 x11-inch casserole dish or into individual molds; freeze. Remove from freezer 10 to 15 minutes before cutting into squares or unmolding. Serve on lettuce leaves. **Yield:** 6 to 8 servings

Note: *Can be multiplied for a holiday gathering of 60 as easily as 6.*

Debra Dobbins Burleson '79

FROZEN BANANA-CRANBERRY SALAD

"Made by four generations of our family"

2 large or 3 small bananas, mashed
1 (16-ounce) can whole cranberry sauce
1 (8-ounce) can crushed pineapple, drained

½ cup mayonnaise, optional
½ cup chopped nuts, optional
1 (8-ounce) carton frozen whipped topping, thawed

Combine bananas, cranberry sauce, and pineapple. Stir in remaining ingredients. Spoon into a mold, loaf pan, or individual paper-lined muffin tins. Freeze. **Yield:** 12 muffin-tin servings

 Note: *For a reduced-fat version, omit mayonnaise and nuts, and use light whipped topping.*

Lynda Miller Southwick '65

 ## FROZEN HEART'S DELIGHT SALAD

1 (16-ounce) can pitted black sweet cherries, drained
1 (10-ounce) can mandarin oranges, drained
1 (8-ounce) can crushed pineapple, drained

¾ cup chopped pecans
1 (8-ounce) carton sour cream
1 (8-ounce) package cream cheese, softened
½ cup sugar

Combine cherries, oranges, pineapple and pecans. In the blender mix sour cream, cream cheese and sugar. Add to fruit mixture. Pour into mold or individual molds; cover and freeze. **Yield:** 8 to 10 servings

 Note: *Almost fat-free, if you use reduced-fat ingredients.*

Donell Teaff
Wife of Grant Teaff, former Baylor head football coach
and athletic director

THE ELITE'S DRESSING

"This is the original Elite Dressing, served at the Elite Cafe on the Circle in Waco. The dressing was in syrup pitchers on each table along with a basket of saltines. We nibbled crackers and dressing while waiting for our burgers or fried shrimp. We must have eaten gallons." Editor's note: The current management of the Elite says this tradition is still popular.

1 cup mayonnaise-style
  salad dressing
2 egg yolks
1 tablespoon Worcestershire
  sauce
1 tablespoon tarragon
  vinegar

1 tablespoon sugar
2 cups salad oil, divided
1 teaspoon salt
1 teaspoon pepper
1 teaspoon paprika
Juice of 1 large lemon
1 sliced garlic bud

Beat salad dressing. Add egg yolks, Worcestershire sauce, vinegar and sugar; beat well. Slowly add 1 cup of oil. Add salt, pepper, paprika, lemon juice. Add remaining cup of oil. Beat until thick. Add garlic. Leave garlic in dressing as long as desired. **Yield:** About 3½ cups

Submitted by Doris Hollingsworth Gage '47

MY MOTHER-IN-LAW'S MAYONNAISE

"You may never buy mayonnaise again."

2 egg yolks	1 teaspoon salt
2 teaspoons red wine vinegar	4 to 5 dashes hot pepper sauce
2 teaspoons Dijon mustard	Juice of ½ a lemon
1½ cups salad oil	

Using a food processor or blender, mix yolks with vinegar and mustard. Slowly pour in oil. (It will thicken as oil is beaten in.) Add salt, pepper sauce, and lemon juice. Flick blender off and on a few times until thick. Must be refrigerated. **Yield:** Approximately 2 cups

Hint: *Try this on thick, fresh tomato slices in the summertime. Adding chopped fresh basil is a good addition.*

Jo Sparks Salmon '76

HOT MUSTARD

"A blue ribbon winner at the Teton County Fair, Jackson, Wyoming."

2 cups Coleman's dry mustard	4 eggs, beaten
2 cups white vinegar	2 cups sugar
	Dash of salt

Soak dry mustard in vinegar overnight. Beat eggs, sugar, and salt together; add to vinegar mixture. In top of a double boiler, cook over low heat for approximately 15 to 18 minutes, or until mixture resembles a custard. Pour immediately into jars and seal. Mustard will keep in refrigerator indefinitely. **Yield:** 2 pints

Hint: *Pour into 4-ounce jars and give as a small "neighbor" gift.*

Gretchen Peterson Thomas '45

CALIENTE DRESSING

¼ cup oil
2 tablespoons tarragon
   vinegar

2 tablespoons sugar
½ teaspoon salt
1 teaspoon hot pepper sauce

Combine ingredients, mixing well. Drizzle over fresh greens.
Yield: About ½ cup

*Hint: Red-tipped lettuce, mandarin oranges, and toasted pecans
are especially good tossed with this dressing.*

Gary David Willson
Husband of Andrea Wilkes Willson '91

HONEY POPPY SEED DRESSING

⅔ cup sugar
1 teaspoon dry mustard
1 teaspoon paprika
½ teaspoon salt
⅓ cup honey
3 tablespoons lemon juice

3 tablespoons white wine
   vinegar
2 teaspoons grated onion
1 cup vegetable oil
1 tablespoon poppy seed

Mix first 4 ingredients in container of electric blender. Add honey,
lemon juice, vinegar, and onion, and blend well. With blender
running, slowly add oil. Stir in poppy seed. Store in refrigerator
in a jar with a tight lid. Will keep at least a week. **Yield**: 1 pint

Hint: Wonderful over fresh melon balls.

The Cookbook Committee

Main Dishes

*D*uring my high school days, the local hot spot was the A&W Root Beer stand. It was a kind of place where you'd pull up in your car and they would come out and put a tray on the window. We would go there just to sit and talk and hang out.

My girlfriends and I liked to go there to stare at the boys, and we'd try to come up with real sophisticated schemes for starting conversations with the ones we thought were cute.

It's remarkable how exciting a root beer stand can be when a group of girls start conniving, and I imagine we looked pretty silly most of the time.

I also remember one of my first dates was at the Elite Cafe. I thought that going to the Elite Cafe on a date was a big deal. It was one of the few restaurants that stayed open late, and everybody would go there and have a cup of coffee and a piece of pie before they went home. I still remember that I ordered a platter of fried shrimp. I think I knew enough not to eat the tails, but I'm not entirely sure.

You have to understand that until that date, I had probably been into a restaurant about a half dozen times in my life. The few times my father and mother and I went out to eat, we went to Charlie Lugo's Cafe and my Daddy would order a dozen tamales with chili poured all over them. We would all have tamales, which was a tasty and inexpensive dinner.

I think the only other times I went out to eat would have been at lunch in high school, when we would leave the campus and sit at a counter. You wouldn't be caught dead carrying your lunch in high school. I was a senior and I had to keep up appearances.

Most of all, I think those special meals and special times in Waco remind me of my family and friends who shared such good times together. No matter how long I'm away, when I'm sitting in those familiar restaurants or eating my favorite meals, it always reminds me how good it is to be back home.

The Honorable Ann Willis Richards '54
Governor, State of Texas

⏱ TEMPTING TENDERLOIN

1 (8-pound) tenderloin
4 ounces Kitchen Bouquet
8 ounces Italian salad
    dressing

2 cups herb-seasoned
    stuffing mix

Trim any fat from meat; liberally brush all sides with Kitchen Bouquet and Italian dressing. Roll loin in stuffing crumbs, pressing as much as possible onto the meat's surface. Place meat in roasting pan that has been lined with foil. Spoon remaining stuffing over and around meat. Place in cold oven and roast at 400° for 30 to 35 minutes. Let tenderloin rest 5 minutes before slicing. Cut into ¾-inch slices, diagonally across meat. Serve 2 to 3 slices per person with a spoonful of stuffing. **Yield**: 8 servings

Jan Reedy, PhD '94
Wife of Chuck Reedy, Baylor head football coach

"If you accept a dinner invitation, you have a moral obligation to be amusing."

The Duchess of Windsor

SAVORY EYE OF ROUND ROAST

"As this turned on the rotisserie, the kitchen never smelled better!"

¾ cup soy sauce
¼ cup Worcestershire sauce
2 tablespoons dry mustard
1 teaspoon salt
1 tablespoon black pepper
½ cup wine vinegar

2 garlic cloves, crushed
⅓ cup lemon juice
1 teaspoon oregano,
  crumbled
1½ cups salad oil
1 5-pound eye of round roast

Combine first 9 ingredients in a blender. Very slowly add salad oil, a tablespoon at a time, with blender running on medium speed. (This slow addition of oil makes a thick marinade that can be spread on the roast.)

Spread marinade over all sides of roast. Place roast and any extra marinade in a zip-lock bag, refrigerate, and marinate for at least 6 to 8 hours, or overnight if possible. Turn bag several times while marinating.

Put roast on rotisserie; pour marinade into rotisserie drip pan. Cook roast to medium rare. Let roast rest 15 minutes before slicing; serve with marinade as a gravy. **Yield**: 6 to 8 servings

Note: *May be cooked, covered with foil, in the oven at 300° for 2 hours; then 30 minutes uncovered at 350° to brown.*

Patricia Inman Halsell '57

VEAL SENTINO
"An elegant company dinner"

8 asparagus spears
4 scaloppine veal, pounded
Salt and pepper to taste
¼ cup flour
7 tablespoons butter,
    divided

¼ pound mushrooms (about
    2 cups sliced)
4 thin slices Swiss cheese
Juice of 1 lemon

Clean asparagus and cook in boiling water 2 or 3 minutes until crisp-tender. Drain, and set aside. Sprinkle veal with salt and pepper, and dredge in flour. In large skillet, brown veal in 2 tablespoons butter until golden, about 2 minutes. Remove from skillet. Melt remaining 5 tablespoons butter in same skillet, and sauté mushrooms until brown. Arrange veal in single layer in 7x11-inch baking dish. Top with sautéed mushrooms. Arrange 2 asparagus spears on each slice of veal, and cover with cheese slice. Broil in hot broiler just until cheese melts. Remove to warm plates. Mix lemon juice with melted butter left in skillet from cooking mushrooms. Pour sauce over veal. **Yield**: 4 servings

Hint: *Serve with buttered noodles, grilled tomatoes, and a green vegetable.*

Martha Durr Lemon '59, MSEd '69

SAVAGE STIR-FRY STEAK

½ cup soy sauce
3 tablespoons minced onion
1 garlic clove, minced
2 tablespoons sugar
¼ teaspoon ground ginger

¼ cup dry white wine
2 to 2½ pounds sirloin steak,
   thinly sliced
1 tablespoon vegetable oil

Combine first 6 ingredients, and mix well. Pour marinade over meat and cover. Let stand for 2 hours or overnight in the refrigerator. Drain marinade. Pour oil in wok, and heat on medium-high heat. Place ½ of steak in wok and stir-fry for 3 minutes or until tender. Push meat up the sides of wok, and stir-fry remaining steak. Reduce heat to low and serve from wok. Serve with rice, snow peas, and a mandarin orange salad. **Yield**: 4 to 5 servings

Hint: *A wonderful marinade for rib-eye or T-bone steaks to be cooked on the grill.*

Paige McCann Savage '88

5-HOUR STEW

2 pounds stew meat, cut into
   bite-size pieces
5 carrots, sliced
1 onion, cut into small
   wedges
2 to 3 ribs celery, sliced
2 large potatoes, peeled and
   cut into pieces

1 green pepper, cut into
   strips
1 (16-ounce) can tomatoes
1 tablespoon sugar
1 tablespoon salt
3 tablespoons minute
   tapioca or corn starch

Combine meat with vegetables, seasonings, and tapioca in a Dutch oven with a tight lid. Cover and bake at 250° for 5 hours. Do not peek! **Yield**: 8 to 10 servings

Note: *Can be prepared in crockpot and cooked on low all day.*

Denna Johnson
Wife of Darrel Johnson, Baylor head basketball coach

NO-PEEP DINNER

2 pounds lean boneless stew
  meat, cut in bite-size
  pieces
1 (10¾-ounce) can mushroom
  soup
1 (4-ounce) can mushroom
  stems and pieces

Pepper to taste
¼ cup water
1 (1-ounce) envelope dry
  onion soup mix
½ cup red wine

Place stew meat in 2½-quart casserole. Combine soup, mushrooms, and pepper; use no salt. Pour over meat. Add remaining ingredients. Cover and bake at 325° for 3 hours. Do not "peep" while cooking. Serve over rice or noodles. **Yield**: 8 servings

Note: *This recipe is a great one for busy cooks because it can be left on "time bake" in the oven, or set the crockpot on low and cook it all day.*

Betty Beniteau Bell '59

Bill and I were both missionary kids (MK's). He grew up in Buenos Aires, and I spent my childhood in Brazil. When we came to Baylor as students, we enjoyed the kindness of many people who had us into their homes.

During the mid-1970s, when the first of our many nephews and nieces started coming to Baylor (at one point there were nine of them here), we decided that a good way for all of us to get to know each other would be to feed them (and their friends) once a week, so we began our tradition of "Thursday nighters," a time to include international students, other missionary kids, and our own friends and family members.

Every Thursday night for many years we made supper and waited to see who came. Sometimes there were a dozen there, sometimes more than twenty. Conversation—often a mixture of several languages— and laughter filled our house each Thursday night, and memories of those occasions continue to enrich our lives.

Thelma Smith Cooper '57, MM '59
Baylor School of Music

TEX'S JERKY

Jerky can be made of almost any meat, from beef to venison to pork. Slice meat with the grain into ⅛-inch thick strips about 1 inch wide. For health precautions, if wild meat or wild pork is used, boil raw meat slices just long enough to remove the red color. Select lean meat, the leaner the better; no marbling is ideal. Remove all fat and gristle.

For each pound of meat (after trimming) use:
Salt 1 large handful (1 heaping tablespoon)
Black pepper ½ handful (¾ tablespoon)
Chili powder ½ handful (¾ tablespoon)
Garlic powder ¼ handful (1 rounded teaspoon)
Onion powder ¼ handful (1 rounded teaspoon)
Cayenne pepper to taste (Be careful)
Liquid smoke ⅓ ounce (3 dashes or to taste)

Place meat slices in shallow glass baking dishes. Dissolve in water, and add enough water to just cover meat. Marinate overnight (more won't hurt). Drain marinated meat well. Dry in the sun if climate permits, or in a very low (250°) oven with the door ajar. Dry until strips are black and crack when bent, but don't break. If dried in the sun, spread cheesecloth over meat to screen from insects. It should be either brought in or covered at night to keep the meat dry. If dried in the oven, place strips on oven racks, not touching. Put a drip pan below.

Note: *Properly cured jerky will keep in sealed plastic bags or jars for at least a year.*

Phil Barclay '57

"You've got two choices for dinner: take it or leave it."

A quote seen in a modern kitchen

SOUTH TEXAS BEEF FAJITAS
"A real Texas winner."

1 (1½-pound) beef skirt or
round steak
¼ to ½ cup fresh lime juice
¼ cup tequila, optional
3 to 4 cloves garlic, finely
minced
1 teaspoon salt
½ teaspoon freshly-ground
black pepper
1 small onion, thinly sliced
into rings

1 tablespoon vegetable oil
1 green pepper, cut into
strips
12 flour tortillas, warmed
Guacamole
Pico de gallo or picante
sauce
Shredded Cheddar cheese
Sour cream

Cut beef into 4 pieces. Put in plastic zip-lock bag with lime juice, tequila, garlic, salt and pepper. Close bag securely, and marinate in refrigerator for 2 to 3 hours or overnight.

In heavy, cast-iron skillet, sauté onion in oil for 2 minutes. Add green pepper, and cook for 2 more minutes or until vegetables are crisp-tender.

Drain marinade from meat, saving some to use as basting sauce. Broil steak over coals (mesquite to be authentic), basting several times with reserved marinade while grilling, or fry in heavy, cast-iron skillet over medium-high heat. Cook for 3 to 4 minutes per side. Carve into thin slices across grain. Quickly stir beef and vegetables together in skillet, and cook for 1 to 2 minutes or until heated through. Fill warmed tortillas with beef and vegetables. Add any or all of last 4 ingredients. **Yield**: 4 servings

Hint: *Add ¼ teaspoon rosemary, 1 teaspoon oregano, ¼ teaspoon thyme, and 1 chopped green onion to marinade for a change of flavor.*

Carol Watson Barclay '60

EL PASO SMOKED BRISKET

5 to 6 pounds boneless brisket	¾ cup liquid smoke
1 teaspoon salt	1 cup ketchup
½ teaspoon pepper	3 tablespoons brown sugar
½ teaspoon garlic powder	2 tablespoons
⅛ teaspoon paprika	Worcestershire sauce
	4 dashes hot pepper sauce

Trim brisket, and place on large piece of heavy foil. Mix remaining ingredients in a medium-size bowl. Spread ½ of seasoning mixture on all sides of meat. Fold foil tightly around brisket. Bake on a cookie sheet at 250° for 5 or 6 hours. Carefully remove from foil. Let meat rest about 20 minutes before slicing. Heat remaining ½ of sauce to serve with brisket. **Yield**: 12 servings

Holly Beth Ford '81

 ## MOCK FILETS
" A real family favorite"

1 pound ground beef	¼ cup lemon juice
1 cup cracker crumbs	1 teaspoon seasoned salt
1 egg, beaten	¼ teaspoon pepper
⅓ cup ketchup	Bacon slices

Combine all ingredients except bacon; mix well and shape into patties. Wrap a bacon strip around each patty, and secure with wooden pick. Place on broiler pan. Bake at 375° for 20 minutes. **Yield**: 6 to 8 servings

Hint: *Take these frozen and before baking to friends with new babies or to friends who are home from the hospital or who have just moved. It's nice for them because it's not a casserole!*

Marilyn Wyrick Ingram '72

DR PEPPER MEAT LOAF
"This is a Baylor must!"

1½ pound ground beef (or
    ground turkey)
2 eggs
1½ cups breadcrumbs
2 (8-ounce) cans tomato
    sauce, divided
1 tablespoon instant onion
    flakes
1 teaspoon onion salt

½ teaspoon salt
⅛ teaspoon black pepper
⅔ cup barbecue sauce
1 tablespoon Worcestershire
    sauce
1½ tablespoons prepared
    mustard
⅓ cup brown sugar
¼ cup Dr Pepper

Thoroughly mix ground beef, eggs, breadcrumbs, and 1 can of
tomato sauce. Add onion flakes, onion salt, salt, and pepper. Form
into loaf shape and place in large, deep 3-quart casserole dish.
Mix second can of tomato sauce, barbecue sauce, Worcestershire
sauce, mustard, brown sugar, and Dr Pepper (for that special
Baylor flavor). Cover meat loaf with ½ of sauce. Bake, covered, at
350° for 20 minutes. Remove from oven and pour remaining sauce
over meat loaf. Continue to bake, uncovered, for 45 minutes or
until done. **Yield**: 6 to 8 servings

Charles (Chuck) Hicks '77

*Waco is the "home of Dr Pepper," since the soft drink was invented
in the 1880s at the Old Corner Drug Store, not too far from the
Baylor campus. Baylor folks have always had a special fondness for
the beverage. It's even a favorite of the bear cub mascots, who like
nothing better than to sit back on their haunches and polish off a
bottle of Dr Pepper. (One year they tried to get him to drink 7-Up,
but it gave him a stomach ache.)*

*As a Baylor student, I never dreamed that I would one day be the
curator of the Dr Pepper Museum, which is now housed in the old
bottling plant, built in 1906 at the corner of 5th and Mary Streets.*

Millie Gholson Walker '58

AMERICAN MEAT LOAF
"Different and good"

1 pound ground beef
1 egg
1 cup crushed cheese-
  flavored snack crackers
1 bottle chili sauce, divided

3 tablespoons dried onion
  soup mix
1 tablespoon Worcestershire
  sauce
1 teaspoon garlic powder
1 teaspoon black pepper

Mix meat, egg, crackers, ½ cup of chili sauce, onion soup, Worcestershire sauce, and garlic powder. Form into a loaf in a casserole dish. Top with remaining chili sauce. Bake at 400° for 50 to 60 minutes. Remove from oven, and sprinkle with black pepper while still hot. **Yield**: 4 to 6 servings

Hint: For a southwest version, substitute seasoned corn chips for crackers and picante sauce for chili sauce. Add 1 cup grated sharp Cheddar cheese. Serve with sour cream.

Madelyn Jones, Baylor Registrar

TEXAS STYLE BURRITOS
"My children loved this."

2 pounds ground meat
1 small onion, chopped
1 (15-ounce) can ranch-style
  beans, mashed
2 (8-ounce) cans tomato
  sauce
1 tablespoon chili powder
1 teaspoon garlic powder
1 teaspoon salt

Pepper to taste
2 (4-ounce) cans chopped
  green chiles
2 to 3 dozen flour tortillas
1½ cups grated Cheddar
  cheese
1½ cups grated Monterey
  Jack cheese

Brown meat and onion in a large skillet. Drain well. Add next 7 ingredients, and simmer for 20 to 30 minutes. Spoon mixture into tortillas, top with Cheddar cheese and roll up. Place seam-side down in a large greased baking dish or 2 9x13-inch baking dishes. Spoon remaining meat over top of burritos. Top with Monterey Jack cheese. Cover dish tightly with foil. Bake at 350° for 10 to 15 minutes. **Yield**: 12 to 15 servings

Ellen Dawne Cleveland '92

🕐 SANTE FE GREEN CHILE SAUCE

"A once-a-week standard in my home."

2 (13-ounce) containers
  frozen green chiles or
  7 (4-ounce) cans chopped
  green chiles
3 to 5 small garlic cloves,
  crushed

½ teaspoon dried oregano
½ teaspoon pepper
1 cube chicken bouillon,
  optional
½ cup water

Combine ingredients and simmer until hot, about 15 to 20 minutes. **Yield**: 2 to 4 servings

Hint: *Great over chicken, cheese, or bean burritos and enchiladas. Especially delicious with Monterey Jack cheese. Or stir in melted pasteurized process cheese for a dip to serve with fresh vegetables or chips.*

Cheryl Schellinger Nace '83

🕐 MEXICAN CORN BREAD CASSEROLE

1 cup cornmeal
1 cup milk
2 eggs, well beaten
½ teaspoon baking soda
¾ teaspoon salt
1 (16-ounce) can cream-style
  corn

1 onion, chopped
1 pound ground beef
1 to 2 jalapeño peppers,
  chopped
2 cups grated Cheddar
  cheese

Mix first 6 ingredients and set aside. Brown onion with ground beef until meat is done. Add jalapeños and cheese. Pour ½ of batter into a shallow greased 2-quart casserole dish. Add meat mixture. Cover with remaining batter. Bake at 350° for 45 minutes. **Yield**: 4 to 6 servings

Brenda McDougal Ramey
Employee, Baylor Alumni Association and Baylor mom

FIESTA BY DESIGN

A favorite from our first cookbook, Flavor Favorites, *and still a winner with our testers now!*

2 (12-ounce) packages corn chips, crushed
1 (14-ounce) box instant rice, cooked according to directions
Meat Sauce
1 pound sharp Cheddar cheese, grated
2 heads lettuce, chopped

7 medium tomatoes, chopped
3 medium onions, chopped
1 (6-ounce) jar sliced green olives
1 cup pecans, chopped
1 (7-ounce) package coconut
1 (24-ounce) jar picante sauce

Place each ingredient in a bowl or plate. Arrange on buffet table in order listed. Let each person "design" his own "fiesta" plate, beginning with crushed corn chips as a base. **Yield**: 20 servings

Meat Sauce:
4 pounds ground beef
3 onions, chopped
1 (28-ounce) can whole, peeled tomatoes
1 (16-ounce) can tomato sauce
2 (1-pound) cans tomato puree

2 to 3 tablespoons chili powder
1 to 2 tablespoons powdered garlic
4 teaspoons salt
1 (46-ounce) can ranch-style beans
Cumin powder, optional

Brown meat and onions in large Dutch oven; drain excess fat. Add remaining ingredients, and simmer 1 hour. (Add a little water if sauce gets too thick.)

Hint: *Sour cream, chopped avocados, sliced ripe olives, chili sauce or other favorite condiments may be offered. Meat sauce can be prepared the day before.*

Judy Allen Mitchell '43

MOUSSAKA

Editor's note: Nick's Restaurant has long been a favorite gathering spot for Baylorites—from romantic young coeds to dyed-in-the-wool sports fans. This recipe is one of Nick's specialties.

3 medium eggplants,
   unpeeled, and thickly
   sliced
Butter for frying
4 tablespoons butter
2 pounds ground beef
3 large onions, chopped fine
3 tablespoons tomato paste
½ cup red wine

3 tablespoons chopped
   parsley
¼ teaspoon cinnamon
Salt and pepper
2 eggs, slightly beaten
¾ cup fine, dry breadcrumbs
1 cup freshly-grated
   Parmesan cheese
White Sauce

Fry eggplant slices quickly in butter on each side until light brown. Heat 4 tablespoons butter in large skillet, and sauté meat until brown. Add onions, and cook for 10 minutes longer. Mix tomato paste with wine. Add tomato paste, parsley, cinnamon, salt and pepper. Simmer over low heat, stirring frequently until all liquid has been absorbed. Remove from heat; when cool, mix in the eggs.

Assemble casserole in a buttered 9x13x2-inch baking dish or oblong roasting pan. Sprinkle ¼ cup of breadcrumbs over bottom of dish. Combine remaining ½ cup breadcrumbs with Parmesan cheese. Layer dish with ½ of eggplant, ½ of White Sauce, ½ of cheese, and all of meat sauce. Repeat layering in the same order, ending with cheese. (The White Sauce forms a "crust" on top of Moussaka.) Bake at 375° for 1 hour or until top is golden. Allow to set for 10 minutes before serving. Cut in squares. **Yield**: 8 servings

White Sauce:
4 tablespoons butter
6 tablespoons flour
2 cups hot rich milk

2 egg yolks, well beaten
½ teaspoon salt
Dash of nutmeg

For white sauce, melt butter and blend in flour, stirring steadily. When mixture begins to bubble, add milk slowly, stirring constantly. Continue cooking over low heat until smooth and thickened. Remove from heat, and add salt and nutmeg.

Nick Klaras '52

SPICY SUPPER-IN-A-HURRY

1 pound lean ground meat
1 (1¼-ounce) package taco
  seasoning
1 (15-ounce) can pinto beans
  with jalapeños, undrained

1 (11-ounce) can tomato and
  rice soup
1 (10¾-ounce) can cream of
  celery soup
1 (8-ounce) package, noodles
Grated cheese

In a large skillet brown meat; drain well. Add taco seasoning, beans, and soups. Mix well and heat for 10 to 15 minutes over medium heat. Cook noodles in boiling, salted water; drain. Serve noodles on individual plates, spoon meat sauce over noodles, and top with grated cheese. **Yield**: 6 to 8 servings

Thurman Hugh Saxon '62

MISS TEXAS CASSEROLE

1 pound ground beef
2 teaspoons salt
2 teaspoons sugar
1 (16-ounce) can tomatoes
1 (8-ounce) can tomato sauce
½ teaspoon garlic powder
¼ teaspoon black pepper

1 (8-ounce) package egg
  noodles, cooked
1 cup sour cream
1 (3-ounce) package cream
  cheese, softened
6 green onions, chopped
  with tops
1 cup grated Cheddar cheese

Brown beef in skillet. Add next 6 ingredients. Cook over low heat for 15 minutes, covered. Combine cooked and drained noodles with sour cream, cream cheese, and green onions. In a greased 3-quart casserole, arrange in layers, beginning with ½ of noodle-cheese mixture, following with ½ of meat mixture. Repeat layers. Top with grated cheese. Bake at 350° for 25 to 30 minutes or until cheese is bubbly. **Yield**: 6 to 8 servings

My mother, Martha Jo Cooke Rutherford '59, gave me this recipe when I moved into my first apartment my junior year at Baylor. Little did I know it would become a favorite casserole for all my roommates and their friends too!

Sarah Rutherford Starr '88, MA '90

PORK MEDALLIONS IN MUSTARD SAUCE

"Easy, but impressive enough for guests."

3 tablespoons vegetable oil
1 tablespoon coarse-grained
   mustard
½ teaspoon salt
½ teaspoon pepper

2 (¾-pound) pork
   tenderloins
¼ cup dry white wine
Mustard Seed Sauce

Combine first 4 ingredients, stirring well. Rub mixture over pork; place in a plastic zip-lock bag, closing well, and refrigerate 8 hours.

Place tenderloins on rack in a shallow roasting pan. Insert meat thermometer into thickest part of meat. Bake at 375° for 25 minutes, or until meat thermometer registers 160°. Baste every 10 minutes with wine.

Slice tenderloins into ¾-inch slices, and arrange 4 slices on each dinner plate. Spoon Mustard Seed Sauce around pork on each plate. **Yield**: 4 servings

Mustard Seed Sauce:
1¾ cup whipping cream
¼ cup coarse-grained
   mustard

¼ teaspoon salt
⅛ teaspoon white pepper

Heat whipping cream in a heavy saucepan until reduced to 1¼ cups, about 15 minutes. Do not boil. Stir in remaining ingredients, and heat 1 minute.

Roxanne Nemmer Gottlick '79

LEMON PORK CHOPS

"Easy—and everyone loved it!"

4 very thick butterfly pork
   chops
Salt and pepper to taste
1 large onion, sliced

1 large lemon, sliced
1 green bell pepper, sliced
2 cups tomato juice

Sear chops in a skillet with no fat. When chops are brown on both sides, salt and pepper to taste; add onion, lemon, and green pepper. Pour tomato juice over all. Simmer covered for 1 hour. Serve over steamed buttered rice. **Yield**: 4 servings

Vanessa Wienecke Beard '79

CUBAN PORK ROAST

1 (6 to 7-pound) loin of pork
1 large onion, thinly sliced
3 bay leaves
2 teaspoons salt
½ cup lemon juice

¾ cup soy sauce
¾ cup sugar
¾ teaspoon powdered ginger
2 cloves garlic, minced

Place pork and all ingredients into a zip-lock bag. Turn bag over several times until ingredients are mixed. Refrigerate about 12 hours, turning bag occasionally. Place pork uncovered in a shallow baking pan, saving marinade. Arrange onion rings from marinade around pork. Insert meat thermometer, and roast at 325°, basting often with reserved marinade. Cook until thermometer registers 185°, 2 to 3 hours depending on thickness of roast. Remove meat from pan, and cool 15 minutes before slicing. Add pan juices to any remaining marinade; heat to boiling, and boil 2 to 3 minutes. Serve over pork roast slices. **Yield**: 12 to 14 servings

Hint: *Teams nicely with black beans and rice or with a hot fruit compote.*

Edythe Galvan Hoeltzel '71

PORK CHILE VERDE

1 pound pork tenderloin, cut in ½-inch cubes	1½ teaspoons ground cumin
1 medium yellow onion, chopped	1 teaspoon chili powder
	2 cloves garlic, minced
1 large green pepper, chopped	½ teaspoon crushed dried red chiles
1 tablespoon olive oil	Salt and pepper to taste
2 small green jalapeño peppers, seeded, deveined, and diced	2 cups low-sodium chicken broth

Sauté pork, onion, and green pepper in olive oil until pork is cooked through. Add remaining ingredients, and simmer 1 hour. Turn heat to high, and boil until liquid is reduced to desired consistency. (Thicken with cornstarch or flour if desired.) Serve hot on top of bean burritos. Add choices of grated cheese, tomatoes, red onions, lettuce, low-fat sour cream, and salsa. **Yield**: 6 servings

Note: *May be frozen.*

John T. Hull '66

 ## BUDDY'S RED BEANS AND RICE
"Even children like it."

½ cup chopped onion	1 teaspoon Worcestershire sauce
½ cup chopped celery	
¼ cup chopped green pepper	½ pound link sausage, sliced
1 tablespoon margarine	1 (15-ounce) can kidney beans, drained and liquid reserved
1 tablespoon chopped parsley	
1 bay leaf	3 to 4 drops hot pepper sauce
1½ tablespoons ketchup	Pinch of sugar
	Hot cooked rice

Sauté onion, celery, and green pepper in margarine in a large skillet. Add next 5 ingredients and liquid from beans. Cook 15 minutes. Add beans, hot pepper sauce, and sugar; cook 5 minutes. Remove bay leaf before serving. Serve over hot cooked rice. **Yield**: 3 to 4 servings

Lois Butcher Huckaby '81

POULET EN PAPILLOTE
"A lovely presentation"

4 chicken breasts, skinned
and boned
1 (10-ounce) bag fresh
spinach, washed and
stems removed
3 ounces Feta cheese
2 tablespoons chicken broth
1 teaspoon arrowroot
½ cup skimmed milk
1 egg, lightly beaten
2 teaspoons unsalted butter
¼ teaspoon salt
Dash of cayenne pepper

Place chicken breasts in enough water to cover, and add bay leaf and whole pepper corns. Simmer for 35 to 45 minutes, just until tender. While chicken cooks, wilt spinach in a saucepan over high heat for 1 minute. Squeeze excess liquid from spinach. Mix spinach and Feta cheese. Set aside.

While chicken is cooking, dissolve arrowroot in warm chicken broth. (Two teaspoons flour may be substituted for arrowroot). Set aside. Warm milk in saucepan until small bubbles appear. Add a few tablespoons warm milk to slightly beaten egg, then add egg to the milk. Stir in dissolved arrowroot and heat until thickened, stirring constantly for about 3 minutes. Add butter, salt, and pepper.

When cooked chicken is cool enough to handle, split chicken breasts to make a pocket for spinach and cheese filling. Stuff chicken breasts with mixture.

Cut parchment paper into 4 heart shapes, with each half of the heart slightly larger than the chicken breasts. Place a stuffed chicken breast on one side of each heart, and fold heart in half. Seal edges by folding and pleating. Set packages in a greased 9x13-inch baking dish, and bake for 12 minutes. Remove from parchment paper. Place on serving plate and cover with sauce. **Yield**: 4 servings

Note: *Squares of foil may be used in place of parchment paper hearts.*

Lois Wroten Boatwright '59

CHICKEN BREASTS LOMBARDY

6 whole chicken breasts,
  boned, skinned, and
  quartered
½ cup flour
1 cup butter or margarine,
  divided
Salt and pepper to taste
1½ cups sliced mushrooms

¾ cup Marsala or dry white
  wine
½ cup chicken stock or broth
½ teaspoon salt
⅛ teaspoon pepper
½ cup shredded Fontina or
  mozzarella cheese
½ cup grated Parmesan
  cheese

Place each piece of chicken between 2 sheets of wax paper. Flatten to ⅛-inch thickness, using meat mallet or rolling pin. Dredge chicken lightly in flour. Place 4 pieces at a time in 2 tablespoons melted butter in a large skillet. Cook over low heat 3 to 4 minutes on each side, or until golden brown. Place chicken in a greased 9x13-inch baking dish, overlapping edges. Sprinkle with salt and pepper to taste. Repeat procedure with remaining chicken, adding 2 tablespoons butter to skillet each time. Reserve drippings in skillet and set aside.

Sauté mushrooms in ¼ cup butter until tender; drain. Sprinkle evenly over chicken. Stir wine and chicken stock into drippings in skillet. Simmer 10 minutes, stirring occasionally to loosen cooked bits on bottom of skillet. Stir in salt and pepper. Spoon about ⅓ of sauce evenly over chicken. Reserve remaining sauce. Combine cheeses, and sprinkle over chicken. Bake at 450° for 10 to 12 minutes. Place under broiler 1 to 2 minutes or until lightly browned. Serve with reserved sauce. **Yield**: 8 servings

Hint: *Serve with cooked white or brown rice, or with a rice pilaf.*

Lynn Goelzer Engelke '79

POULET MAISON

8 (8-ounce) chicken breasts,
  skinned and boned
Salt and pepper
Flour
2 eggs, slightly beaten
2 tablespoons Triple Sec
1½ cups breadcrumbs
2 cloves garlic, minced
2 tablespoons paprika
½ cup Parmesan cheese
1½ tablespoons minced
  parsley
Melted butter
Chicken stock
Cumberland Sauce

Pound chicken breasts to flatten. Sprinkle with salt and pepper, and dredge in flour. Mix eggs and Triple Sec in a pie plate. Mix breadcrumbs and next 4 ingredients in a second pie plate.

Dip chicken breasts in egg mixture, then in breadcrumb coating. Roll each breast like a jelly roll, and place in buttered pan. Brush each breast generously with melted butter. Bake at 350° for 30 minutes. Then pour chicken stock in pan to cover rolls halfway. Bake 45 minutes longer, basting occasionally. Serve with Cumberland Sauce. **Yield**: 8 servings

Note: *Can be made ahead and frozen*

Cumberland Sauce:
6 tablespoons + 2 teaspoons
  red currant jelly
2 tablespoons sherry
2 tablespoons Madeira
4 tablespoons fresh orange
  juice
2 tablespoons fresh lemon
  juice
1 teaspoon dry mustard
1 teaspoon paprika
1 teaspoon ground ginger
3 teaspoons freshly-grated
  orange rind

Heat jelly until melted; blend in wines, juices, and seasonings. Serve at room temperature.

Claudia Burton Johnson, a Baylor mom

CHICKEN DIJON

"We were served this dish in Brisbane, Australia, and brought back the recipe to share."

4 chicken breasts, boned and
    skinned
2 tablespoons Dijon mustard

½ cup mayonnaise
1 cup grated Monterey Jack
    cheese

Place chicken breasts in greased 9x13-inch baking dish. Mix mustard and mayonnaise; spread over chicken breasts. Sprinkle with grated cheese. Cover loosely with foil and bake at 400° for 45 minutes. Remove foil and bake 10 minutes longer or until brown. **Yield:** 4 servings

Hint: *Very easy to adapt to any number.*

Carol Hunter Wells '69

BROCCOLI CHICKEN

4 to 6 chicken breasts
1 tablespoon butter or
    margarine
1 (10-ounce) can broccoli
    cheese soup

½ cup water or milk
2 cups fresh broccoli
    flowerets
Salt and pepper to taste

In a large skillet, brown chicken breasts on both sides in margarine. Place chicken in 9x13-inch baking dish. In a small bowl, whisk soup and milk together. Stir in broccoli, and salt and pepper. Pour sauce over chicken in baking dish. Cover and bake at 350° for 10 to 15 minutes. Serve over cooked rice. **Yield:** 4 to 6 servings

Wayne H. Morgan '56

CASHEW CHICKEN

6 boneless, skinless chicken
   breast halves
¼ cup soy sauce
2 tablespoons cornstarch
½ teaspoon sugar
½ teaspoon salt
4 tablespoons oil, divided
1 cup cashew nuts
2 (6-ounce) packages frozen
   Chinese pea pods

½ pound fresh mushrooms,
   sliced
1 cup chicken stock
1 (8-ounce) can water
   chestnuts, drained and
   sliced
4 green onions, sliced,
   including some tops
Hot cooked rice

Cut chicken into bite-size pieces. In a small bowl, mix soy sauce, cornstarch, sugar, and salt until well blended; set aside. In an electric skillet at 350°, or a wok, or a large heavy skillet, heat 1 tablespoon oil. Add nuts, cooking for 1 minute or until brown, stirring constantly. Remove nuts; drain, and set aside. To the skillet, add remaining oil and heat. Add chicken, and stir-fry until meat looks opaque. Stir in pea pods, mushrooms, and stock. Cover and simmer 2 minutes. Add water chestnuts and soy sauce mixture. Cover and cook until sauce is thickened. Uncover and cook 1 minute. Mix in onions and sprinkle with nuts. Serve over hot rice. **Yield:** 4 to 6 servings

Marcy Koch Sosnowski '87

No matter how long you've been away—six weeks or sixty years—when you go back to the place you grew up, you always say, "I'm going home."

Overheard at a cookbook planning meeting

TANGY BAKED CHICKEN

4 boneless, skinless chicken
  breast halves (4-ounces
  each)
⅛ teaspoon ground red
  pepper or ground chile
  powder

¼ teaspoon black pepper
¼ cup reduced-calorie
  Catalina salad dressing
1 tablespoon Dijon mustard
1 teaspoon Worcestershire
  sauce

Rinse chicken; pat dry with paper towels. Combine red and black
peppers; rub over chicken breasts. Combine salad dressing, mustard, and Worcestershire sauce. Lightly brush both sides of
chicken breasts with mixture. Place chicken in a shallow baking
dish or pan. Bake uncovered at 375° for 20 to 25 minutes, or until
chicken is no longer pink. In a small saucepan, heat any remaining dressing mixture just to boiling; serve with chicken. **Yield:** 4
servings

Dixie Cavitt Soong '82

CHICKEN ITALIANA

1½ cups fine dry
  breadcrumbs
½ cup grated Parmesan
  cheese
¼ teaspoon garlic powder

Salt and pepper to taste
6 boneless chicken breasts
½ cup cooking oil
1½ cups spaghetti sauce
6 slices mozzarella cheese

Mix breadcrumbs, Parmesan cheese, garlic powder, salt, and pepper. Dip chicken in oil, shake off excess, and coat with breadcrumb
mixture. Heat remaining oil in large skillet; brown chicken on
both sides. Place chicken in greased 9x13-inch baking dish. Cover
with spaghetti sauce. Bake covered at 350° for 45 minutes. Remove from oven and place a slice of mozzarella cheese on each
chicken breast. Let sit until cheese melts, or return to oven for 3
minutes until cheese melts. Serve with linguini or any favorite
pasta. **Yield:** 6 servings

Note: *Can be begun ahead of time and finished later.*

Nancy Mitchell Pearce '71

BAKED CHICKEN ANY-WAY-YOU-LIKE-IT

"Start with this basic mildly-flavored baked chicken breast, and complete the dish with your own creative taste-touches."

2 pounds frozen boneless, skinless chicken breasts (6 or 7), thawed
¾ cup fat-free sour cream

1 cup wheat breadcrumbs
Salt and pepper
Liquid margarine
⅓ cup white cooking wine

Wash chicken breasts, and pat dry. Coat 1 side of breasts with sour cream. Sprinkle with breadcrumbs, salt, and pepper. Place chicken, coated-side down, in buttered baking dish. (For low fat, use vegetable cooking spray in place of margarine.) Coat tops of chicken with sour cream, breadcrumbs, salt and pepper. Drizzle liquid margarine over prepared chicken. Cover with foil. Bake at 350° for 45 minutes. Remove foil, and pour cooking wine over chicken. Continue baking uncovered 15 minutes.

Serve each chicken breast with a spoonful of chutney or apricot preserves. Or sprinkle with Parmesan cheese and capers. Or top with picante sauce or salsa, and garnish with thin slices of avocado. Or top with a fresh tomato slice and a sprinkle of grated Mozzarella cheese and chopped fresh basil. **Yield**: 6 to 7 servings

Note: *Easily doubled. Freezes well. For crumbs, process slices of day-old wheat bread in blender, and store in plastic bag in freezer.*

Joy Copeland Reynolds '74
Wife of Baylor President, Dr. Herbert H. Reynolds

GRILLED CHICKEN WITH SUMMER SALSA

1 cup chopped fresh plums
1 cup chopped fresh peaches
½ cup chopped fresh
  pineapple
¼ cup chopped red bell
  pepper
2½ tablespoons white wine
  vinegar

1½ tablespoons minced
  cilantro
1 teaspoon sugar
⅛ to ¼ teaspoon chili
  powder
6 skinned, boned chicken
  breast halves
Salt and pepper, optional

Combine first 8 ingredients in a glass bowl; mix gently but thoroughly. Refrigerate several hours. Sprinkle chicken breasts with salt and pepper, if desired. Grill chicken over medium-hot coals for 10 to 12 minutes, turning frequently. Serve chicken with salsa. **Yield:** 6 servings

Marilyn Wyrick Ingram '72

MARY'S HERBED CHICKEN

4 chicken breasts
¼ cup margarine or butter
⅔ cup fresh mushrooms,
  sliced
1 (10¾-ounce) can cream of
  chicken soup
¾ cup sherry or cooking
  sauterne

2 tablespoons chopped green
  pepper
½ teaspoon thyme
1 (5-ounce) can water
  chestnuts, drained and
  sliced

Season chicken lightly with salt and pepper. In a large skillet, brown chicken in margarine or butter. Arrange chicken in 2-quart baking dish. Quickly sauté mushrooms in skillet drippings. Add soup and wine slowly, stirring until smooth. Add remaining ingredients. Heat to boiling, and pour over chicken. Cover and bake at 350° for 25 minutes. Uncover and continue baking for 25 to 30 minutes, or until chicken is tender. Serve with rice. **Yield:** 4 servings

Hint: *Sauce may be doubled if you like lots of gravy.*

Helen Hargrove Hastings '52

CASSEROLE CASSANDRA
"This is super good."

1 (6-ounce) jar marinated
  artichoke hearts
3 pounds chicken, breasts &
  thighs
2 (16-ounce) cans stewed
  tomatoes, drained and
  juice reserved
1½ cups raw rice

1 cup white wine
1 tablespoon Beau Monde
  seasoning
1 teaspoon Italian herb
  seasoning
½ cup sliced, stuffed green
  olives

Drain marinade off artichoke hearts into a large skillet. Sauté
chicken in marinade until golden. (This will splatter and pop!)
Break up tomatoes into smaller pieces if they are large. Pour most
of tomatoes into a 3-quart casserole with a tight-fitting lid, saving a few tomato pieces with the drained juice. Pour raw rice over
tomatoes.

Remove chicken pieces to casserole as browned. Place drained
artichoke hearts over chicken. Remove all but 2 tablespoons of
oil from skillet. Stir in tomato juice, wine, and seasonings. Heat
to boiling, and pour over chicken. Add sliced olives. Cover and
bake at 350° for 45 to 55 minutes. **Yield**: 6 servings

The Cookbook Committee

WICKED CHICKEN

2 chickens, cut into serving
  pieces, or 8 whole chicken
  breasts
2 (10¾-ounce) cans of cream
  of mushroom soup

1 pint sour cream
1 cup sherry
Paprika

Place chicken in flat baking dish. Mix soup, sour cream, and sherry
and pour over chicken. Sprinkle paprika on top. Bake, covered,
at 350° for 1½ hours. Serve over rice, noodles, or with baked potato. **Yield:** 10 to 12 servings

*My father, Dr. Stanley Wilkes, pastor and former Baylor trustee,
named this recipe—a family favorite for its quick and easy preparation, especially on Sundays!*

Doris Jean Wilkes Johnson '52

EASY OVEN BAR-B-Q CHICKEN

1 large onion, chopped
3 tablespoons vinegar
3 tablespoons brown sugar
Juice of 1 lemon
1 cup ketchup
1 tablespoon horseradish or
  prepared mustard

½ teaspoon salt
¼ teaspoon cayenne pepper
2 fryers, cut into serving
  pieces
Flour, salt, and shortening
  for browning chicken

Combine first 6 ingredients in saucepan; simmer over low heat for 10 to 15 minutes.

Lightly salt chicken pieces, dredge in flour, and brown in shortening until lightly browned. Transfer to a greased, shallow 3-quart dish. Pour sauce over chicken, and cook at 350° for 1 hour, covered loosely. **Yield**: 6 to 8 servings

This is believed to be an original Texana recipe passed down through the generations by great-grandparents who came to East Texas about 1848. This could be what the Baylorites ate at Washington-on-the-Brazos.

LaVerne Wellborn Wentworth '49, MA '54

CHICKEN FLURETTE

From Baylor's Home Economics Department in 1962, and ranked high with our testers today.

1 (12-ounce) box wild rice mix with seasonings, cooked
1 baked chicken, skinned, boned, and cut into fairly large pieces
8 ounces mushrooms, sautéed in butter
1 (2-ounce) can sliced ripe olives

¾ stick margarine
¼ cup flour
2 cups half-and-half
2 cups grated Cheddar cheese, divided
¼ cup margarine
½ cup cracker crumbs
¼ cup slivered almonds

Spray 9x12-inch casserole with non-stick vegetable spray. Layer with cooked rice, cooked chicken, mushrooms, and olives. Make a sauce by melting margarine in small saucepan over low heat. Mix in flour until smooth; slowly add half-and-half. Cook while stirring until sauce is thick. Add 1 cup cheese and heat until melted. Pour sauce over layers in casserole. Mix ¼ cup melted margarine with cracker crumbs, remaining cheese, and almonds. Sprinkle over casserole. Bake at 350° until bubbly, about 30 minutes. May freeze and bake later. **Yield:** 6 to 8 servings

Gloria Turner DuBose '62

ENCHILADAS DE POLLO

"Deluxe chicken enchiladas with a different flare"

4 boneless, skinless chicken
  breasts, cooked
½ medium onion, chopped
1 tablespoon butter
2 cups Monterey Jack cheese,
  grated and divided
1 (4-ounce) can green chiles
1 (13-ounce) can tomatoes,
  drained

¼ cup cilantro leaves
¾ cup whipping cream,
  unwhipped
1 egg
Salt to taste
¼ cup vegetable oil
12 corn tortillas

Shred chicken with 2 forks or with fingers. Lightly sauté chopped onion in butter in medium skillet, or microwave in a small cup for 45 seconds. Mix chicken, onion, and 1 cup cheese; set aside. In a blender or food processor, combine green chiles, tomatoes, cilantro, whipping cream, and egg; blend until smooth. Add salt to taste. Set aside.

Heat vegetable oil in a skillet. Carefully place 1 tortilla at a time in hot oil. Hold in oil 3 to 5 seconds until softened. Quickly turn tortillas and soften other side. Drain over skillet or on paper towels. (To reduce fat content, tortillas can be softened in hot chicken broth.)

Place equal amounts of chicken mixture on each tortilla, about ⅓ cup. Roll each tortilla tightly; place seam-side down in a lightly-greased 9x13-inch baking dish. Pour the chile-cream mixture over enchiladas, and sprinkle evenly with remaining cup of grated cheese. Bake at 350° for 20 minutes, or until heated through and bubbly. Serve with guacamole, sour cream, shredded lettuce, and chopped tomatoes. **Yield**: 4 to 6 servings

Susan Reed Fletcher '85

MOM'S CHICKEN AND RICE

"A favorite of my mother's and special to me."

1 cup raw rice
1 (10¾-ounce) can cream of
    mushroom soup
1 (10¾-ounce) can cream of
    chicken soup
1 (14½-ounce) can chicken
    broth

½ cup margarine, melted
Salt and pepper
1 chicken, cut in serving
    pieces, or 4 to 6 chicken
    breasts

Spread uncooked rice in a greased 9x13-inch baking dish. Mix soups and broth, and pour over rice. Dip cut-up chicken in melted butter, season with salt and pepper, and place on top of rice. Cover with foil and bake at 325° for 2 hours. Remove foil, and bake for 20 to 30 minutes longer for chicken to brown. Use any remaining melted butter and baste chicken pieces as needed. **Yield:** 4 to 6 servings

Note: *A wonderfully simple dish to fix for company or potluck dinners.*

Marilyn Jeanne Jones '82

 # LIGHT TEX-MEX STUFFED PEPPERS

"For two"

2 medium bell peppers (red,
    yellow, or green)
1 cup chopped cooked
    chicken breast
½ cup picante sauce
1 cup cooked Spanish rice
    (may use Spanish rice
    boxed mix)

½ cup whole kernel corn,
    drained
½ cup (2 ounces) shredded
    Cheddar cheese
¼ cup sliced green onions
2 tablespoons sliced ripe
    olives, drained
¼ teaspoon salt

Cut peppers in half lengthwise; remove seeds. Parboil 4 minutes; drain well. Place in shallow baking dish. Combine remaining ingredients; mix well. Spoon into pepper halves. Cover loosely with foil and bake at 350° for 20 to 25 minutes. Top with additional picante to serve. **Yield:** 2 servings

Ken Casner '53

CRESCENT CHICKEN SQUARES

"The girls in my luncheon group thought this was a winner."

2 (3-ounce) packages cream
cheese with chives,
softened
6 tablespoons butter,
divided
5 (5-ounce) cans boned
chicken (or 4 cups cubed
cooked chicken)

½ teaspoon salt
¼ teaspoon pepper
4 tablespoons milk
2 tablespoons diced
pimiento
2 (8-ounce) cans crescent
dinner rolls
Italian breadcrumbs

In medium bowl, blend cream cheese and 4 tablespoons butter until smooth. Add the next 5 ingredients; mix well. Separate crescent dough into 8 rectangles (4 in each can); firmly press perforations to seal. Spoon ½ cup chicken mixture onto center of each rectangle. Pull 4 corners of dough to top center of chicken mixture; twist slightly and seal edges. Melt remaining 2 tablespoons butter; brush tops of dough packets. Sprinkle with breadcrumbs. Place on cookie sheet. Bake at 350° for 25 minutes or until golden brown. **Yield:** 8 servings

Hint: *Can use 2 packages of plain cream cheese and add 2 tablespoons fresh or frozen chives.*

Pat Parchman Franklin '64

POPPY SEED CHICKEN

"Start this the night before."

4 chicken breasts, cooked
and diced
1 (10½-ounce) can cream of
mushroom soup
1 (16-ounce) carton sour
cream

½ cup cooking sherry
4 tablespoons poppy seeds
1 sleeve round buttery
crackers, crushed
4 tablespoons melted butter

The night before, combine first 5 ingredients. Pour in a 2½-quart casserole dish, and cover with plastic wrap. Refrigerate overnight. Just before baking, sprinkle crackers over top of casserole, and drizzle with melted butter. Bake at 375° for 25 to 30 minutes. **Yield:** 6 servings

Jennifer Lee Willis '93

AZTEC CHICKEN

2 tablespoons oil
¼ cup chopped onion
2 tablespoons minced garlic
1 (16-ounce) can whole
   tomatoes, pureed
1½ teaspoons salt
1 tablespoon butter
3 cups fresh or frozen corn
   kernels

3½ cups chopped zucchini
⅓ cup water
10 corn tortillas
Oil for frying tortillas
1 cup half-and-half
4 cups cooked diced chicken
3 cups grated Monterey Jack
   cheese

Heat oil in a skillet; sauté onion and garlic until tender. Add pureed tomatoes and salt; cook over medium heat for 5 minutes, stirring often. Cover and cook over low heat for 10 more minutes. Set aside.

Melt butter in a large saucepan. Add corn and zucchini, and cook for 2 minutes. Add water, cover and cook over low heat for 8 minutes or until zucchini is tender. Set aside. Heat ¼-inch oil in a medium saucepan. Fry tortillas one at a time for 15 to 20 seconds on each side just to soften. Drain well on paper towels and set aside.

Place a layer of vegetables on bottom of greased 9x13-inch baking dish. Top vegetables with 5 of the corn tortillas. Cover with tomato sauce. Add half of remaining vegetables, ½ cup of half-and-half, half of diced chicken, and half of cheese. Repeat layers, finishing with cheese. Bake at 375°, uncovered, for 10 to 15 minutes until cheese begins to melt. **Yield**: 6 to 8 servings

Note: *To reduce fat intake, tortillas can be softened in hot chicken broth. Dish can be prepared ahead and baked later.*

Hilda Chapa '83

CRESCENT PECAN CHICKEN BAKE

½ cup chopped celery
½ cup chopped onion
4 tablespoons butter,
  divided
3 cups cubed cooked chicken
  breasts (4 to 6 breasts)
1 (10¾-ounce) can cream of
  chicken soup
1 (10¾-ounce) can cream of
  mushroom soup
1 (8-ounce) can sliced water
  chestnuts, drained

1 (4-ounce) can sliced
  mushrooms, drained
⅔ cup mayonnaise
½ cup sour cream
¼ teaspoon curry powder
1 (8-ounce) can crescent
  dinner rolls
⅔ cup shredded Cheddar
  cheese
½ cup chopped pecans

In a large skillet, sauté celery and onion in 2 tablespoons butter. Add next 8 ingredients. Heat, but do not boil. Pour into 9x13-inch baking dish. (Can be frozen at this point).

Separate rolls into 4 rectangles; place dough on chicken mixture. Melt remaining 2 tablespoons butter, and brush over dough. Sprinkle with cheese and chopped pecans. Bake at 375° for 20 to 25 minutes until crust is deep golden brown. **Yield**: 8 to 12 servings

Hint: *Reheats nicely and is still delicious.*

Virginia King Speasmaker '67

VERSATILE CHICKEN POT PIE

"A family-pleasing way to recycle the leftovers"

1 (10½-ounce) can cream of
  mushroom soup
1 (10¾-ounce) can cream of
  chicken soup
1 (10¾-ounce) can cream of
  celery soup
3 chicken breasts, cooked,
  boned, and chopped

1 (10-ounce) package frozen
  peas, slightly thawed
3 ribs celery, chopped
3 medium carrots, chopped
½ cup chopped onion
½ cup melted butter or
  margarine
1 cup flour
1 cup milk

In a large bowl combine soups, chicken, and vegetables. Pour
mixture in a lightly-greased 9x13-inch baking dish. Melt butter
in small saucepan. Stir in flour, and cook for 2 to 3 minutes until
bubbly. Add milk slowly and stir constantly until thickened and
smooth. Pour evenly over chicken mixture. Bake at 350° for 1 hour
or until topping is brown and gravy is bubbling. **Yield:** 8 to 10
servings

Note: *A basic recipe. Use other meats and vegetables. Add spices,
herbs, and seasonings of your choice. But great just like it is, too.*

Martha Newton Garber '71

"I cannot eat alone; it's not the same. Food is meant to be shared."

**The late Martha Emmons '21
Baylor Department of English**

CHICKEN PORTUGUESE

2 skinless whole chicken
  breasts, halved
2 onions, divided
¾ teaspoon cumin, divided
3 cloves garlic, divided
1 tablespoon butter
1 green pepper, chopped
1 poblano chile pepper,
  chopped
1 to 2 fresh jalapeño peppers
  to taste, seeded, deveined,
  and chopped
1 (15-ounce) can tomatoes,
  drained
1 teaspoon chili powder
1 (4-ounce) can green chiles
¼ cup chicken stock,
  reserved
¾ pound pasteurized process
  cheese, cubed
½ cup sour cream (or more to
  taste)
Fried tortilla strips, chips, or
  hot cooked rice

In a Dutch oven, cover chicken with water. Add 1 onion cut in quarters, ½ teaspoon of cumin, and 2 garlic cloves. Simmer until tender. Cool in stock; reserve ¼ cup stock. Remove chicken from bones and cut into bite-size pieces. Set aside.

Chop remaining onion, and garlic clove; sauté in butter with green pepper, poblano pepper, and jalapeño. Add tomatoes, chili powder, remaining ¼ teaspoon cumin, green chiles, ¼ cup reserved stock, cheese, and chicken. Simmer, stirring constantly. When heated through, turn off heat and stir in sour cream. (Taste and add more sautéed jalapeños if desired.) Serve over tortilla strips, tortilla chips, or rice. **Yield**: Serves 6

Note: *A great dish to serve a crowd because it is easily doubled or tripled. If poblano chile peppers are not available, increase the amount of canned green chiles.*

Carol Watson Barclay '60

SPICY CHILE CHICKEN STEW

6 chicken breasts, boned and skinned
1 medium onion, chopped
1 medium green pepper, chopped
2 cloves garlic, minced
1 tablespoon vegetable oil
2 (14½-ounce) cans stewed tomatoes, undrained and chopped

1 (15-ounce) can pinto beans, drained
⅔ cup picante sauce
1 teaspoon ground red New Mexico chile powder
1 teaspoon ground cumin
½ teaspoon salt

Cut chicken into 1-inch pieces. Heat oil in Dutch oven; add chicken, onion, green pepper, and garlic. Sauté until chicken is lightly browned and vegetables are tender. Add tomatoes and remaining ingredients. Cover, reduce heat, and simmer 20 minutes. Serve with a choice of shredded cheese, sour cream, diced avocado, sliced green onions, and corn chips or tortillas. **Yield:** 6 servings

Note: *Use Chimayo brand red chile powder if available in your area. If no New Mexico red chile is available, use commercial chili powder.*

Gloriana Simmons Parchman '54

GREEN CHILE CHICKEN ENCHILADAS

1 (10¾-ounce) can cream of
 chicken soup
1 (10½-ounce) cream of
 mushroom soup
1 (7-ounce) can chopped
 green chiles
2 cups sour cream
1 small onion, finely
 chopped
1 bunch green onion tops,
 chopped

1 (4½-ounce) can sliced ripe
 olives, drained
¾ pound Monterey Jack
 cheese, grated
¾ pound Cheddar cheese,
 grated
5 large chicken breasts,
 cooked, boned, and
 chopped
12 large flour tortillas

Combine soups, chiles, sour cream, onion, olives, and part of green onion tops (saving some for topping). Mix grated cheeses, and add ½ to sour cream filling mixture. Measure out 1½ cup of filling, and set aside. Add chopped chicken to remaining filling.

   Soften 2 or 3 tortillas at a time for a few seconds in microwave. Fill each tortilla down the center with 3 heaping tablespoons of chicken mixture, and roll up tightly. Place seam-side down in large greased shallow pan. Pour reserved sauce over top. Sprinkle with remaining cheese, green onion tops, and paprika. Refrigerate overnight. Bake at 350° for 45 minutes. **Yield**: 8 to 10 servings

Note: *Must be refrigerated overnight before baking.*

Sandra Fleming Ferguson '71

EL PESCADO DE PRICE

"The best new recipe I have tried in years"

4 orange roughy fillets
Creole seasoning
1 (5-ounce) package Spanish
  rice
1⅔ cup water
1 green pepper, sliced
  crosswise
2 large carrots, chopped

2 celery ribs, chopped
1 lemon, sliced thin
Red chile powder, optional
1 cup sharp Cheddar cheese,
  grated
1 cup jalapeño Monterey
  Jack cheese, grated

Sprinkle fillets with creole seasoning. Pour rice into 9x13-inch baking dish and mix with water. Add ½ of vegetables on top of rice. Place seasoned fillets on vegetables. If desired, sprinkle on red chile powder. Place lemon slices on top. Add remaining vegetables around the edge of dish. Bake, covered, at 425° for 1 hour. Remove lid and top with grated cheese. Bake for 5 minutes longer to melt cheese. **Yield:** 4 servings

Note: *A wonderful spicy fish that does not need a lot of fuss or constant attention while cooking.*

Susan Gothard Easley '80

CREAMY BAKED FISH FILLETS

1 cup sour cream
¼ cup grated Parmesan
  cheese
1 tablespoon lemon juice
1 egg, hard-cooked and
  mashed
½ teaspoon salt, or to taste

2 to 3 drops hot pepper
  sauce
1 tomato, chopped fine
1 small onion, finely
  chopped
2 pounds fish fillets (perch,
  sole, snapper or cod)
Paprika

In a medium bowl combine first 8 ingredients, mixing well with a wooden spoon to blend. In 1 or 2 greased 9x13-inch baking dishes, place fillets in a single layer. Spoon cream mixture over fish. Sprinkle with paprika. Bake at 350° for 20 minutes. **Yield:** 6 to 8 servings

Louanna Ruth Werchan '85

⏱ BAKED RED SNAPPER

¼ cup olive oil	1 cup chopped green pepper
1 onion, chopped	2 tomatoes, peeled and
1 teaspoon coriander seeds	chopped
1 teaspoon cumin seeds	½ cup lime juice
Pinch of cayenne	½ cup dry white wine
½ cup chopped dates	2 pounds whole red snapper

In a medium saucepan, heat oil. Sauté onion, coriander, cumin, and cayenne for 5 minutes. Blend well. Stir in the next 5 ingredients, and bring to a boil. Set aside. Wash fish and pat dry. Place in a buttered 9x13-inch baking dish, and pour sauce over. Bake at 375° for 30 minutes or until fish flakes easily. **Yield:** 4 to 6 servings

Hint: *Wonderful sauce to serve on fish fillets cooked on the grill.*

Marguerite Shearer Fleener '90

CAESAR SWORDFISH

2 pounds swordfish steaks,	¼ cup freshly-grated
1-inch thick	Parmesan cheese
⅓ cup reduced-calorie	2 tablespoons Caesar salad-
Caesar salad dressing	style croutons
18 small Romaine lettuce	
leaves	

Place swordfish steaks in a shallow dish. Pour salad dressing over steaks. Cover and refrigerate 1 hour, turning once. Remove steaks from marinade; set aside.

Coat grill rack with vegetable cooking spray. Place steaks on grill 4 to 5 inches above medium hot coals. Grill, brushing with marinade and turning once, just until fish begins to flake when tested with a fork, allowing about 8 to 10 minutes on each side.

To serve, cut steaks in 6 serving-size pieces. Arrange 3 lettuce leaves on individual serving plates; place swordfish on lettuce. Sprinkle each with Parmesan and croutons. **Yield**: 6 servings

Marilyn Wyrick Ingram '72

BLACKENED SEAFOOD WITH A ZIP

1 tablespoon paprika
1 teaspoon salt
1 teaspoon onion powder
1 teaspoon garlic powder
½ to ¾ teaspoon black
    pepper
½ to ¾ teaspoon white
    pepper
¼ to ½ teaspoon cayenne
    pepper

½ teaspoon dried thyme
    leaves
⅛ teaspoon dried oregano
    leaves
1 cup margarine or butter,
    divide and melted
2 pounds fish fillets, ½ to ¾
    inch thick

Mix first 9 ingredients in a flat pan. Heat a large cast-iron skillet over high heat. (Do not use a lightweight or non-stick skillet.) Turn on hood vent. Pour about 3 tablespoons margarine in skillet. Dip each fish portion in remaining melted margarine, then in dry ingredients, patting them in by hand. Cook fish on each side for 2 to 3 minutes, being careful when turning. (The fish will looked charred. There will be some smoke, but not excessive.) This recipe may be cooked outdoors if preferred. **Yield:** 5 to 6 servings

Hint: *Boneless chicken is equally successful with this recipe. The spices can be doubled, stored in a tightly sealed jar, and kept on hand.*

The Cookbook Committee

GERMAN-STYLE BAKED FISH FILLETS

"The best baked fish I've eaten. A very interesting flavor combination."

1½ pounds skinless fish
   fillets
½ cup chopped onion
2 tablespoons margarine or
   oil
1 (27-ounce) can sauerkraut,
   well-drained
½ cup water

½ teaspoon caraway seed
½ teaspoon garlic salt
1 (3-ounce) package cream
   cheese, cubed
½ cup grated sharp Cheddar
   cheese
1 tablespoon chopped fresh
   parsley

Cut fish in serving-size portions. Sauté onion in margarine in large skillet until tender. Add sauerkraut, water, caraway seed, and garlic salt. Cover and simmer for 10 minutes or until flavors are well blended. Top with fish pieces. Arrange cream cheese cubes about the mixture. Cover and simmer for 7 minutes or until fish is opaque. Sprinkle with grated cheese and allow cheese to melt. Sprinkle with parsley. Serve with dark rye bread and a crisp salad. **Yield:** 4 servings

Note: *May be baked in oven instead of cooked on top of range. Bake at 350° for 10 minutes for each inch the fish fillet is thick.*

Carol Watson Barclay '60

"Eating on the porch has for me all the excitement of foreign travel. To me, the greatest joy of a dining-car or a table in a steamship on the river, lake or sea is that you can see so much while you eat. The landscape changes more rapidly than the course, and you, if you properly protract your meal, can devour fifty or so miles of field and forest or waves, without having them included in the check. Likewise, on a porch, you can see a panorama of interest."

Dorothy Scarborough
1896 Baylor alumna and award-winning novelist

ORANGE ROUGHY WITH DUXELLES

"A quick, elegant favorite...for company or family."

3 tablespoons butter-
   flavored margarine
1 (8-ounce) package fresh
   mushrooms, coarsely
   chopped
½ to ¾ cup chopped shallots
   or red onion

¼ cup dry sherry
1 teaspoon lemon-pepper
   seasoning, divided
4 large orange roughy fillets
Paprika

Early in the day, or the day before, make the duxelles. In non-stick skillet, melt margarine and add chopped mushrooms and shallots. Cook over medium heat, stirring often. When most moisture has evaporated, add dry sherry and ½ teaspoon lemon pepper seasoning. Cook, stirring occasionally, until sherry is reduced by ⅓. Set aside to serve over fish fillets.

Season fillets with remaining lemon-pepper seasoning and paprika. Cook on a stove-top grill or in a lightly-oiled non-stick skillet until browned on both sides and flakes easily with a fork. Remove to serving plates and top with duxelles. Serve immediately.
Yield: 4 servings

Note: *Works well with many types of fish and even beef.*

Nancy Harrison Guy '60

BAKED FISH FILLETS WITH MUSTARD AND HERBS

8 fish fillets, about 2 pounds
2 tablespoons Dijon
  mustard
¾ cup fine dry breadcrumbs
½ teaspoon seasoned salt
¼ teaspoon thyme
⅛ teaspoon freshly-ground
  black pepper

3 to 4 tablespoons bottled
  Italian salad dressing or
  vinaigrette
8 tablespoons (1 stick)
  butter
8 lemon wedges
Chopped fresh parsley

Arrange fish fillets in single layer in shallow pan. Spread mustard evenly over fillets. Combine breadcrumbs, salt, thyme and pepper in small bowl. Sprinkle breadcrumb mixture evenly over fillets. Drizzle salad dressing over crumbs. Bake fish at 450° for about 5 to 7 minutes, or until fish flakes easily with a fork. Dot each with 1 tablespoon of butter, and top with lemon wedge. **Yield:** 4 to 6 servings

The Cookbook Committee

SHRIMP CURRY INDIAN DELIGHT

1 large onion, sliced and
  diced
1 clove garlic, minced
4 tablespoons butter
4 tablespoons flour
1 tablespoon curry powder
  (or more to taste)
4 cups chicken bouillon or
  stock

1 teaspoon hot pepper sauce
½ teaspoon salt
⅛ teaspoon white pepper
⅛ teaspoon ginger powder
1 pound boiled shrimp,
  peeled and deveined
Hot cooked rice or pasta

In a large skillet sauté onion and garlic in butter until onion is clear. Stir in flour mixed with curry powder. Slowly add stock, stirring constantly. Add pepper sauce. Bring to a boil, still stirring. Cook in a double boiler over simmering water for 20 to 25 minutes. Add salt, pepper and ginger. Heat shrimp in sauce. Serve over rice or pasta. **Yield:** 4 servings

Orlin Corey '50

MRS. ROGERS' CREOLE SHRIMP

1 cup sliced onions
½ cup chopped celery
1 clove garlic, minced
3 tablespoons butter or
   margarine
1 tablespoon flour
1 teaspoon salt
1 teaspoon sugar

2 to 3 teaspoons chili
   powder
1 cup water, divided
2 cups canned tomatoes
2 cups fresh or frozen raw
   shrimp, peeled
4 cups cooked rice

In large skillet, cook onions, celery and garlic in butter about 10 minutes. Combine flour, salt, sugar and chili powder, and mix with ¼ cup water. Add remaining water. Stir flour mixture into onions and celery in skillet. Simmer, uncovered, 15 minutes. Add tomatoes and shrimp. Cook over medium heat until shrimp is pink, about 5 to 8 minutes. Put rice in individual bowls and pour shrimp creole over. **Yield:** 4 to 6 servings

Thirty-five years ago, my Baylor roommate's mother, Mrs. Rogers, gave me her recipe for shrimp creole. I remember Mrs. Rogers making a rice ring, filling the center with the creole, and serving it at the table. It was such a pretty dish. I have made it all these years for my family. Now my daughters are making it for theirs—all never knowing the lady whose recipe it was.

Ethel Ann de Cordova Porter '58

⏱ SHRIMP CURRY IN-A-MICROWAVE-MINUTE

1 tablespoon margarine
1 (10½-ounce) can cream of
  shrimp soup
1 cup sour cream
2 tablespoons instant
  minced onion
½ teaspoon curry powder
1 cup canned or frozen
  shrimp

Hot cooked rice
Chopped peanuts
Crumbled bacon
Onion rings
Pineapple chunks
Chopped tomato
Chopped green onions

In a covered dish, place butter and shrimp soup. Heat in microwave on high for 2 minutes. Stir in sour cream, minced onion, curry powder, and shrimp. Cover and heat through, 3 to 4 minutes, stirring once or twice. Serve over rice with choice of condiments. **Yield:** 4 to 6 servings

Hint: *Substitute crabmeat for shrimp.*

Martha Mitchell Carroll '69

⏱ SPICY SHRIMP CASSEROLE

1 onion, chopped
1 green pepper, chopped
6 tablespoons margarine or
  butter
1 (10½-ounce) can French
  onion soup

1 (10¾-ounce) can cream of
  chicken soup
1 (10-ounce) can chopped
  tomatoes and green chiles
2 cups instant rice
1 to 1½ pounds raw shrimp,
  peeled

In small skillet or saucepan sauté onion and green pepper in butter. Combine soups, tomatoes and chiles, rice, and shrimp. Add sautéed onion and pepper and mix well. Pour into lightly greased 9x11-inch baking dish. Bake at 350° for 30 minutes. Reduce temperature to 325°, and bake for 30 more minutes. **Yield:** 6 to 8 servings

Hint: *Freezes well and tastes even better the next day.*

Cindy Waltman Schuhmann '84

SHRIMP AND RICE CASSEROLE

6 tablespoons chopped
  green pepper
6 tablespoons chopped
  onion
6 tablespoons melted butter
  or margarine
3 (10½-ounce) cans cream of
  mushroom soup
3 tablespoons lemon juice

½ teaspoon Worcestershire
  sauce
½ teaspoon dry mustard
½ cup grated sharp Cheddar
  cheese
Salt and pepper to taste
3 cups cooked white rice
3 cups cooked wild rice
2 pounds cooked shrimp,
  peeled and deveined

Sauté green pepper and onion lightly in butter. Add soup and next 5 ingredients. Combine with rice and shrimp. Turn into a buttered 10x15-inch baking dish. Bake at 375° for 35 to 40 minutes. **Yield:** 8 to 12 servings

Hint: *Use precooked, shelled, frozen shrimp to put together this very quickly. Can be mixed and refrigerated the night before baking.*

Sandra Stoesser Wallace '59

GULF FRIED SHRIMP

1 pound large raw shrimp,
  cleaned
2 eggs
1 cup milk

1 cup flour
1½ teaspoon garlic salt
36 saltine crackers, crushed

Split shrimp down the back to "butterfly." In a small bowl, beat eggs and add milk. In a second small bowl, mix flour and garlic salt. Put cracker crumbs in a third bowl. Dip shrimp, one at a time, into seasoned flour, then into egg and milk mixture, then into cracker crumbs. Fry in deep fat until golden brown. Serve with cocktail sauce, ketchup, or tartar sauce. **Yield:** 4 to 6 servings

Note: *Try fish fillet nuggets, too.*

Cynthia Duran Herin '69

CREAMED OYSTERS IN PASTRY SHELLS
"Easy and different"

2 (16-ounce) jars raw
  oysters, undrained
5 green onions, chopped

3 sprigs parsley, chopped
Thick White Sauce
8 small patty shells

Pour oysters with their liquid into a medium saucepan. Add just enough water to cover. Boil oysters until edges curl. Add oysters and water in which they were cooked, onion and parsley to Thick White Sauce. Pour into heated patty shells when ready to serve.
Yield: 4 to 6 servings

Thick White Sauce:
2 tablespoons butter
2 tablespoons flour
1 cup milk or half-and-half

½ teaspoon salt
⅛ teaspoon pepper, if
  desired

In small saucepan melt butter and stir in flour. Cook until flour is cooked, about 2 to 3 minutes, stirring constantly. Gradually stir in milk and continue stirring until mixture boils and thickens. Cook about 3 minutes longer. Add seasoning. Place in double boiler to keep hot. Cover tightly until served.

Lanelle Andrews Barfield '50

PASTA WITH SAUSAGE AND PEPPERS

2 pounds sweet Italian
  sausage
3 tablespoons olive oil
1 cup finely-chopped yellow
  onion
3 sweet red peppers, ribs and
  seeds removed, cut into
  medium-size julienne
  pieces
1 cup dry red wine
1 (35-ounce) can Italian plum
  tomatoes, including
  liquid
1 cup water

1 tablespoon dried oregano
1 teaspoon dried thyme
Salt and freshly-ground
  black pepper, to taste
½ teaspoon dried red pepper
  flakes
1 teaspoon fennel seeds
½ cup chopped Italian
  parsley
6 or more garlic cloves,
  peeled and finely
  chopped
2 pounds pasta (ziti or
  rigatoni), cooked

Pierce Italian sausage links all over with the tines of a fork. In a saucepan with ½-inch of water, simmer uncovered for about 20 minutes. The pot will boil dry and sausages will begin to fry in their own fat. Turn occasionally, cooking for another 10 minutes, or until they are well browned. Drain sausages well on paper towels.

Discard sausage drippings, but do not wash pot. Add olive oil and onions. Over low heat cook covered until tender, about 25 minutes. Add peppers and cook uncovered over medium heat for another 5 minutes, stirring often. Add wine, tomatoes, water, oregano, and thyme; season to taste with salt, black pepper, and red pepper flakes. Bring to a boil, reduce heat and simmer, partially covered for 30 minutes.

Slice sausages into ½-inch thick rounds. Add sausages and fennel seeds to sauce, and simmer uncovered for another 20 minutes. Add parsley and chopped garlic. Simmer for another 5 minutes. Serve over pasta, with a dollop of ricotta, fresh Parmesan cheese, and fresh black pepper. **Yield**: 10 to 12 servings

Claudia Burton Johnson, a Baylor mom

CRAZY SPAGHETTI

"If you like Chinese food, you'll like this."

1 pound ground meat
1 large onion, chopped
1 (5-ounce) bottle soy sauce
1 medium head cabbage,
    shredded
1 (4-ounce) can mushrooms

1 (16-ounce) can bean
    sprouts
1 (8-ounce) can water
    chestnuts
1 (16-ounce) package
    spaghetti, cooked and
    drained

Brown meat with onion in very large skillet or Dutch oven. Drain off fat. Pour ½ of soy sauce over meat. Add cabbage; cover and simmer about 5 minutes. Add mushrooms, bean sprouts, water chestnuts, and remaining soy sauce. Cover and simmer 3 minutes longer. Add cooked spaghetti. Cover and cook over low heat just to heat through. **Yield:** 8 servings

Betty Skinner Dison '46

TINA PIAZZA'S ITALIAN SPAGHETTI

1 onion, chopped
4 tablespoons olive oil
1 pound ground chuck
4 cloves garlic, minced
Salt and pepper, to taste
½ teaspoon oregano
½ teaspoon basil

3 (6-ounce) cans tomato paste
3 teaspoons sugar
6 (6-ounce) cans water
1 (16-ounce) package
    spaghetti, cooked
Parmesan cheese or Romano
    cheese, grated

In a large Dutch oven sauté onion lightly in oil just until tender. Add meat and brown slightly. Add garlic, salt, pepper, oregano, basil, and tomato paste; stir well and simmer 1 to 2 minutes. Add sugar and water. Cook covered for 1 hour. (If sauce is not thick enough, remove lid and cook slowly a little longer.) Serve over cooked spaghetti and top with grated Parmesan or Romano cheese. **Yield:** 6 to 8 servings

Ken King '67

ITALIAN STUFFED SHELLS

"Serve with a green salad and garlic toast."

1 (16-ounce) package jumbo
    pasta shells
½ pound Italian sausage
1 (10-ounce) package frozen
    spinach, thawed and
    squeezed dry
½ pound small curd cottage
    cheese, drained
3 crushed garlic cloves

Juice of ½ lemon
⅓ cup grated Romano cheese
Salt and coarsely-ground
    pepper, to taste
½ teaspoon oregano
1 egg, beaten
2½ cups spaghetti sauce
2 cups grated Mozzarella
    cheese

Boil shells until tender, but still firm. Rinse in cold water and drain. Sauté sausage and break into small pieces. Mix sausage with spinach and next 6 ingredients. Add egg and mix well. Spoon ½ cup sauce into baking dish. Fill shells with sausage mixture, placing filling-side up on top of sauce. Gently spoon remaining spaghetti sauce over each shell, and sprinkle with grated Mozzarella cheese. Bake at 350° for about 30 minutes until heated through and cheese is melted. **Yield**: 4 servings

Hint: *Can be completely prepared the day before serving and reheated.*

Carol Spearman '74

BURRO RUSSO

1 cup sweet butter
4 tablespoons tomato paste
½ cup heavy cream
½ teaspoon leaf sage,
    crumbled, or ¾ teaspoon
    powdered sage
1½ teaspoon Hungarian
    sweet paprika

Salt to taste
2 to 4 cloves garlic, crushed
¾ cup freshly-grated
    Parmesan cheese
1 (16-ounce) package pasta,
    cooked and drained

In a medium skillet melt butter; whisk in tomato paste and cream. Crumble sage between palms, and add together with paprika, garlic, and salt. Simmer 2 to 3 minutes. Whisk in Parmesan and pour over hot pasta. **Yield**: 6 to 8 servings

Julia Teegerstrom White '90

🕐 SHRIMP FETTUCINE

"Very impressive dish, and it's so easy."

1 (16-ounce) package fettucine	3 tablespoons butter
1½ pounds shrimp, peeled and deveined	1 (16-ounce) carton sour cream
6 cloves garlic, divided and crushed	½ cup butter, softened
	1 (4-ounce) block Parmesan cheese, grated

Cook fettucine in boiling, salted water until done but still slightly firm. Set aside.

Sauté shrimp and 3 cloves of crushed garlic in 3 tablespoons butter in large skillet until shrimp are pink, about 3 to 5 minutes. (Do not overcook shrimp or they will be tough.) Remove skillet from heat, and set aside.

In medium bowl, mix sour cream, ½ cup butter, remaining 3 cloves of crushed garlic and grated cheese. Add to shrimp in skillet and return to low heat just until cheese is melted. Stir into fettucine carefully. Turn into a greased 2½-quart casserole. Bake at 350° for 15 about minutes to warm thoroughly. **Yield:** 6 to 8 servings

Hint: *Serve with a green salad and garlic bread.*

Millicent Hislop Shankle '65

PASTA PRIMAVERA

1 pound broccoli
2 small zucchini
½ pound fresh asparagus
1 (16-ounce) package
  linguini
1 large clove garlic, chopped
1 pint cherry tomatoes,
  halved
¼ cup olive oil
1 teaspoon dried leaf basil,
  crumbled

½ pound fresh mushrooms,
  sliced
½ cup frozen green peas
¼ cup chopped fresh parsley
1½ teaspoons salt
¼ teaspoon black pepper
¼ teaspoon crushed red
  pepper
¼ cup butter
¾ cup heavy cream
⅔ cup freshly-grated
  Parmesan cheese

Wash and trim broccoli, zucchini, and asparagus. Cut broccoli into bite-size pieces; cut zucchini into thin slices; cut asparagus into 1-inch pieces. Cook in boiling, salted water until crisp-tender. Drain; put in a large bowl. Cook and drain linguini. Sauté garlic and tomatoes in oil in large skillet for 2 minutes. Stir in basil and mushrooms; cook 3 minutes. Stir in peas, parsley, salt, pepper, and red pepper; cook 1 minute. Add mixture to vegetables in bowl. In same skillet melt butter. Add cream and grated cheese, and stir constantly until smooth over medium heat. Add linguini; toss to coat. Stir in vegetables, and heat gently just until hot. **Yield:** 6 to 8 servings

Hint: *Add fresh boiled shrimp, or cubes of cooked ham or chicken. Serve with crisp bread sticks.*

Frances Durham Prather '44

SPINACH-ZUCCHINI VEGETABLE LASAGNA

1 (32-ounce) jar spaghetti
  sauce with mushrooms
  and onions
1½ cups water
1 (10-ounce) package frozen
  chopped spinach, thawed
  and squeezed dry
1 (16-ounce) carton cottage
  cheese

2 cups grated Mozzarella
  cheese
½ cup Parmesan cheese
2 eggs
8 ounces uncooked lasagna
  noodles
3 medium zucchini, sliced
  thin

In medium saucepan combine spaghetti sauce and water, and simmer. Mix spinach with cottage cheese, Mozzarella cheese, Parmesan cheese, and eggs. Pour 1 cup sauce into a 9x13-inch baking dish. (Use a deeper pan if available, or put a baking sheet under the dish in case of spillovers.) Layer 3 lasagna noodles over sauce. Cover with 1½ cups sauce. Spread ½ spinach filling over sauce; top with ½ sliced zucchini. Repeat noodles, sauce, filling, and zucchini. Top with remaining noodles and sauce. Cover with foil. Bake at 350° for 55 to 60 minutes. Remove foil and bake 10 minutes longer. Let stand 10 minutes before cutting. **Yield**: 8 servings

Note: *Use low-fat cottage cheese and Mozzarella cheese, and egg substitute. It's best to use half regular and half low-fat Mozzarella, because regular cheese melts better. Freezes well.*

Holly Zumwalt Taylor '90

LAZY-DAY OVERNIGHT LASAGNA
"This is perfect for busy families."

1 pound mild Italian sausage
   or ground beef
1 (32-ounce) jar prepared
   spaghetti sauce
1 cup water
1 (15-ounce) carton ricotta
   cheese
2 tablespoons fresh chives,
   chopped

½ teaspoon oregano leaves
1 egg
8 ounces uncooked lasagne
   noodles
1 (16-ounce) package sliced
   Mozzarella cheese
2 tablespoons grated
   Parmesan cheese

In large skillet, brown sausage; drain well. Add spaghetti sauce and water; blend, and simmer 5 minutes. In medium bowl, combine ricotta cheese, chives, oregano, and egg; mix well. In bottom of ungreased 9x13-inch baking dish or lasagna pan, spread 1½ cups of meat sauce. Top with ½ of noodles, ½ of ricotta cheese mixture, and ½ of Mozzarella cheese. Repeat with remaining noodles, ricotta cheese, and Mozzarella cheese. Top with remaining meat sauce, and sprinkle with Parmesan cheese. Cover and refrigerate overnight.

To bake, uncover baking dish, and bake at 350° for 50 to 60 minutes, or until noodles are tender and casserole is bubbly. Let stand 15 minutes before serving. **Yield**: 12 servings

Phyllis Wyrick Patterson '74

I prepared lasagna for Keven the night we were engaged at the Quadrangle (by the Christ statue). We had returned from Thanksgiving vacation early and few restaurants were open, so I prepared dinner. I didn't know he was going to propose. In fact, he was acting so strange, I thought he was going to break up with me. I had prepared the dish a hundred times before and he always ate every bit of it. That night, he could hardly eat a bite.

Keven told me he proposed to me on campus because he wanted it to be a special place we could go back to even when we were old. I guess that is why Baylor is so special. It is a place you can always go back to and call home.

Caroline Franklin Brelsford '90

GREEN CHILE CHEESE CASSEROLE

"The perfect brunch item for morning wedding showers."

2 (4-ounce) cans diced green chiles	4 eggs, separated
1 pound grated Cheddar cheese	⅔ cup evaporated milk
1 pound grated Monterey Jack cheese	1 teaspoon flour
	½ teaspoon salt
	⅛ teaspoon pepper
	2 tomatoes, sliced

Remove seeds and drain chiles. Combine chiles and cheese. Turn into a well-buttered 9x13-inch baking dish. Beat egg whites until soft peaks form. Set aside. Combine egg yolks, milk, flour, salt, and pepper. Gently fold egg whites into yolk mixture. Pour over cheese. Toss lightly and spread evenly into the dish. Bake at 325° for 30 minutes. Remove from oven, and arrange tomato slices on top. Bake 30 minutes more. **Yield**: 6 to 8 servings

Ellen Stoesser Byrd '64

CHEESY EGG CASSEROLE

"An excellent do-ahead dish for breakfast."

1 pound diced, cooked ham	1 teaspoon salt
2 cups milk	1 teaspoon dry mustard
6 slices bread, cubed	8 ounces Cheddar cheese, grated
6 eggs, beaten	

Combine all ingredients, and pour into a buttered 9x13-inch baking dish. Refrigerate overnight. Bake at 325° for 1 hour. **Yield**: 6 to 8 servings

Note: *Must be prepared a day ahead. Meat may vary: use 1 pound of bacon that has been fried and crumbled, or 1 pound of sausage, browned and crumbled.*

Martha Moody Stephens '59

EGGS FANTASTIC

"Tastes like a western omelet."

6 eggs
3 tablespoons sour cream
1 pound pork sausage
1 medium onion, chopped
8 ounces fresh mushrooms,
   sliced
6 tablespoons picante sauce
1 (8-ounce) box pasteurized
   process cheese, cubed

2 cups grated Cheddar
   cheese
2 cups grated Mozzarella
   cheese
Paprika, optional
Chili powder, optional
Garlic salt

Blend eggs with sour cream. Pour into a well-greased 9x12-inch baking pan. Bake at 400° for 4 to 7 minutes until set.

In a medium skillet, brown sausage, onion, and fresh mushrooms until meat is done. Drain well. When eggs are set, spread picante sauce over the top. Spoon on meat mixture. Combine cheeses and layer over meat. Sprinkle with paprika or chili powder, and garlic salt. Bake at 350° for 30 minutes or until cheese melts. **Yield**: 8 servings

Louanna Ruth Werchan '85

BRUNCH ENCHILADAS

1 pound hot bulk sausage
1 onion, chopped
8 eggs, scrambled

4 cups grated Monterey Jack
   cheese
1 dozen flour tortillas
1 (8-ounce) jar picante sauce

Brown sausage with onion. Add cheese and scrambled eggs. Spoon onto steamed and softened flour tortillas. Roll into enchiladas. Place seam-side down in lightly-greased baking dish. Refrigerate until ready to use. Heat covered in a 350°oven for 20 minutes, or uncovered on high in a microwave for 3 minutes. Spoon picante sauce over enchiladas when serving. **Yield**: 6 to 8 servings

Nancy Hudson Fields '73

SOUTHWESTERN GREEN CHILE OMELETTE

1 whole egg	White pepper to taste
¾ cup egg substitute	4 to 6 dashes hot pepper
1 (12-ounce) can evaporated	sauce
skim milk + water to	2 cups grated reduced-fat
make 2 cups	Cheddar cheese
½ cup flour	1 (4-ounce) can chopped
½ teaspoon salt	green chiles

Beat eggs until foamy in a large bowl. Beat in milk, flour, salt and pepper, and hot pepper sauce. Stir in cheese and chiles. Pour into a 2-quart (8x12-inch) baking dish that has been coated with non-stick vegetable spray. Bake at 350° for 50 to 60 minutes until the center is set and brown. Serve hot with jalapeño peppers and salsa. **Yield**: 4 servings

Hint: *As a light supper with corn tortillas, pintos or refried beans, and pico de gallo.*

Mary Chambers Hull '67

CHRISTMAS MORNING QUICHE

"The father prepares this for the family every year. He certainly has made Christmas morning easy for the mother. (Of course, she cooks the rest of the day!)"

1 pound bulk sausage	6 eggs
2 unbaked (9-inch) pie shells	2 cups sour cream
2 cups grated Cheddar	½ teaspoon salt
cheese, divided	

In a medium skillet, cook sausage until crumbled and brown. Drain well. Divide sausage between the 2 pie shells, covering the bottom of each. Sprinkle 1 cup of grated cheese over sausage in each shell. Beat eggs, and add sour cream and salt. Pour ½ of egg mixture into each shell. Bake at 350° for 35 to 40 minutes. **Yield**: 12 servings

Diane Waters Davis '66

ZUCCHINI QUICHE IN A HURRY

4 cups thinly-sliced zucchini
1 cup chopped onion
½ cup margarine
½ cup chopped parsley
½ teaspoon salt
½ teaspoon pepper
¼ teaspoon garlic powder
¼ teaspoon basil

¼ teaspoon oregano
2 eggs, well beaten
2 cups grated Mozzarella
  cheese
1 (8-ounce) package crescent
  dinner rolls
2 teaspoons Dijon mustard

Sauté zucchini and onion in margarine about 10 minutes. Combine parsley and seasonings and add to zucchini mixture. Blend eggs and cheese in a medium bowl. Spread roll dough in a 11-inch quiche pan or a 7x11-inch glass baking dish. Spread mustard over dough. Spoon zucchini mixture into dish. Pour egg mixture over all. Bake at 375° for 18 to 20 minutes **Yield**: 6 to 8 servings

Carrie Anna Millard Pearce, MSEd '70

CHILE RELLEÑOS

2 (4-ounce) cans whole green
  chiles
1 (8-ounce) package
  Monterey Jack cheese, cut
  into ½x½x2-inch strips
½ cup milk

1 egg, slightly beaten
½ cup flour
½ teaspoon baking powder
¼ teaspoon salt
⅓ cup corn meal
Cooking oil

Rinse whole chiles and remove any seeds. Drain well on paper towels. Stuff each chile with strips of cheese, using all the cheese. Place on paper towels, and drain again in refrigerator for 1 hour before cooking.

Blend milk and egg. Add sifted dry ingredients and mix well. Dip each chile in batter, being sure that all sides are coated. Fry quickly in hot cooking oil in a medium skillet, a few at a time, until all are cooked. Drain on paper towels. Serve hot with salsa or picante sauce. **Yield**: 6 servings

Sandra Bobo Karnes '60

Vegetables

I come from a long line of ranchers and farmers, and when I was grow-ing up, our freezer was always full of the beef my granddad sent. My mother broiled those steaks to tender perfection. In my memory, at least, we ate steak several times a week.

It's true that the wonder of steaks was balanced by the ongoing hor-ror of vegetables from our garden. Some years we cultivated half an acre, and my parents were determined not to waste even the yellow squash and zucchini. My mother tried to make these palatable in every possible way, but it was a doomed effort. Boys can recognize squash in any conceivable incarnation.

Her experiments with other vegetables were more successful: I still cook turnips with butter and sugar, and not too long ago, I cooked up a mess of fried okra from my own garden. Things have come full circle.

Now if only I could raise some cattle.

Greg Garrett
Baylor Assistant Professor of English

⏱ FRESH ASPARAGUS STIR-FRY

1½ pounds fresh asparagus
2 tablespoons olive oil
2 tablespoons sesame oil

1 tablespoon finely-chopped
  fresh ginger
1 tablespoon soy sauce
1 cup cashew pieces, toasted

Snap off tough lower end of asparagus spears. Cut remaining asparagus into bite-size pieces. Heat oils in wok or electric skillet. When hot, stir-fry ginger 1 minute. Toss in asparagus and stir-fry 4 to 5 minutes. Do not overcook. Asparagus should be crisp-tender. Add soy sauce and cashews. Serve immediately. **Yield:** 4 servings

Marguerite Shearer Fleener '90

⏱ ASPARAGUS CASSEROLE

2 (15-ounce) cans asparagus,
  cut in 2-inch pieces
1 teaspoon salt
1 (2-ounce) jar chopped
  pimiento
1 cup grated sharp Cheddar
  cheese

1 cup milk
⅛ teaspoon white pepper
3 eggs, beaten
1¼ cups buttered
  breadcrumbs

Mix first 7 ingredients. Pour in buttered 2-quart baking dish. Top with buttered breadcrumbs. Bake at 350° for 30 minutes. **Yield:** 6 to 8 servings

Hint: *Freezes well before baking.*

Carolyn Griffin Keathley '65

GREEK GREEN BEANS

1 medium onion, sliced	1 (16-ounce) can tomatoes
1 tablespoon oil	¼ teaspoon nutmeg
2 (16-ounce) cans green	1 tablespoon dried parsley
beans, drained and rinsed	

Microwave onion in cooking oil in a covered casserole for 3 minutes. Add remaining ingredients and microwave for 15 minutes on medium high. **Yield:** 6 to 8 servings

Note: *Beans may also be simmered, covered, over direct heat for 30 to 45 minutes. Or baked, covered at 350° for 1 hour.*

Kelly Korene Soter '89

SWEET AND SOUR GREEN BEANS

"The beans change texture and become crunchy. Delicious!"

3 (16-ounce) cans cut green	1 cup firmly-packed light
beans, drained & rinsed	brown sugar
¼ cup margarine	1 (6-ounce) can frozen
	limeade, thawed

Pour beans into a large bowl. Melt margarine in saucepan. Add sugar and limeade, and bring to a boil. Pour over beans, stirring carefully. Refrigerate, covered, for 24 hours. When ready to serve, reheat, drain, and serve hot. **Yield:** 8 servings

Note: *May be made several days ahead. Marinade may be frozen and used again.*

Vera Wilcoxson Scirratt '54

BAKED FIVE-BEAN CASSEROLE

"Travels well to potluck suppers"

3 medium onions, chopped
2 tablespoons butter or
　margarine
1 (16-ounce) can cut green
　beans, drained
1 (16-ounce) can butter
　beans, drained
1 (16-ounce) can kidney
　beans, drained

1 (16-ounce) can lima beans,
　drained
1 (20-ounce) can pork and
　beans
¾ cup firmly-packed brown
　sugar
½ cup vinegar
½ teaspoon garlic salt
1 teaspoon dry mustard

Sauté onions in butter. Add onions to remaining ingredients in a large bowl. Mix well. Pour into a 9x13-inch baking dish. Bake at 350° for 60 to 90 minutes or until sauce cooks down. **Yield:** 12 servings

Debbie Russell Hembree '74

 # MEXICALI BEANS

"Not a spicy dish, but one with unusual flavor. It grows on you with each bite."

3 (15-ounce) cans ranch-style
　beans, drained and rinsed
1 cup chopped celery
½ cup chopped green pepper
½ cup chopped onion
2 small, firm tomatoes,
　chopped

1 (4-ounce) can chopped
　green chiles
2 cups grated Cheddar
　cheese
1 teaspoon cumin
1 teaspoon salt
1 cup mayonnaise
1 cup crushed tortilla chips

In a large bowl combine all ingredients, except tortilla chips. Mix carefully and well. Pour into 9x13-inch baking dish. Top with crushed chips. Bake at 350° for 40 to 45 minutes. Allow additional baking time if it has been refrigerated before cooking. **Yield:** 6 to 8 servings

Hint: *Best when made the day before, refrigerated, and baked later. Serve with hamburgers or grilled chicken.*

Emily Eichelberger Harrell '67

BROWN BEANS BY BULLOCK

It shouldn't be necessary to have a recipe for cooking a pot of pinto beans. But it must be. I've come to that conclusion after the many times I've been served mushy pintos that don't even deserve to be recycled on a nacho.

Soaking beans overnight is the Number One killer of a good pot of beans. Don't do it. This old soaking overnight mistake is a hangover from the days when beans were sold in bulk straight from the fields without washing. Today's packaged beans are free of dirt and rocks and need only a little rinsing.

The second enemy of a good pot of pintos is cooking them too long in the name of making them just soft enough to eat. How long they cook isn't the answer—how they cook is.

Put your beans in a pot and cover them at least three times higher with water. Bring to a rapid boil for five minutes covered. After five minutes of boiling, turn out the fire and *Do not open the lid*. If you open the lid, forget it. You've ruined it.

Let the covered pot set for one hour. Then turn the fire back on just a little higher than a simmer. When the pot starts boiling again and the lid starts jumping around and sputtering over on the stove, put in a tablespoon of oil. This will cut down the sputtering.

After a couple of hours—a little longer if you're busy doing something else—you should need to add more water. Add only *hot* water. Never put cold water in boiling food.

This is also a good time to add some onion, a slab of salt pork or whatever else you like. The salt pork sold in most markets today is so sorry that you get about the same good out of a couple of strips of bacon.

Now turn the fire down to simmer, and thicken the juice. A tablespoon or two of brown sugar works fine. It doesn't taste in the beans. Some folks like to use two or three tablespoons of masa flour worked into a paste. You can taste this in the beans, but it is good. Incidentally, if you don't keep masa flour around, you can get the same effect by pulverizing a handful of Fritos.

Now the beans can simmer until they are exactly like you want them. They will not get mushy.

At this point you can also decide if you want just plain beans or if you want to go another route. If you like something off in the sweet direction, put in some more brown sugar or a little molasses.

Continued on next page

Brown Beans by Bullock (continued)

If you want something with a little zing, put in whatever is your favorite, or barbecue sauce, steak sauce, chili powder, jalapeños or the like.

When all this is simmered in good, you're ready to eat. If you're planning ahead, you can now put the beans in the icebox and warm 'em up when ready. Just warm them; don't cook 'em to death. They won't get mushy, but the juice will get thick.

Good eating!

The Honorable Bob Bullock, JD '58
Lieutenant Governor, State of Texas

HERB GARDEN VEGETABLE PIE

1½ cups flour
1½ teaspoons sugar
1 teaspoon salt
½ cup vegetable oil
2 tablespoons cold milk
½ cup freshly-grated
  Parmesan cheese
½ pound broccoli flowerets
  (about 2 stalks)
2 cups grated Monterey Jack
  cheese
½ cup freshly-grated
  Parmesan cheese
2 tablespoons flour

¼ teaspoon pepper
1 teaspoon dried basil, or 3
  teaspoons chopped fresh
  basil
½ teaspoon dried thyme, or
  1½ teaspooons chopped
  fresh thyme
½ cup chopped green onions
  (about 1 bunch)
2 fresh tomatoes, thinly
  sliced
¼ cup unsalted butter,
  melted

Combine first 6 ingredients for crust. Shape into a ball, and press evenly into a 9-inch pie pan. Boil broccoli 3 minutes in salted water. Rinse with cold water and drain. Combine cheeses, flour, pepper, basil, thyme, and onion. Put ½ of mixture in pie shell. Layer broccoli, then tomatoes, on top. Add remaining cheese mixture. Pour butter over pie. Bake at 350° for 30 minutes. Let stand a few minutes before slicing. Serve warm or at room temperature. **Yield:** 6 to 8 servings

Linda Gale Thompson White '64
Wife of The Honorable Mark White '62, JD '65
Former Governor, State of Texas

STIR-FRY CABBAGE WITH TOMATOES

1 tablespoon oil
2 medium onions, sliced
1 medium head cabbage,
  coarsely shredded

2 teaspoons sugar
Salt and pepper to taste
2 medium tomatoes,
  chopped in large pieces

In hot oil in a large skillet or wok, sauté onions for 2 to 3 minutes. Add cabbage and seasonings. Stir-fry until cabbage is crisp-tender. Do not overcook. Add tomatoes and heat through. **Yield:** 6 to 8 servings

Note: *May use halved cherry tomatoes.*

Carolyn Logsdon Wilkes '60

MINTED CARROTS

⅓ cup sliced water chestnuts
2 tablespoons margarine,
  melted and divided
2 cups sliced cooked carrots,
  drained

⅓ cup sifted powdered sugar
1 teaspoon dried mint or 1
  tablespoon chopped fresh
  mint leaves
¼ teaspoon cinnamon

Sauté water chestnuts in 1 tablespoon margarine for 5 minutes. Combine with carrots in a 1-quart casserole. Pour remaining tablespoon of margarine over carrots. Mix powdered sugar, mint leaves, and cinnamon; sprinkle over carrots. Bake covered at 350° for 20 minutes. Stir several times during baking. **Yield:** 2 to 4 servings

Barbara Ann Byrom Driver '54

SINFULLY SIMPLE CARROTS

1 pound bag carrots, coarsely
  grated
1 tablespoon sugar
½ teaspoon salt

⅛ teaspoon pepper
4 tablespoons butter or
  margarine

Put grated carrots in lightly-greased 2-quart casserole. Sprinkle sugar, salt, and pepper over carrots and toss. Dot with butter. Cover and bake at 350° for 1 hour. **Yield:** 5 to 6 servings

Mona Rogers Burchette '58

CREAMY VEGETABLE MEDLEY

1 (32-ounce) bag frozen
    mixed vegetables
1 tablespoon butter or
    margarine
½ teaspoon salt
¼ teaspoon garlic salt

½ cup butter or margarine
⅓ cup flour
¾ cup sour cream
¼ cup Parmesan cheese
Buttered breadcrumbs

Cook vegetables in boiling water according to package directions, adding 1 tablespoon butter, salt and garlic salt to water. Drain and save water.

    Melt ½ cup butter in saucepan. Add flour, stirring constantly to make a paste and cook for 2 minutes. Add reserved vegetable cooking water. Cook until mixture thickens. Add sour cream and cheese. Pour over mixed vegetables and blend. Pour into a 9x13-inch baking dish. Top with buttered breadcrumbs. Bake at 350° for 30 to 35 minutes. **Yield**: 8 to 10 servings.

 Note: *To make this recipe lower in fat, use liquid butter substitute, fat-free sour cream and fat-free Parmesan cheese. Also, use this sauce with any leftover vegetables you might have.*

Suzanne Richardson Keener '74

⏱ SPICY HOMINY IN A SKILLET

½ cup coarsely chopped
    onion
½ cup coarsely chopped
    green pepper
1 tablespoon butter, melted
1 (14½-ounce) can white or
    golden hominy, drained

1 (16-ounce) can tomatoes,
    undrained and chopped
1 (1¼-ounce) package taco
    seasoning mix
⅛ teaspoon hot pepper sauce
½ cup water
1 cup grated Cheddar cheese

In a 10-inch skillet, sauté onion and green pepper in butter until tender. Stir in remaining ingredients, except cheese. Simmer, stirring occasionally, until slightly thickened, approximately 25 minutes. Top with cheese, and let stand 5 minutes before serving. **Yield:** 4 to 6 servings

Jan Cranford Herrstrom '74

GARDEN CASSEROLE

"A delicious way to use garden veggies"

3 cups chicken broth
1 teaspoon salt or to taste
½ teaspoon basil
½ teaspoon thyme
1 cup uncooked brown rice
2 to 4 tablespoons oil
1½ cups diced eggplant
    (about ½ pound)
½ cup chopped onion

1 clove garlic, crushed
1 cup sliced zucchini (about
    ¼ pound)
½ cup chopped green pepper
1 large tomato, cubed
1 cup grated Swiss cheese
1 cup grated Monterey Jack
    cheese

Bring broth to a boil; add seasonings and rice. Cover and simmer about 50 minutes or until liquid is absorbed. Sauté eggplant, onion, and garlic in oil until tender. Combine rice and all vegetables; spoon ½ of mixture into a greased 2-quart casserole. Combine cheeses, and sprinkle 1½ cups over vegetables. Repeat layers, ending with remaining ½ cup of cheese. Bake at 325° for approximately 25 minutes or until heated through. **Yield:** 6 to 8 servings

The Cookbook Committee

CORN AND RICE CASSEROLE

1 large onion, chopped
½ cup chopped green pepper
¼ cup butter or margarine,
    melted
1 (17-ounce) can cream style
    corn
1 cup instant rice, cooked

1 (2-ounce) jar pimiento,
    drained
1 tablespoon sugar
1 egg, slightly beaten
1 cup grated Cheddar cheese
Salt and pepper to taste

Sauté onion and green pepper in butter. In a large bowl combine remaining ingredients. Add onion and peppers, and mix well. Pour into a greased 1½-quart casserole. Bake at 350° for 30 minutes. **Yield:** 6 to 8 servings

Suzanne Richardson Keener '74

☉ FAVORITE CORN BAKE

"Good with jalapeño peppers added, and maybe some cheese."

1 (17-ounce) can cream style
   corn
1 (16-ounce) can whole
   kernel corn, drained
½ cup margarine, melted

1 egg, beaten
1 (8½-ounce) package corn
   muffin mix
1 cup sour cream

Mix all ingredients. Pour into a buttered 9 x13-inch baking pan. Bake at 350° for 30 minutes. **Yield:** 8 to 10 servings

Peggy Simmons Kemble '59

☉ HAYS MAIZE

½ cup butter, melted
1 (3-ounce) package cream
   cheese, softened

2 (16-ounce) cans whole
   kernel corn, drained
¼ cup picante sauce

Beat butter and cream cheese, mixing well. Add corn and picante sauce. Bake at 350° for 20 minutes, uncovered, in a 1½-quart baking dish. Serve hot. **Yield:** 8 servings

Frances Hujar Stacy '77, JD '79

☉ HOT AND CHEESY CORN BAKE

2 tablespoons butter or
   margarine
1 (8-ounce) package cream
   cheese
2 (16-ounce) cans whole
   kernel corn, drained

1 (4-ounce) can chopped
   green chiles
¼ cup milk
Dash of cayenne pepper
¼ teaspoon salt, optional
¼ teaspoon garlic salt

Melt butter or margarine with cream cheese over low heat or in microwave. Combine remaining ingredients, and stir in cream cheese mixture. Pour into a 2-quart baking dish. Bake uncovered at 350° for 20 to 25 minutes. **Yield:** 6 to 8 servings

Sondra Blalock Adair '72

VEGETABLE MEDLEY IN CASSEROLE

"Convenient when fresh garden vegetables are out of season "

1 cup chopped onion
1 cup chopped celery
3 tablespoons butter
2 (10-ounce) packages frozen
 mixed vegetables, cooked
 and drained
1 cup grated Cheddar cheese

1 cup mayonnaise
1 (11-ounce) can white shoe
 peg corn
¼ pound round buttery
 crackers, crushed
½ cup butter, melted

In a large skillet sauté onion and celery in butter until tender. Stir in next 4 ingredients. Place in buttered 9x13-inch baking dish. Mix cracker crumbs with ½ cup melted butter. Use as topping for casserole. Bake at 350° for 30 minutes. **Yield:** 8 to 10 servings

Hint: *Serve with grilled chicken or beef.*

Doris Jean Wilkes Johnson '52

"Better is a dinner of vegetables where love is than a fatted ox and hatred with it." Proverbs 15:17

MUSHROOMS FLORENTINE

¼ cup chopped onion
¼ cup melted butter
1 pound fresh mushrooms,
 sliced
2 (10-ounce) packages frozen
 chopped spinach, cooked
 and squeezed dry

1 teaspoon salt
Dash of lemon pepper
1 cup grated Cheddar cheese,
 divided
Garlic powder

Sauté onions in butter until slightly cooked. Add mushrooms, and sauté until brown. Line a 9x13-inch baking dish with spinach. Sprinkle with salt and a dash of lemon pepper. Spread ½ of cheese over the top. Spoon on mushrooms and onions. Season lightly with garlic powder. Cover with remaining cheese. Bake at 350° for 20 minutes or until hot. **Yield:** 8 servings

Pat Belew Powell '65

ELEGANT PARMESAN-STUFFED MUSHROOMS
"Great flavor"

16 large mushroom caps
¼ cup grated Parmesan
   cheese
½ cup flavored breadcrumbs

1 tablespoon oil
16 slivers of margarine
Watercress or parsley to
   garnish

Arrange mushroom caps in a well greased 9x13-inch baking pan. Mix cheese, breadcrumbs, and oil; fill each mushroom cap. Place sliver of margarine on top of each cap. Bake at 350° for 30 minutes. Arrange on plates and garnish with parsley. **Yield:** 6 to 8 servings

Hint: *Freshly-grated Parmesan cheese is a must.*

Fonda Graves Paxton '81

BAKED SWEET ONIONS
"You can't beat Vidalias from Georgia for this recipe."

2 to 3 large Vidalia onions,
   peeled and sliced
½ cup butter or margarine

20 to 25 round buttery
   crackers, crushed
¼ cup grated Parmesan
   cheese

Sauté onions in butter or margarine until transparent. Spread ½ of onions into a 2-quart casserole. Top with ½ the crackers, then with ½ the cheese. Repeat layers, ending with cheese. Bake at 325° for 30 minutes. **Yield:** 6 to 8 servings.

Note: *Substitute 1015s or other sweet onion for Vidalias.*

Martha McCullough Park '85

ORIENTAL PEAS

1 small onion, minced
2 tablespoons finely-
  chopped green pepper
1 cup celery, sliced
½ cup margarine or butter
2 (15-ounce) cans sweet peas,
  drained
1 (8-ounce) can sliced water
  chestnuts, drained
1 (2-ounce) jar chopped
  pimientos, drained
1 (10½-ounce) can cream of
  mushroom soup
Round buttery crackers,
  crushed
2 tablespoons butter, melted

In a large skillet, sauté onion, green pepper, and celery in butter until soft. Stir in peas, water chestnuts, and pimientos. Layer ½ of mixture in buttered 2-quart casserole. Top with ½ of undiluted soup. Repeat layers. Top with cracker crumbs, and drizzle with melted butter. Bake at 350° for 30 minutes until hot and bubbly.
Yield: 8 to 10 servings

Carolyn Griffin Keathley '65

SOUTH TEXAS PARTY PEAS

1 (16-ounce) package frozen
  green peas
1 (6-ounce) jar sliced
  mushrooms, drained
1 (4-ounce) jar chopped
  pimientos, drained
¼ cup margarine
1 (8-ounce) can water
  chestnuts, drained and
  thinly sliced
1 tablespoon sugar
½ teaspoon salt
¼ teaspoon white pepper
4 tablespoons water
3 tablespoons cornstarch
½ cup milk
1 (8-ounce) jar Mexican-
  flavored pasteurized
  process cheese spread

In a large saucepan, combine first 9 ingredients. Bring to a boil; reduce heat and simmer 5 to 10 minutes. In a small bowl mix cornstarch and milk, stirring well. Pour over vegetables and stir. Cook over low heat just until mixture thickens. Add cheese spread, and stir just until melted. **Yield:** 8 to 10 servings

Carol Watson Barclay '60

EASY CHEESY POTATOES

1 (32-ounce) bag frozen hash
   browns

1 (16-ounce) box pasteurized
   process cheese, cubed
2 cups mayonnaise

Mix 3 ingredients together. Spoon into a greased 9x13-inch baking dish. Cover with foil. Bake at 300° for 1 to 1½ hours. Stir several times during baking to prevent burning. **Yield:** 8 to 10 servings

Jan Reedy, PhD '94
Wife of Chuck Reedy, Baylor head football coach

TWICE-BAKED POTATO CASSEROLE

6 medium potatoes
2 cups sour cream
1 bunch green onions, finely
   chopped

1 cup grated sharp Cheddar
   cheese
½ cup butter, melted

Bake potatoes at 400° for approximately 1 hour. When cool, peel potatoes and grate coarsely. Combine all ingredients. Pour in a 9x13-inch greased baking dish. Bake at 350° for 45 minutes. **Yield:** 8 servings

Mina Jones O'Bannon '55

GREEN AND GOLD PARTY POTATO CASSEROLE

8 medium potatoes (about 2½ pounds)
1 (8-ounce) container sour cream
2 tablespoons milk
4 tablespoons margarine or butter, divided
1¾ teaspoon salt
¼ teaspoon pepper

5 yellow squash, sliced, cooked and drained
1 large egg, slightly beaten
1 (10-ounce) package frozen chopped spinach, thawed and squeezed dry
2 teaspoons grated onion
¼ cup shredded Cheddar cheese

In 5-quart saucepan cook whole potatoes in water to cover for 25 to 30 minutes, until fork tender. Drain; cool potatoes slightly, and peel. In a large bowl, using an electric mixer, beat potatoes, sour cream, milk, 2 tablespoons margarine, 1½ teaspoon salt and ⅛ teaspoon pepper until smooth and fluffy; set aside.

In small bowl, mix squash with 1 tablespoon margarine and ⅛ teaspoon salt. Set aside. In another small bowl, mix egg with spinach, grated onion, 1 tablespoon margarine and ⅛ teaspoon salt. Mix well.

In deep casserole or soufflé dish, evenly layer with ⅓ of mashed potato mixture, all of squash, another ⅓ of potatoes, all of spinach, and last add remaining potatoes. Bake at 350° for 40 minutes or until heated through. Remove from oven. Sprinkle cheese on top, and let stand until cheese melts. **Yield**: 12 servings

Maydell Pickett Wyrick '33

The first big stuffed potato I ever ate was in 1960 at the Hickory Stick in Waco. That was also the year I had my first taste of Black-Bottom Pie at Sam Coates' restaurant. What a good year for food!

Bob Anne McMullan Senter '63

AVOCADO RICE

1 onion, chopped
1 clove garlic, minced
3 tablespoons butter
1 cup rice, uncooked
½ teaspoon saffron, optional

2½ cups chicken broth
1 teaspoon salt
Dash of pepper
2 avocados

In a large skillet sauté onion and garlic in butter until tender. Add rice, and sauté until rice is slightly browned. Add saffron, broth, salt, and pepper. Bring to a boil; reduce heat and simmer, covered, for 20 minutes or until rice is tender. Peel and chop avocados, and add to cooked rice just before serving. **Yield:** 6 to 8 servings

Hint: *A pleasant change from Spanish rice on a Mexican food menu.*

Ruth Stoesser Seaberg '62

SAUSAGE-RICE DRESSING
"A delicious accompaniment for pork, chicken, or turkey."

1 pound bulk sausage
½ cup chopped onion
1 cup chopped celery
1 cup raw rice

1 (2-envelope size) box
    chicken noodle soup mix
4½ cups water
½ cup slivered almonds

Brown sausage, onion, and celery in skillet. Drain well. Spoon sausage mixture into a 2-quart casserole dish. Add rice, soup mix and water, stirring until soup mix is partially dissolved. Bake at 350°, uncovered, approximately 1 hour. Fluff rice with a fork, and sprinkle almonds over top before serving. **Yield:** 6 to 8 servings

Susie McDonald Robinson '65

BROWN RICE PILAF WITH RAISINS AND NUTS

¼ cup chopped onion
2 tablespoons butter
1 tablespoon oil
1 cup raw brown rice
2½ cups chicken stock or
    water

¼ teaspoon black pepper
½ cup yellow raisins
½ cup dry white wine
¾ cup almonds, sliced and
    toasted

Sauté onions in butter and oil until clear. Add rice and cook over low heat for 3 minutes, stirring constantly, until lightly browned. Add chicken stock. Season with pepper. Bring to a boil. Cover, reduce heat, and simmer for 45 minutes. While rice cooks, plump raisins in white wine for about 45 minutes. Drain. When rice is cooked, stir in raisins and toasted almonds. **Yield:** 4 servings

Note: *One (14½-ounce) can of clear chicken broth may be used for the stock. Add water to make 2½ cups.*

Marian Haile Williams '72

⏱ OREGANO RICE

½ cup margarine
1 medium onion, chopped
1 (10-ounce) can consomme
¾ cup water

1 teaspoon oregano, crushed
1 (4-ounce) can mushroom
    pieces
1 cup raw rice

In a large skillet, sauté onion in margarine until clear. Add remaining ingredients. Pour into a greased 2-quart casserole dish. Bake, covered, at 350° for 1 hour. **Yield:** 4 to 6 servings

Sharon Elaine Howard '73

SOPA DE ARROZ

2 tablespoons cooking oil
1 cup long-grain raw rice
½ cup chopped onion
1 teaspoon salt (omit if broth
  is salted)

1 (16-ounce) can tomatoes,
  undrained
2 cups chicken broth

Heat oil in large skillet. Stir in raw rice. Stirring constantly, sauté rice over medium heat until every grain is brown. Add onion, salt, tomatoes and chicken broth. Reduce heat. Cover skillet tightly, and steam for 25 to 30 minutes until all liquid is absorbed. **Yield:** 4 to 6 servings

Note: *Many variations to this dish. Add 1 cup frozen green peas 3 to 4 minutes before end of cooking time. Add 1 cup chopped, cooked chicken or pork. Add chopped parsley or chopped green pepper. Sprinkle cooked rice with grated Parmesan or Cheddar cheese.*

My husband's parents were missionaries to Mexico and this recipe was one of the pluses of their tenure. All of the Cheavenses (five "original" alumni plus numerous offspring) have enjoyed it and consider it their own specialty.

Alice Dawson Cheavens '29

ORIENTAL RICE ALMONDINE

1 (6-ounce) package long-
  grain and wild rice mix
1 cup chopped onion
1 cup chopped celery
3 tablespoons margarine
2 tablespoons soy sauce

1 (3-ounce) can mushrooms,
  stems and pieces, drained
1 (5-ounce) can water
  chestnuts, drained and
  sliced
⅓ cup slivered almonds,
  toasted

Cook rice according to package directions. Sauté onion and celery in margarine until tender. Mix remaining ingredients. Stir into rice. Pour into a 1½-quart greased casserole dish. Bake at 350° for 20 minutes or until hot. **Yield:** 8 servings

Fran Booth Porter '54

SPINACH BALLS ON TOMATO SLICES

2 (10-ounce) packages frozen
  chopped spinach, cooked
  and squeezed dry
2 cups dry breadcrumbs or
  stuffing mix
1 medium onion, chopped
  fine
2 eggs, beaten

¾ cup butter or margarine,
  melted
½ cup Parmesan cheese
1½ teaspoons garlic salt
1 teaspoon thyme
½ teaspoon pepper
5 ripe tomatoes

Mix all ingredients into drained spinach. Make into individual balls using a ¼-cup measure to form balls. (An ice cream scoop works well.) Freeze on a cookie sheet; when frozen, store in ziplock bags in freezer. When ready to use, place each spinach ball on a thick slice of tomato. Bake at 350° for 20 to 25 minutes, or until heated through. **Yield:** 15 servings

Hint: *Make ahead and freeze.*

Kay Nethery Elliott '64

GREEN AND GOLD SPINACH
"Quick, easy, and the little ones will eat something green!"

1 (10¾-ounce) can cream of
  potato soup
⅓ cup milk
¼ teaspoon nutmeg
⅛ teaspoon salt

2 (10-ounce) packages frozen
  chopped spinach, cooked
  and squeezed dry
½ cup grated Cheddar cheese

In a medium bowl combine soup with milk. Add nutmeg and salt. Stir in cooked spinach. Pour into a 7x11-inch baking dish. Bake at 350° for 30 minutes or until hot. Top with cheese. Return to oven just long enough for cheese to melt. **Yield:** 6 to 8 servings

Candyce Rasner Jones '81

ELEGANT SPINACH WITH SHRIMP

"Delightful"

2 (10-ounce) packages
   frozen, chopped spinach
1 (3-ounce) package cream
   cheese with chives,
   softened
3 tablespoons butter or
   margarine

1 (10½-ounce) can cream of
   shrimp soup
Juice of ½ lemon
¾ cup bread or cracker
   crumbs
2 tablespoons butter, melted

Cook spinach according to package directions; drain well. While spinach is still hot, stir in cream cheese and butter. Add soup and lemon juice, and mix well. Pour into a buttered 2-quart casserole. Toss crumbs with melted butter, and sprinkle over top of casserole. Bake at 375° about 30 minutes or until bubbly. **Yield:** 8 to 10 servings

Joy Copeland Reynolds '74
Wife of Baylor President, Dr. Herbert H. Reynolds

ITALIAN SPINACH

"Also great over cooked pasta for a simple supper"

4 tablespoons olive oil
2 medium yellow onions,
   coarsely chopped
4 heaping tablespoons
   chopped garlic
Lemon-pepper seasoning

3 tablespoons dry sherry
3 to 4 tablespoons seasoned
   rice vinegar
3 (10-ounce) packages frozen
   chopped or leaf spinach

Heat olive oil in a large skillet. Add onion and garlic, and sauté until onion is transparent. Add seasonings and heat through. Add spinach and heat, breaking up frozen packages. Mix well. Cover, and cook over low heat, stirring occasionally, for 20 to 25 minutes. **Yield:** 6 to 8 servings

Note: *Can be prepared early and kept warm. It gets better with time.*

Nancy Harrison Guy '60

CHILE-CHEESE SQUASH BAKE

5 yellow squash, sliced
2 teaspoons instant minced
  onion
6 tablespoons butter,
  divided
½ cup canned tomatoes with
  green chiles

1 cup grated Cheddar or
  Monterey Jack cheese
Salt and pepper to taste
Cracker crumbs or crushed
  corn chips

Cook squash with instant onion in salted water. Drain very well.
Add 4 tablespoons of butter, tomatoes, cheese, salt, and pepper.
Stir to blend. Pour into a buttered 1½-quart casserole. Melt remaining butter, pour over squash and sprinkle with cracker
crumbs or corn chips. Bake at 350° about 30 minutes or until bubbly. **Yield:** 6 servings

Doris Davis Sosnowski '62

THE BLACK-EYED PEA RESTAURANT'S BAKED SQUASH

"The best squash casserole I've eaten."

5 pounds medium yellow
  squash, thickly-sliced
2 eggs, beaten
1 cup whole wheat
  breadcrumbs
½ cup butter or margarine

¼ cup sugar
2 tablespoons chopped
  onion
½ teaspoon salt
¼ teaspoon pepper

Cook squash in a large saucepan with enough water to cover.
Cook until tender. Drain well and mash. Drain again. Combine
squash with remaining ingredients. Turn into a 3-quart casserole
that has been lightly greased or sprayed with non-stick vegetable
spray. Top with additional bread crumbs. Bake at 350° about 20
minutes or until lightly browned. **Yield:** 10 servings

Hint: *Packaged herb-seasoned dressing mix may be used for
breadcrumbs.*

Martha Durr Lemon '59, MSEd '69

BAKED PECAN SQUASH IN MICROWAVE

"Don't like squash? This is different!"

4 tablespoons butter,
divided
¼ cup round buttery cracker
crumbs
¼ cup chopped pecans
1 tablespoon water
Dash of salt
1 pound yellow squash,
sliced

¼ cup mayonnaise
1 egg, beaten
½ cup shredded Cheddar
cheese
1½ teaspoons sugar
½ teaspoon instant minced
onion

In a 1-quart casserole, microwave 2 tablespoons butter on high for 30 seconds until melted. Add crumbs and pecans. Microwave on high for 2 minutes, stirring after 1 minute. Pour crumbs onto wax paper and set aside. In same casserole, place water, salt and squash. Cover. Microwave on high for 8 to 10 minutes until tender, stirring after 4 minutes. Drain well.

Mix together mayonnaise, egg, cheese, remaining 2 tablespoons melted butter, sugar, and onion. Pour over squash, mixing well. Microwave on medium for 4 minutes. Stir and cover squash with crumb topping. Microwave on medium 2 to 4 minutes more until center is set. Let stand 5 minutes before serving. **Yield**: 4 servings

Hint: *Mix zucchini and yellow squash for added color interest.*

Dorothy Jane Beck Irwin '43

Thanksgiving in Louisiana was always a memorable time for me and my family. Mother must have cooked for days, preparing many of the foods which she knew we loved. Since mother's death I try to bring the tastes of her kitchen into my home with her favorites that she enjoyed cooking for us each year. The memories of this special holiday spent in Bastrop flood back into our minds as we gather in Waco.

Julia Nell (Judy) McConathy Graves '60

BAKED SQUASH MEDLEY

3 yellow squash, cut in
  ½-inch slices
3 zucchini squash, cut in
  ½-inch slices
Salt and pepper to taste
Garlic salt to taste

3 tablespoons butter or light
  margarine, melted
1 cup grated Cheddar cheese
2 medium tomatoes, sliced
2 cups corn flake crumbs

Cook squash in boiling water, or steam, for 8 to 10 minutes. Drain
well and chop coarsely; drain again. Season with salt, pepper,
and garlic salt. Butter a 9x13-inch baking dish or spray with non-
stick vegetable spray . Pour squash into dish; drizzle with melted
butter. Cover with grated cheese. Arrange tomato slices on top.
Sprinkle with corn flake crumbs. Bake uncovered at 350° for 20
minutes or until hot. **Yield:** 6 to 8 servings

Carolyn Logsdon Wilkes '60

BLUE RIBBON SWEET POTATO SOUFFLE

4 to 6 sweet potatoes
1¼ cups sugar
½ teaspoon nutmeg
½ teaspoon cinnamon

2 eggs, beaten
1 cup milk
¼ cup + 2 tablespoons
  margarine, melted

Bake or boil whole potatoes until done. When cool enough to
handle, peel and mash well. Add sugar, spices, eggs, milk and
margarine; mix well. Pour into 2-quart greased casserole dish.
Bake at 400° for 20 to 25 minutes. While soufflé is baking, mix
Topping ingredients. Remove casserole from oven, and spread
Topping evenly over potatoes. Bake 10 minutes longer. **Yield:** 4
to 6 servings

Topping:
¾ cup crushed cornflakes
½ cup chopped nuts
½ cup firmly-packed brown
  sugar

¼ cup + 2 tablespoons butter
  or margarine, melted

Mix all ingredients together.

Anita O'Quinn Baker '60, MSEd '79

GLAZED YAMS IN SHERRY 'N CREAM

8 medium yams	⅓ cup heavy cream
2 cups sugar	2 teaspoons sherry
1 cup water	1 teaspoon salt

Cook unpeeled yams in boiling water for 10 minutes. While yams are cooking, combine sugar and 1 cup water in a large skillet; bring to a boil. Lower heat, and boil gently for 8 minutes. Remove from heat.

Drain yams, peel and cut in half lengthwise. Drop into syrup in skillet. Cook slowly 10 minutes, turning frequently. When yams begin to lighten in color, remove from heat, and drain off ½ of syrup.

In a small saucepan, combine cream, sherry, and salt; heat through. Pour over yams. Bake at 350° until yams are glazed. **Yield**: 8 to 12 servings

Frances Durham Prather '44

"I think sweet potatoes give me more constant pleasure than any other form of food, and a world without them would be less joyous for me than it is."

Dorothy Scarborough
1896 Baylor alumna and award-winning novelist

GLAZED YAMS AND GRANNY SMITH APPLES

"We introduced our visiting international students to Thanksgiving and sweet potatoes with this recipe."

4 large yams
4 Granny Smith apples,
  peeled, cored, sliced
¼ cup butter, divided
4 tablespoons brown sugar

1 teaspoon cinnamon
1 teaspoon nutmeg
¼ teaspoon salt
¼ teaspoon pepper

Place unpeeled yams in large saucepan with water to cover. Boil until almost tender, about 20 minutes. Remove from heat, and cool slightly. Peel and cut yams into ¼-inch thick slices.

Butter a shallow 2-quart baking dish. Layer bottom of dish with ½ the yams, followed by ½ the apple slices. Dot with 2 tablespoons of butter. Sprinkle with 2 tablespoons brown sugar. Mix cinnamon, nutmeg, salt, and pepper. Sprinkle ½ of seasoning mixture over casserole. Repeat layering. Cover and bake at 325° for 30 minutes. Remove cover; continue baking for an additional 25 to 30 minutes, or until the apples are soft and yams are brown and glazed. **Yield**: 9 servings

Note: *Rome, McIntosh, or any cooking apple may be substituted.*

Diane Gajdica Deily '80

PRALINE SWEET POTATOES
"A favorite recipe of many"

4 to 6 medium sweet
   potatoes or yams
½ to 1 cup sugar, to taste
½ teaspoon salt
½ cup milk

1 teaspoon vanilla
2 eggs, slightly beaten
⅓ cup butter, softened
Praline Topping

Bake potatoes at 350° until done, about 1½ hours. When cool enough to handle, peel potatoes. Mash with an electric mixer. Add least amount of sugar; taste potatoes, and adjust for desired sweetness. Add remaining ingredients , mixing well after each addition. Pour into a 2-quart casserole dish that has been buttered or sprayed with non-stick vegetable spray. Top with Praline Topping. Bake, uncovered, at 350° for 30 minutes. **Yield:** 6 servings

Praline Topping:
1 cup brown sugar
⅓ cup flour

½ cup butter, melted
1 cup chopped walnuts

Mix all ingredients together.

When our children were very young, many of our fellow church families who were also away from families and "home" would have wonderful potluck holiday meals. Not only did this give us a sense of having a large family, but it also provided some great shared recipes. When I use these recipes today, I remember those wonderful friends who crossed our path years ago.

Eileen Erickson Bright '69

MARINATED TOMATOES ITALIA

3 large tomatoes
⅓ cup olive oil
¼ cup red wine vinegar
1 teaspoon salt
¼ teaspoon pepper
¼ teaspoon garlic powder

1 tablespoon chopped
  parsley
1 teaspoon dried basil
1 teaspoon dried dill weed
Liberal dash of cayenne
2 tablespoons finely-
  chopped onions

Cut tomatoes into thick slices, and arrange in shallow dish. Combine remaining ingredients. Whisk until salt dissolves. Pour over tomato slices. Cover and marinate in refrigerator for several hours or overnight. **Yield:** 6 servings

The Cookbook Committee

All the fine praise,
All the good wishes,
Will never replace
Help with the dishes.

Anonymous

Breads

I can remember, as a child, setting the table for company, running stubby fingers around the flowers on the cool, white plates.

Mother said they were forget-me-nots, the little blue flowers standing in a circle around Grandma's china. She told me how this grandmother, who died before I was born, often took her china to church dinners and community gatherings. She claimed, "I'd rather have it broken being used than just gathering dust in the cabinet."

I sometimes wonder, Grandma, how many times your china has been used during its ninety-four years. I wonder how many hundred of Mother's hot dinner rolls have sat perched on the edge of a crowded plate — waiting for the butter to be passed around — as friends and family sat elbow-to-elbow at a laughter- and story-filled table.

A few years ago Mother gave me the forget-me-not china; I now had a home of my own. Carefully I washed it and put it away, afraid my two small boys might damage it. Then I remembered.

Now, one Sunday each month is our Sabbath Sunday — a time to cease, to celebrate. While Buddy and I prepare the simple meal, our boys carefully set the table with the crystal and Grandma's china. After hands are held and grace is said, we eat by the light of a single candle, telling stories. Sometimes the stories are new — our memories in the making. But sometimes the room is filled with the unseen presence of friends and family to whom we are connected, those who have shared our table and our lives, those we can never forget.

Judy Henderson Prather '73

TEXAS WHOLE WHEAT BREAD

1 teaspoon sugar
1 cup lukewarm water
2 (¼-ounce) packages dry
    yeast
1 cup powdered milk
4 cups whole wheat flour,
    divided
3 tablespoons safflower oil
    or any unsaturated oil

3 tablespoons honey
1 tablespoon butter
    flavoring
2 cups hot water
1 tablespoon salt
4 cups unbleached white
    flour

Dissolve sugar in lukewarm water; add yeast and let stand until it foams up to fill a 2-cup measuring cup. (The action of the yeast in sugared water is rather fast, so be sure your other ingredients are ready to use.) Mix powdered milk and 2 cups of whole wheat flour. Dissolve oil, honey, and butter flavoring in 2 cups of hot water. Add powdered milk mixture, beating until most of the lumps dissolve. Make sure this mixture cools to lukewarm before adding the yeast mixture. Then add yeast mixture. Beat until well mixed. Let rise in a warm place until it is bubbly or until it rises about an inch in the mixing bowl, 15 to 20 minutes. Add salt; beat in remaining 2 cups of whole wheat flour. Add white flour, 1 cup at a time, until dough becomes thick enough to handle. Turn out on a floured surface, and knead until smooth.

Put in a greased bowl; turn the greased side of the dough up and cover. Let rise until about double in size. Shape into 3 loaves. Place in well-greased 9x5-inch pans. Let rise until doubled in bulk, 45 to 60 minutes. Bake at 400° for 10 minutes; reduce heat to 350° and bake 30 minutes. Remove loaves from pans, and place on a wire rack to cool. **Yield**: 3 loaves

Hint: *An interesting subtlety can be added to the taste of the bread by replacing 1 cup of the whole wheat flour with ½ cup of wheat germ and ½ cup of rye flour.*

"Making bread is one of the most rewarding challenges for a person inclined to give it a try. My own bread baking began when I wrote to Barbara Kilgore [wife of Dr. Jack Kilgore, Baylor philosophy professor] and asked for her recipe. I gave it a try and it worked to a charm."

Dr. Bill Cooper '54
Dean, Baylor College of Arts and Sciences

LITTLE BRAIDED HERB BREADS

½ cup sugar
3 packages quick-rise active
    yeast
6 to 6½ cups flour, divided
1 cup milk
½ cup water

6 tablespoons butter or
    margarine
3 eggs
¼ cup grated Parmesan
    cheese
1½ teaspoons thyme leaves

Combine sugar, yeast, and 2 cups of flour in large bowl. Heat milk, water, and butter or margarine in 2-quart saucepan over low heat until very warm (120° to 130°). (Butter or margarine does not need to melt completely.) Gradually beat liquid into dry ingredients until just blended, using low speed on mixer. On medium speed, beat 2 minutes, occasionally scraping bowl with rubber spatula. Beat in eggs, cheese, thyme, and 1 cup flour to make a thick batter. Continue beating 2 minutes, scraping bowl often. With wooden spoon, stir in 3 cups flour to make a soft dough.

Turn dough onto lightly-floured surface, and knead about 10 minutes until smooth and elastic, working in about ½ cup more flour while kneading. Shape dough into a ball and place in large greased bowl, turning dough over so that top is greased. Cover with towel; let rise about 30 minutes in warm place (80° to 85°), away from draft, until doubled in size. (Dough is doubled when two fingers pressed lightly into it leave a dent). Punch down dough, and turn onto lightly floured surface. Cover with bowl, and let rest for 15 minutes for easier shaping.

Cut dough into 9 equal pieces. With floured hands, roll 1 dough piece into an 18-inch-long rope. Repeat with 2 more dough pieces. Place 3 ropes side by side and loosely braid. (Braid should be about 12 inches long.) Cut braid crosswise in half. Pinch cut ends and tuck under to seal, making 2 small braided loaves. Place each loaf, seam side down, in a greased 5¾x3¼-inch loaf pan. Repeat with remaining dough. Cover with towel and let rise in warm place until doubled, about 15 minutes. Bake loaves at 400° for 15 minutes or until golden brown. Loaves will sound hollow when lightly tapped with fingers. Remove from pans immediately; cool on wire racks. **Yield**: 6 loaves; 4 servings each

Kelly Korene Soter '89

BASIC REFRIGERATOR ROLLS

1 cup shortening
1 cup sugar
1½ teaspoons salt
2 cups water, divided
2 eggs, beaten

2 (¼-ounce) packages dry
  yeast
6 cups flour, unsifted
Margarine, melted

Combine shortening, sugar, and salt. Bring 1 cup of the water to a boil, and stir into shortening mixture, blending well. Cool slightly, and add eggs. In a small bowl, mix yeast and 1 cup warm water according to package directions. Add to shortening mixture. Mix in flour, a little at a time, blending well after each addition. Knead 5 to 10 minutes on lightly-floured surface.

Turn dough into a very large greased glass or crockery bowl (do not use stainless steel). Brush top with melted margarine; cover loosely with plastic wrap and refrigerate at least 4 hours.

At least 3 hours before baking, place a portion of dough on a floured surface and allow to warm slightly, about 30 minutes. Roll dough out to about ¼-inch thick, and cut into small rounds with biscuit cutter. Brush with melted margarine and fold over for Parkerhouse rolls. Place in a shallow greased pan. Allow to rise at room temperature for 2 hours or until double in size. Bake at 425° for 8 to 10 minutes. **Yield**: About 4 dozen

Hint: *When rolling out, use extra flour from a shaker to make dough easy to handle. Refrigerated dough will keep 7 to 10 days.*

Betty Stoesser Ritchie '66

ALL-BRAN YEAST ROLLS

1 cup water
½ cup shortening
6 tablespoons sugar
½ cup all-bran cereal
¾ teaspoon salt

1 (¼-ounce) package dry
    yeast
1 egg, well beaten
3 cups sifted flour

Bring water to a boil. Pour ½ cup into a large bowl; set aside other ½ cup to cool. Mix shortening, sugar, bran cereal, and salt in bowl with boiling water. Stir until sugar is dissolved. Cool to lukewarm.

Dissolve yeast in the remaining ½ cup water that has cooled to lukewarm. Add egg. Stir yeast mixture into bran mixture. Stir in flour. Chill, covered, in refrigerator at least 2 hours. Turn dough onto lightly-floured surface, and knead until smooth, about 5 minutes, adding small amounts of flour as needed. Divide and shape as desired. Let rise in greased pan until double in bulk. Bake at 400° about 8 to 10 minutes or until richly browned. **Yield**: About 3 dozen

Frances Newland '83

SAUSAGE BREAKFAST BREAD

"Bake this in 1-pound coffee cans"

1 link sausage,
    approximately 1 pound
4 cups flour, divided
1 (¼-ounce) package yeast
½ cup milk

½ cup water
¼ cup sugar
½ cup margarine
1 teaspoon salt
2 eggs, slightly beaten

Cook sausage. Remove casing, crumble, and blot out excess grease. Mix 2 cups flour with yeast. In small saucepan, stir milk, water, sugar, margarine and salt over low heat until margarine melts. Cool 5 minutes and add to flour. Stir in remaining flour, eggs and sausage. Dough will be stiff; turn into lightly-floured surface and knead until smooth and elastic, about 5 to 8 minutes.

Coat insides of 2 1-pound coffee cans with cooking oil. Divide dough in half. Put in cans and cover with plastic lids. Let dough rise until within 1 inch of the top of can. Remove lids. Bake at 375° for 35 minutes or until loaf sounds hollow when tapped. **Yield**: 2 loaves

Marilyn Sebesta '71

HERBED CHEDDAR BUNDT BREAD

Our testers gave this bread a 5-star rating.

¼ cup butter, softened
1 teaspoon minced onion
1 cup grated longhorn
   Cheddar cheese
¼ teaspoon marjoram
¼ teaspoon thyme
2½ cups flour, divided
2 tablespoons sugar

1 teaspoon salt
2 (¼-ounce) packages yeast
½ cup milk, warmed
½ cup water
¼ cup butter
1 egg, beaten
1 tablespoon poppy seeds

In a small bowl, mix first 5 ingredients for filling; set aside. Combine 1½ cups flour, sugar, salt, and yeast. Combine warm milk, water, and butter; add to flour mixture. Stir in egg. Blend with mixer for about 3 minutes; gradually add remaining flour. Stir by hand for stiff batter. Spoon ½ of batter into greased bundt pan and sprinkle with poppy seeds. Spoon cheese filling over batter. Add remaining batter. Cover and let rise in a warm place for 1 hour. Bake at 400° for 35 to 40 minutes. Remove from pan immediately. **Yield:** 1 large loaf

Becky A. Dyer '69

Never trust a skinny cook.
Kitchen graffiti

OLD WORLD POTATO BREAD

3½ cups flour, divided	2 teaspoons salt
¾ cup mashed potato, fresh or instant	3 tablespoons margarine
2 (¼-ounce) packages yeast	1½ cups warm water
2 tablespoons sugar	1 cup whole wheat flour
	1 tablespoon flour, optional

Combine 1½ cups flour, mashed potato, yeast, sugar and salt. Melt margarine in very warm water. Gradually add to flour mixture. Beat 2 minutes on high. Stir in whole wheat flour and enough of the remaining 2 cups flour to make a soft dough. Turn out onto lightly-floured surface, and knead 6 to 8 minutes until smooth. Place dough in a greased bowl; cover and let rise until doubled in bulk.

Divide dough in half; roll out to 8x12-inch rectangle. Roll up from small side; pinch seam closed, and place on greased baking sheet. Flatten slightly. Let rise again until doubled. Score loaves with 3 cuts (¼-inch thick) and dust lightly with 1 tablespoon flour, if desired. Bake at 400° until done, about 25 minutes. **Yield**: 2 loaves

Hint: *To use instant potato, bring ½ cup water + 3 tablespoons milk to a boil. Add ½ cup instant mashed potatoes.*

Wanda May LeMaster, MSEd '83

My mother managed the lumber yard that she and my father owned. Because she was at work, I began cooking mid-day meals for the family by the time I was eight, getting step-by-step instructions from Mother by phone. Fortunately, I had few disasters, but the one I remember best was my first attempt at mashed potatoes.

Being very busy that day, Mother gave me all the instructions at once. I followed them carefully, but the result wasn't what I expected. They were kind of watery and gray. I called her; she agreed that I had followed the instructions. Then she asked, "Judy, did you drain the potatoes before you mashed them?"

She never said anything about draining them —I swear she didn't!

Judy Henderson Prather '73

KOLACHES

"As good as ones from any Czech bakery."

3 (¼-ounce) packages dry
   yeast
¾ cup sugar, divided
1 cup warm water (105° to
   115°)
8 cups flour, divided

2 cups milk
1 cup margarine, melted
2 eggs, beaten
1 teaspoon salt
Filling variations

Dissolve yeast and 1 tablespoon sugar in warm water in a large bowl. Add 1 cup flour, and stir well; cover and let rise in a warm place (85°), free from drafts, 1 hour or until doubled in bulk.

Scald milk; let cool to luke warm (105° to 115°). Stir yeast mixture down; add milk, margarine, eggs, and salt, stirring well. Add enough remaining flour to make a soft dough. Cover and repeat rising procedure, for 1 hour or until doubled in bulk.

Punch dough down, and let rest 5 minutes. Turn out onto a floured surface, and roll to ½-inch thickness. Cut with a 2½-inch biscuit cutter. Place on lightly-greased baking sheets. Make indentation in the center of each roll using thumb; fill indentation with 1 teaspoon of desired filling.

Cover and repeat rising procedure 30 to 45 minutes or until doubled in bulk. Bake at 375° for 20 minutes or until brown. **Yield**: About 6 dozen

Cheese Filling:
½ (12-ounce) carton cottage
   cheese
1 single-serving container
   prepared tapioca pudding

1 egg yolk
1 teaspoon lemon juice
⅓ cup sugar

Combine cottage cheese and pudding. Let set 30 minutes. Stir in remaining ingredients, mixing well.

Apricot Filling:
1 (6-ounce) package dried
   apricots

¾ (16-ounce) can sliced
   peaches, drained
⅓ cup sugar

Cook apricots in small amount of water until apricots are tender. Add peaches and sugar. Mash with a fork until smooth.

Hint: *A drinking glass makes a good-size cutter for the dough.*

Shala Mills Bannister '84

CINNAMON PECAN ROLLS
"Needs only one rising"

1 cup buttermilk
¼ cup sugar
1 teaspoon salt
¼ cup shortening
1 teaspoon vanilla
½ teaspoon butter flavoring
⅓ cup warm water
2 (¼-ounce) packages yeast
1 egg

3 cups sifted flour
½ cup margarine, softened
 and divided
1 cup firmly-packed brown
 sugar
½ cup chopped pecans
2 teaspoons cinnamon
Icing

Warm buttermilk slightly, and stir in next 5 ingredients. Let cool to lukewarm. Measure very warm water into large bowl. Sprinkle in yeast, and stir to dissolve. Add buttermilk mixture, egg and flour; beat well. Turn onto floured board and knead a few seconds to form a smooth ball. Cover with a damp cloth, and let rest for 5 minutes.

Combine 4 tablespoons margarine, brown sugar, pecans, and cinnamon. Divide dough into 2 equal parts. Roll each portion into a 9x18-inch rectangle. Spread each rectangle with 2 tablespoons margarine and sprinkle with brown sugar mixture. Beginning on long side, roll like a jelly roll. Cut each roll into twelve 1½-inch slices. Place in greased muffin tins or 9x13-inch pan. Cover and let rise in a warm, draft-free place until doubled, about 1 hour. Bake at 375° for 12 to 15 minutes. Top with Icing while rolls are still hot. **Yield**: 2 dozen rolls

Icing:
2 cups powdered sugar,
 sifted
3 tablespoons milk

1 teaspoon vanilla
½ teaspoon butter flavoring

Blend all ingredients together well.

Betty Rogers Bryant '58

"I'm convinced that heaven will smell like home-baked bread."
Overheard at a cookbook planning meeting

EGGLESS AUTUMN BREAD

3 cups flour
1 cup whole wheat flour
2 cups sugar
1 tablespoon baking soda
1 teaspoon salt
2 teaspoons cinnamon
1 teaspoon cloves

3 cups fresh-baked butternut
   squash, (about 1 medium-
   large squash)
¾ cup oil
¾ cup raisins
¾ cup chopped pecans

Stir dry ingredients together. Add squash and oil, and mix with an electric mixer. Stir in raisins and nuts. (Batter will be stiff and heavy.) Pour into 2 9x5-inch loaf pans lined with wax paper. Bake at 350° for about 1 hour and 15 minutes or until tester inserted in center comes out clean. Cool 5 minutes in pans. Turn out on racks, and remove wax paper. **Yield**: 2 loaves

Hint: *Canned pumpkin can be substituted for the fresh-baked butternut squash, but you can tell the difference.*

Corwinna McCharen Barnette '60

APRICOT NUT BREAD

Delicious with morning coffee.

1 cup dried apricots, cut in
   quarters
1¼ cups sugar, divided
2 tablespoons shortening
1 egg, beaten
½ cup orange juice

2 cups sifted flour
2 teaspoons baking powder
½ teaspoon baking soda
1 teaspoon salt
1 cup chopped nuts

Cover dried apricots with water, and set aside to soak for 20 minutes. Cream 1 cup sugar, shortening, and egg. Stir in remaining sugar and orange juice. Add dry ingredients; blend well. Drain apricots, and add with nuts. Bake in greased and floured 8x4-inch loaf pan at 350° for 1 hour. **Yield**: 1 loaf

Jessie Lee Wolfe Janes '38

ORANGE PECAN BREAD

"This 'quick' bread takes longer than most, but is worth the effort."

½ cup butter or margarine, softened	1½ teaspoons baking powder
¾ cup sugar	¼ teaspoon baking soda
2 eggs, separated	Pinch of salt
Grated rind of 1 large orange	½ cup fresh orange juice
1½ cups flour	1 cup chopped pecans
	Orange Glaze

Cream butter; add sugar gradually, beating with an electric mixer until light. Beat in egg yolks, 1 at a time, and add grated orange rind. Mix dry ingredients and add to batter alternately with orange juice, beginning and ending with flour. Stir in pecans. In small bowl, beat egg whites until stiff, and fold carefully into batter. Pour into greased 8x4-inch loaf pan. Bake at 350° on middle rack of oven for 50 to 60 minutes. Spoon or brush Orange Glaze over bread when bread is removed from oven. Cool in pan or on a wire rack. **Yield**: 1 loaf

Orange Glaze:

¼ cup fresh orange juice   ¼ cup sugar

Combine in small saucepan. Simmer gently for 5 minutes, stirring occasionally, until a light syrup forms.

Note: *This makes good muffins, too. Fill 18 to 20 greased muffin tins and bake for 30 minutes.*

The Cookbook Committee

POPPY SEED BREAD

3 cups flour
1½ teaspoons salt
1½ teaspoons baking powder
3 eggs
1½ cups milk
1⅓ cups oil
2¼ cups sugar

1½ tablespoons poppy seeds
1½ teaspoons vanilla
1½ teaspoons almond extract
1½ teaspoons butter
   flavoring
Glaze

In a large bowl sift dry ingredients together. Add remaining ingredients, and mix thoroughly with mixer on medium speed for 2 minutes. Pour into 2 greased and floured 9x5-inch loaf pans. Bake at 350° for 1 hour (325° for glass pans). Cool for 5 minutes. Pour Glaze over bread while still hot. Cool completely, and remove from pans. Wrap in foil and refrigerate. Can be frozen. **Yield:** 2 loaves

Glaze:
¼ cup orange juice
¾ cup powdered sugar
½ teaspoon butter flavoring

½ teaspoon almond extract
½ teaspoon vanilla

Stir ingredients together.

Dr. Liz Schmitz
Wife of Dr. Charles Schmitz,
Dean of Baylor School of Education

GARDEN BUNDT BREAD

½ pound bacon
1 cup finely-chopped green
    pepper
1 cup finely-chopped onion
1 (2-ounce) jar pimiento,
    drained and chopped

½ cup butter, melted
½ cup grated sharp Cheddar
    cheese
3 (8-ounce) cans refrigerator
    biscuits, cut in quarters

Fry bacon till crisp; reserve drippings. Cool and crumble bacon. Sauté green pepper and onion in bacon drippings. Pour off excess drippings. In large bowl, carefully combine bacon, pepper, onion, and remaining ingredients. Spoon into greased bundt pan. Bake at 350° until brown, about 30 minutes. **Yield**: 4 to 6 servings

Hint: *May use 1 pound sausage with sage in place of bacon.*

Wanda J. Rice '52

COFFEE LOVERS' COFFEE CAKE

2 cups flour
2 teaspoons instant coffee
    granules
2 cups firmly-packed brown
    sugar
1 teaspoon ground cinnamon
½ teaspoon salt

¼ teaspoon ground nutmeg
½ cup butter
1 (8-ounce) carton coffee-
    flavored low-fat yogurt
1 teaspoon baking soda
1 egg, beaten

Combine flour and coffee granules in a large bowl. Add brown sugar and next 3 ingredients; stir well. Cut in butter with a pastry blender until mixture resembles coarse meal. Press ½ of crumb mixture into a greased 9-inch square baking pan, and set aside. Combine yogurt and baking soda, stirring well. Add to remaining crumb mixture, stirring just until dry ingredients are moistened. Add egg, stirring gently to combine. Pour yogurt mixture over crumb mixture in pan. Bake at 350° for 45 minutes. **Yield**: One 9-inch coffee cake

Marilyn Wyrick Ingram '72

BANANA NUT ROLL

½ cup butter or margarine,
   softened
2 cups sugar
2 eggs
2 cups flour
1½ teaspoons baking soda
¼ teaspoon salt

¼ cup, plus 2 tablespoons
   buttermilk
1½ cups mashed ripe banana
   (about 3 medium)
1 cup chopped pecans or
   walnuts
1 teaspoon vanilla

Cream butter and sugar, beating well with mixer at medium speed. Add eggs, 1 at a time, and beat well after each. Combine flour, baking soda, and salt. Add to creamed mixture alternately with buttermilk, beginning and ending with flour. Stir in banana, pecans, and vanilla. Spoon batter into 3 greased and floured 1-pound coffee cans. Bake at 350° for 55 minutes, or until a wooden pick inserted in center comes out clean. Cool in cans for 10 minutes; remove to wire rack, and cool completely. **Yield**: 3 rolls

Hint: *As bananas become very ripe, they may be successfully frozen if peeled and wrapped tightly in foil. Package 3 or 4 together for a future batch of bread.*

Peggy O'Neill Strode '74

CREAM CHEESE BREAKFAST BREAD

2 (8-ounce) cans refrigerated
   crescent dinner rolls
2 (8-ounce) packages cream
   cheese, softened

1 cup sugar
1 teaspoon vanilla
1 egg, separated

Unroll 1 can of rolls on the bottom of a 9x12-inch baking dish, and pinch perforations together. Cream together cream cheese, sugar, vanilla, and egg yolk. Spread evenly over roll dough. Unroll second can of rolls, and place dough on top of cream cheese mixture. Mix egg white with 1 teaspoon water. Brush top layer with egg white wash, and sprinkle evenly with a little sugar. Bake at 350° for 30 minutes. Cool before serving. **Yield**: 8 servings

Eleanor Shattles Morris '65

BLUEBERRY COFFEE CAKE
"This is top notch!"

½ cup butter, softened
1 (8-ounce) package cream
   cheese, softened
1¼ cups sugar
2 eggs
1 teaspoon vanilla
2 cups flour

1 teaspoon baking powder
½ teaspoon baking soda
¼ teaspoon salt
⅓ cup milk
1 cup frozen blueberries,
   unthawed, but patted dry
Topping

Cream butter, cream cheese, and sugar until light. Add eggs and vanilla and beat well. Sift dry ingredients; add to creamed mixture alternately with milk. Fold in blueberries. Spread in greased and floured 9x13-inch pan. Sprinkle on Topping. Bake at 350° for 25 to 30 minutes. **Yield**: 18 to 24 servings

Topping:
½ cup firmly-packed brown
   sugar
1 teaspoon cinnamon

½ cup flour
3 tablespoons butter

Mix brown sugar, cinnamon, and flour. Cut in butter until mixture is crumbly.

Frances Adkins Cleveland '67

REUNION COFFEE CAKE

1½ cups sugar
½ cup margarine, softened
½ cup shortening
1 teaspoon vanilla
1 teaspoon almond extract
1 teaspoon butter flavoring
4 eggs

3 cups flour
1½ teaspoons baking powder
½ teaspoon salt
1 (21-ounce) can peach,
    cherry, or apple pie filling
1 cup powdered sugar
1 to 2 tablespoons milk

Blend first 7 ingredients in large mixing bowl on low speed. Beat for 3 minutes on high. Gradually stir in flour, baking powder, and salt. Spread ½ of batter in lightly-greased and floured 10x15-inch pan. Place fruit filling by tablespoons (9 to 12) over batter. Spoon remaining ½ of batter on top of pie filling. Bake at 350° for 30 minutes. Mix powdered sugar and milk, and drizzle over cake when it has cooled. **Yield**: 20 to 24 servings

This coffee cake has been a steady menu item for a retreat enjoyed once a year by several Baylor roommates and their spouses. Tradition began spasmodically at Homecomings during the fifties but has continued quite steadily since the mid-sixties. We're quite proud of this record.

**Contributed by Wynell Gillen Patterson '50
and Jeannine Boyles '50**

APPLE PECAN MUFFINS

½ cup butter
2 cups sugar
2 eggs
1 teaspoon vanilla
2½ cups flour
1 teaspoon baking powder
¾ teaspoon baking soda

1 teaspoon salt
½ teaspoon nutmeg
1 teaspoon cinnamon
3 cups peeled and diced
    Granny Smith apples
1 cup chopped pecans

Cream butter and sugar. Add eggs and vanilla; beat until fluffy. Thoroughly mix all dry ingredients. Slowly add to butter-sugar mixture, mixing only until moistened. Hand stir in pecans and apples. (Mixture may be a little dry; however, apples will provide enough moisture.) Fill greased or lined muffin tins with ¼ cup of mixture. Bake at 350° for 20 minutes or until muffins test done. **Yield**: 18 to 24 muffins

Hint: *These muffins make great gift basket fillers.*

Marilyn Jeanne Jones '82

SWEET APPLETS

1½ cups sifted flour
2 teaspoons baking powder
½ teaspoon salt
½ teaspoon nutmeg
½ cup sugar
⅓ cup shortening
1 egg

⅓ cup milk
1½ cups pared, shredded
    apples (about 3 medium
    apples)
¼ cup butter or margarine,
    melted
½ cup sugar
1 teaspoon cinnamon

Sift first 4 ingredients together and set aside. Cream sugar and shortening. Blend in egg, and mix well. Add milk alternately with dry ingredients. Stir in apples. Fill well-greased miniature muffin tins ⅔ full. Bake at 400° for 20 to 25 minutes until brown. Cool enough to remove from pan. Dip top of muffin into melted butter and then immediately into mixture of sugar and cinnamon. **Yield**: 3 dozen miniature muffins.

Peggy Wilson Dobbins '54

SUGAR-TOP MUFFINS

1 cup flour
1 cup quick-cooking oats
¾ cup brown sugar
1 teaspoon baking powder
1 teaspoon baking soda
1 egg, beaten

¾ cup milk
⅓ cup oil
½ cup chopped nuts
2 teaspoons sugar
¼ teaspoon cinnamon

Combine first 5 ingredients in medium mixing bowl. In a small mixing bowl, mix egg, milk, and oil. Make a well in center of dry ingredients, and add egg mixture. Stir just until dry ingredients are moistened. Add nuts and stir. Fill greased or lined muffin cups ⅔ full. Mix sugar and cinnamon together and sprinkle about ½ teaspoon on top of each muffin. Bake at 375° for 18 to 20 minutes or until golden brown. Serve warm. **Yield**: 12 muffins

Darlene Bobo Caddell '57

RASPBERRY MUFFINS

1½ cups flour
½ teaspoon baking soda
½ teaspoon salt
1½ teaspoons cinnamon
1 cup sugar

1 (12-ounce) package frozen
   unsweetened raspberries,
   thawed
2 eggs, well-beaten
⅔ cup oil
½ cup chopped pecans

Mix dry ingredients in medium bowl. Make a well in the center, and stir in undrained raspberries, eggs, and oil. Mix thoroughly; add pecans. Spoon batter into lightly-greased muffin tins. (Muffin cups will be full. Batter is heavy and won't overflow.) Bake 400° for 15 to 20 minutes. Cool 5 minutes before removing from tins. **Yield**: 12 muffins

Note: *Can be baked in 1 greased and floured 9x5-inch loaf pan at 350° for about 1 hour.*

Judy Lindsey Oberkrom '66

BANANA HEALTH MUFFINS

"Moist, dense, and tasty"

2 cups oat flour
2 tablespoons bran
2 tablespoons wheat germ
1 teaspoon baking soda
¼ teaspoon salt
1 egg, beaten

1 cup mashed bananas
⅓ cup maple syrup
⅓ cup safflower oil
6 tablespoons milk
2 tablespoons vinegar

Mix dry ingredients together in large bowl. Process egg, bananas, and liquid ingredients in food processor until well blended. Mix quickly into dry ingredients. Fill greased muffin tins ⅔ full. Bake at 400° for about 20 minutes. **Yield**: 12 muffins

Note: *For oat flour, grind quick-cooking oats in food processor until fine. Measure as usual.*

Lanette Lemons Whitley '70 and Dennis Whitley '71

SWEET-FROM-FRUIT MUFFINS

Fruit provides the only source of sugar in this tasty muffin.

1 cup chopped dates
½ cup raisins
½ cup chopped prunes
1 cup water
½ cup margarine
¼ teaspoon salt

1 teaspoon baking soda
2 eggs, beaten
1 teaspoon vanilla extract
1 cup flour
½ cup chopped nuts

In a saucepan, combine fruits with water; bring to a boil and boil 5 minutes. Stir in margarine and salt. Set aside to cool. Add remaining ingredients to cooled fruit. Stir until dry ingredients are just moistened. Spoon into greased muffin pans and bake at 350° for 15 minutes. **Yield**: 12 to 15 muffins

Note: *This moist and tasty dessert proves to be a good alternative for those who should not and for those who cannot have "something sweet." Can be baked in 11x7-inch pan for 30 minutes.*

Joan Martin Cook '56

TEA ROOM MUFFINS

"Very simple—everything you need you have on the shelf."

1 cup brown sugar
½ cup flour
¼ teaspoon salt
2 eggs, beaten

2 tablespoons margarine,
   melted
1 teaspoon vanilla
1 cup coarsely-chopped
   pecans

Combine brown sugar, flour, and salt. Add eggs, margarine, and vanilla; mix just until dry ingredients are moistened. Fold in pecans. Fill greased miniature muffin tins ⅔ full. Bake at 400° for 15 minutes. **Yield**: 2 dozen miniature muffins

Lucy Lattimore Mebane '58

A-PEELING MUFFINS

½ cup margarine
1 cup sugar
1 egg
1 cup mashed bananas
1 teaspoon baking soda

1½ cups flour
1 teaspoon nutmeg, optional
1 teaspoon vanilla
½ cup chopped pecans

Cream margarine and gradually add sugar; mix till light and fluffy. Add egg and continue beating; stir in mashed bananas. Mix dry ingredients together, and gradually add to creamed mixture. Stir in vanilla and pecans, and mix until blended. Fill greased or lined muffin tins ¾ full. Bake at 350° for 25 to 30 minutes. **Yield**: 12 muffins

For over fifty years this recipe has been a family tradition. My aunt gave it to my mother who made it for me and my brothers. I made it for my children, and now my daughter makes the recipe. The tradition continues!

Linda Hull Goodwin '60

MRS. CHARLES' SCONES

"A well-traveled recipe, from British Guiana to Moscow to Texas"

2 cups flour
3 teaspoons baking powder
¼ teaspoon salt
⅓ to ½ cup sugar
½ cup shortening

1 egg, well beaten
¾ cup milk
½ teaspoon vanilla
½ cup raisins

Sift dry ingredients. Cut in shortening until mixture is crumbly. Combine egg, milk, and vanilla. Add to flour mixture, mixing only enough to moisten flour. Stir in raisins. Turn onto lightly-floured board, and pat into a round disk about ½ or ¾-inch thick. Cut into 10 or 12 wedges. (The dough will double or triple in size.) Place on lightly-greased cookie sheet. Bake at 400° for about 15 minutes or until light brown. Serve warm with butter and jam. **Yield**: About 1 dozen

Hint: *The dough can also be dropped from a spoon like drop cookies onto a baking sheet.*

F. Rosalee Hayden Meredith '47

CHEESE DROP BISCUITS

2 cups baking mix
⅔ cup milk
½ cup grated sharp Cheddar
   cheese

¼ cup margarine, melted
¼ teaspoon garlic powder

Spray cookie sheet with non-stick vegetable spray. Mix first 3 ingredients, and drop 1 tablespoon dough for each biscuit onto cookie sheet. Bake at 450° for 8 to 10 minutes. Combine melted margarine and garlic powder. Brush the top of each biscuit while warm. **Yield**: Approximately 10 to 12 biscuits

Sue Dickson Davis '52

BAKING POWDER BISCUITS

2 cups flour
4 teaspoons baking powder
½ teaspoon cream of tartar
½ teaspoon salt

2 tablespoons sugar
½ cup shortening
1 egg, beaten
⅔ cup milk

Sift first 5 ingredients together into a bowl. Cut shortening into flour mixture until it is the consistency of cornmeal. Combine beaten egg with milk and slowly pour into flour mixture. Stir to make a stiff dough. Knead 5 times on a floured surface. Roll to ½-inch thickness; cut with 1½-inch cutter, dipped in flour. Bake on a lightly-greased cookie sheet at 425° for 10 to 15 minutes. **Yield**: About 1 dozen biscuits

While I was at Baylor, one of the mainstays of my diets was an order of biscuits with honey from Tanglewood Farms. My friends and I often headed over to Tanglewood to share a plate of those biscuits, a cup of hot coffee, and a heartfelt conversation. Even today, biscuits are "comfort food" for me. Although I do not have Tanglewood's recipe, I do have a recipe just as delicious—my mother-in-law's Baking Powder Biscuits.

Shala Mills Bannister '84

EXTRA SPECIAL HERBED BISCUITS

2½ cups biscuit mix
3 tablespoons Parmesan
   cheese

2 tablespoons Italian
   seasoning, without salt
⅓ cup margarine, divided
⅔ cup milk

Mix together biscuit mix, cheese, and Italian seasoning. Cut in ¼ cup margarine. Add milk and mix lightly until ingredients are blended. Turn dough out onto floured surface, and roll to ½-inch thickness. Cut with large biscuit cutter. Place on ungreased cookie sheet. Melt remaining margarine, and brush tops of biscuits. Bake at 450° for 8 to 10 minutes, or until lightly browned. **Yield**: 8 to 12 biscuits

Sherry Boyd Castello '58

QUICK HERB ROLLS

½ cup butter	2 tablespoons grated
1½ teaspoons parsley flakes	Parmesan cheese
½ teaspoon dill weed	1 (10-ounce) can refrigerator
1 tablespoon onion flakes	buttermilk biscuits

Melt butter in 9-inch cake pan. Mix herbs and cheese together, and stir into butter. Let stand 15 to 30 minutes. Cut biscuits into halves or fourths, and swish around in herb butter to coat all sides. Bake at 425° for 12 to 15 minutes. **Yield**: 6 to 8 servings

Note: *This may be prepared several hours ahead and refrigerated.*

Carol Adams Stutzenbecker '69

EASY CHEESY ROLLS

"Grown men and women have been known to fight over the last piece."

1 (5-ounce) jar sharp	3 drops hot pepper sauce
pasteurized process	2 (1-dozen) packages sesame
cheese spread	or other brown-and-serve
½ cup margarine, softened	rolls

Combine cheese spread, margarine, and pepper sauce. Cut rolls down the center of the top, being careful not to cut through. Place on greased baking sheet. Spread cheese mixture inside and on top of rolls. Bake according to package directions. **Yield**: 2 dozen rolls

Hint: *For an extra rich treat, use only 1 package of rolls but be sure to use all of cheese mixture.*

Kathy Robinson Hillman '73

⏱ QUICK CRESCENT CARAMEL ROLLS

8 tablespoons margarine,
   divided
¾ cup firmly-packed brown
   sugar
¼ cup water

½ cup chopped pecans,
   optional
2 (8-ounce) cans refrigerated
   crescent dinner rolls
¼ cup sugar
2 teaspoons cinnamon

In ungreased 9x13-inch pan, melt 5 tablespoons margarine in oven. Stir in brown sugar, water, and pecans. Set aside. Separate each can of roll dough into 4 rectangles. Pinch perforations together to seal. Spread with 3 tablespoons softened margarine. Combine sugar and cinnamon; sprinkle over dough. Starting at shorter side, roll up each rectangle. Cut each roll into 4 slices, making 32 pieces. Place cut-side down in prepared pan. Bake at 375° for 20 to 25 minutes until golden brown. Invert immediately to remove from pan. Serve warm. **Yield**: 32 rolls

Hint: *To reheat, wrap in foil and warm at 350° for 10 to 15 minutes.*

Cheryl Blalock Shamburger '74

⏱ QUICK BROCCOLI CORNBREAD
"A more moist texture than the traditional cornbread"

2 (8½-ounce) packages
   cornbread mix
1 (16-ounce) package
   chopped frozen broccoli,
   thawed and drained

¾ cup margarine, melted
4 eggs
1 (12-ounce) carton small
   curd cottage cheese

Mix all ingredients. Pour into a well-greased 9x13-inch baking pan. Bake at 375° for 25 to 30 minutes or until firm and lightly brown. **Yield**: 12 to 15 servings

Hint: *Cottage cheese stored upside down will keep fresh twice as long.*

Sarah Rutherford Starr '88

MEXICAN CORNBREAD

2 eggs
1 cup sour cream
⅔ cup salad oil
½ cup cream-style corn
½ cup niblet corn
1½ cups yellow cornmeal
1 teaspoon salt
3 teaspoons baking powder

2 jalapeño peppers,
  deveined, seeded and
  chopped
1 tablespoon chopped green
  pepper
1 tablespoon chopped red
  pepper
1 cup grated sharp Cheddar
  cheese

Beat eggs slightly. Add sour cream, oil, and both kinds of corn. Mix remaining ingredients together in another bowl. Combine the 2 mixtures and pour in a large greased iron skillet. Bake at 350° for 30 minutes. **Yield**: 8 to 10 wedges

Marguerite Shearer Fleener '90

FIREHOUSE JALAPEÑO CORNBREAD

3 cups cornbread mix
3 teaspoons sugar
1 teaspoon baking powder
3 eggs, beaten
2¼ cups milk
½ cup cooking oil
1 large onion, grated

1 (17-ounce) can cream-style
  corn
1½ cup grated Cheddar
  cheese
1 (12-ounce) jar jalapeños,
  chopped and drained.

Mix dry ingredients in large bowl. Blend eggs, milk, and oil. Stir into dry ingredients just until moistened. Stir in remaining ingredients. Bake at 400° for 45 minutes in greased 9x13-inch metal baking pan. **Yield**: 12 to 15 pieces

Note: *Use fewer chopped jalapeños if hot is not desired.*

Michelle Bodine Stevenson '87

SOUTHERN CORN PONES

1 cup white cornmeal
½ teaspoon salt

¾ cup boiling water
Shortening for frying

Combine cornmeal and salt in a bowl. Pour in boiling water and beat until the mixture is smooth. Shape the mixture into flat round cakes. Fry cakes in 1-inch deep shortening. Turn and fry until both sides are crisp and golden. Serve with butter or cane syrup. **Yield**: 8 to 12 pones

Note: *Bacon drippings may be used for frying.*

Millicent (Millie) Hislop Shankle '65

DADDY DON'S SATURDAY MORNING OATMEAL PANCAKES

2 eggs
2 cups buttermilk
3 tablespoons oil
1½ teaspoons baking powder
1½ teaspoons sugar
½ teaspoon salt

½ teaspoon baking soda
1 teaspoon vanilla, optional
1½ cups flour
½ cup quick-cooking
  oatmeal

Beat eggs in mixer bowl. Add buttermilk and oil, and continue mixing. Add other ingredients, and mix only until blended. Pour pancake batter onto a griddle heated to 450°. Turn pancakes when bubbles start to come to the surface, about 30 to 45 seconds. **Yield**: About 12 4-inch pancakes

Note: *For thinner batter, use equal amounts of milk and buttermilk.*

Don Castello '57

"Don has been cooking pancakes for Saturday morning breakfast since our four kids were little. Over the years he has developed his own healthy version using oatmeal. We have endured the stages of this developing recipe, including one gummy honey version; but he's finally perfected the mix!"

Sherry Boyd Castello '58

GERMAN PANCAKES

4 eggs	⅔ cup milk
⅔ cup flour	½ teaspoon salt
1 tablespoon sugar	1 tablespoon butter

Place eggs in a blender and blend on "stir" until light yellow. Turn off blender. Add remaining ingredients. Blend on medium and mix thoroughly. Pour into 2 well-greased 9-inch cake pans. Bake at 400° for 10 minutes, or until sides rise and are brown. Butter each slightly. Sprinkle with lemon juice and powdered sugar; roll up. Cut each rolled pancake in half. Top with fresh fruit in season. **Yield**: 4 large servings

Gary Patrick Wilkes '91

WHOLE WHEAT OVEN PANCAKES
"You bake these pancakes all at one time"

1 cup whole wheat flour	1 egg, beaten
1 cup whole bran cereal	1 cup buttermilk
⅓ cup wheat germ	¼ cup hot water
1½ teaspoons baking powder	¼ cup oil
½ teaspoon baking soda	¼ cup honey

In medium bowl, stir together first 5 ingredients. Add remaining ingredients, and beat with electric mixer till well blended. Spread batter evenly in a greased 10x15-inch baking pan. Bake at 425° for 12 minutes. Cut into rectangles, and serve at once with butter and jam or syrup, if desired. **Yield**: About 8 pancakes

Hint: *Lightly grease measuring cup when measuring honey or other sticky liquids.*

Phyllis Wyrick Patterson '74

MICROWAVE GRANOLA

3 cups regular oatmeal
⅓ cup brown sugar
⅓ cup wheat germ
⅓ cup seeds (sesame,
    pumpkin, etc.)

⅓ cup nuts (pecans, walnuts,
    etc.)
¼ cup vegetable oil
¼ cup honey
1 teaspoon vanilla
1 cup raisins

Microwave oatmeal on high for 3 minutes in large, shallow microwave-safe dish. Add brown sugar, wheat germ, seeds, and nuts. Mix together vegetable oil, honey, and vanilla, and pour over dry mixture, coating it thoroughly. Microwave on high 4 to 5 minutes, stirring twice during cooking. Add raisins, and microwave on high for additional 15 seconds. **Yield**: About 5 cups

Carrie Millard Pearce, MSEd '70

"You have to eat oatmeal or you'll dry up. Anybody knows that."
from the children's book, *Eloise*, by Kay Thompson

STRAWBERRY SYRUP

1 (10-ounce) package frozen
   strawberries, partially
   thawed

2 tablespoons pectin
¾ cup sugar

Place strawberries in 3-quart stainless steel saucepan. Mash to puree. Mix pectin and sugar, and add to berries. Bring to a boil, stirring constantly, and boil 45 seconds. Store in covered plastic container in refrigerator. Serve hot over biscuits or pancakes, or cold as jelly for toast or biscuits. **Yield**: 1 cup

Mollie Carpenter Bedwell '65

PLUM GOOD

2 (16-ounce) cans purple
   plums, drained and juice
   reserved
2 (16-ounce) cans Freestone
   sliced peaches, drained

⅔ cup sugar
½ teaspoon cinnamon
⅛ teaspoon cloves
⅛ teaspoon allspice

Drain plums and save juice. Drain peaches and discard juice. Remove seed from plums and cut fruit in half. Cut peach slices into 2 or 3 pieces each. Put plums and juice, peaches, sugar and spices in saucepan. Bring to a boil. Lower heat, and simmer uncovered until slightly thickened, about 1 hour. Refrigerate 24 hours before serving. **Yield**: 5 to 6 cups

Hint: *Great spread on toast, toasted English muffins, or hot biscuits.*

The Cookbook Committee

"The rule is jam tomorrow and jam yesterday, but never jam today."
from *Alice in Wonderland* by Lewis Carroll

Desserts

My favorite part of the little country church was going home for Sunday lunch. These people could flat do Sunday lunch! The table in the kitchen was bow-legged from it. You'd have four kinds of meat, nineteen different kinds of fresh vegetables—beets that were hot, cold, cubed, sliced, dashed—everyway you could do beets they were beeted. And then you'd have eight or nine different kinds of relishes and chowchows. You had every known color of green pickles. Then they'd have breads—hot rolls, cold rolls, light bread, heavy bread, corn bread that the South could have won the Civil War with. I really believe this—throwing it at the North or feeding it to them, either way. Break off a chunk and defend your country!

Iced tea—now we're talking serious iced tea, here—dark, sweet, rich, heavy-duty, 40-weight. Sunlight could not penetrate this tea. It would run up the glass, brake, and go around!

For dessert, we'd have chocolate meringue pie—maybe one of my all-time favorite desserts! And the farm had hens that were called to meringue and they surrendered—eggs without yolks in them, committed to meringue. You had to take a rack out of the oven to toast the top. It looked like nine Dairy Queen cones on the top—those little curly peaks and those little pebbles that looked like honey leaking around. The meringue was nine inches thick on top of the chocolate filling—chocolate was the reward for wading through the meringue.

I loved it when they'd have all-day singing and dinner on the grounds down at the little country church. That was one of my favorite things. You'd stand on a front porch under a shade elm, and they would come from every direction, boiling up that gray gravel on the road, firing rocks at mail boxes and heifer calves—sailing in. You could easily spot every single car that had a meringue pie. They would top the last hill and cut off the key and just coast into the parking lot. See, these people knew that if they ran in and hit their brakes, the meringue would slide off in the floorboard. They just knew that.

Grady Nutt '57

MOTHER'S FRENCH CHOCOLATE CAKE

2 cups cake flour
2 teaspoons baking powder
½ teaspoon baking soda
½ cup butter
1 cup sugar
2 eggs, separated

3 (1-ounce) squares
  unsweetened chocolate,
  melted
¾ cup coconut
1¼ cups milk
1 teaspoon vanilla
Coconut Butter Frosting
1¼ cups coconut for topping

Sift flour once, add baking powder and baking soda, and sift together three times. Cream butter and sugar until light and fluffy. Beat egg yolks until lemon-colored, and stir into creamed mixture. Add chocolate and ¾ cup coconut, and blend well. Add flour alternately with milk, a small amount at a time, beating after each addition until smooth. Add vanilla. In a small mixing bowl, beat egg whites until stiff but not dry. Fold into batter carefully. Pour into 2 greased and floured 9-inch cake pans. Bake at 325° for 25 to 30 minutes or until cake tester inserted in center comes out clean. Cool 15 minutes in pans. Remove from pans, and cool completely on wire racks. When cool, fill between layers and frost top of cake with Coconut Butter Frosting. Sprinkle top liberally with coconut. **Yield**: 10 to 12 servings

Coconut Butter Frosting:
½ cup butter
2 cups powdered sugar

¼ cup half-and-half
½ teaspoon vanilla

Cream butter, add sugar gradually, and beat until light and fluffy. Thin with cream as mixture thickens. Add vanilla. Frosting should be the consistency of whipped cream.

Mary Wilson Russell McCall '40, MSEd '67
Wife of Baylor President Emeritus, Dr. Abner McCall

NEVAIRE'S CHOCOLATE CREAM CAKE

"Easier to make than it looks . . . delicious!"

1 (4-ounce) package German
    Sweet chocolate
¼ cup boiling water
1 (8-ounce) package cream
    cheese, softened
1 (3-ounce) package cream
    cheese, softened
1 cup butter or margarine,
    softened
2 (16-ounce) boxes powdered
    sugar

¼ cup shortening
3 eggs
2¼ cups flour
1 teaspoon baking soda
½ teaspoon salt
1 cup buttermilk
1 teaspoon vanilla
Grated sweet chocolate for
    garnish

Melt chocolate in boiling water. Set aside, and cool. Beat cream cheese and butter in a large mixing bowl until light and fluffy. Mix in powdered sugar, and beat well. Stir cooled melted chocolate into sugar mixture. Divide into 2 equal parts (approximately 3 cups each).

Set ½ aside to use later as frosting. To the remaining ½, add shortening and eggs, and beat well. Sift together flour, baking soda, and salt. Add flour to cake batter alternately with buttermilk, beginning and ending with flour; beat well after each addition. Add vanilla. Pour into 3 well-greased and floured 8-inch cake pans. Bake at 325° for 30 to 40 minutes. Allow to cool. Remove cake from pans. Using frosting that has been reserved, spread between layers and on top of cake. Sprinkle grated chocolate on top. **Yield**: 12 to 16 servings

Andrea Wilkes Willson '91

⏱ DOTS OF CHOCOLATE CAKE

1 (18½-ounce) box yellow
  cake mix
1 (3-ounce) box vanilla
  instant pudding mix
1 (3-ounce) box chocolate
  instant pudding mix

4 eggs
1 cup water
⅔ cup oil
1 (12-ounce) package semi-
  sweet chocolate chips

In a large mixer bowl, combine mixes, eggs, water, and oil, beating until well blended, about 2 to 3 minutes. Stir in chocolate chips. Pour into greased and floured tube or bundt pan. Bake at 350° for 50 to 60 minutes or until a cake tester inserted in center comes out clean. Cool 15 minutes before removing from pan. **Yield**: 12 servings

Hint: *Use a 10-ounce package of mint chocolate chips in place of plain chocolate chips — wonderful!*

Nancy McKinney
Wife of Dr. Joseph McKinney, Baylor Professor of Economics

EARTHQUAKE CAKE
"It looks like an earthquake hit."

1 cup coconut
1 cup pecans, broken
1 (18½-ounce) German
  chocolate cake mix
½ cup margarine, softened

1 (8-ounce) package cream
  cheese, softened
1 (16-ounce) box powdered
  sugar
1 teaspoon vanilla

Spread coconut and pecans evenly over bottom of greased and floured 9x13x2-inch baking pan. Mix cake according to directions on box. Spread batter over coconut and pecans. Cream last 4 ingredients in large mixer bowl until smooth and creamy. Dot over cake batter. Bake at 350° for 35 to 45 minutes. (As it cools, cake will crack and fall, thus the name.) Cool before cutting. **Yield**: 18 to 24 servings

Darlene Winkelmann Gorham '72

GUILTLESS CHOCOLATE CAKE SQUARES

"Fat free!"

¼ cup cornstarch	½ teaspoon salt
1¼ cup flour	4 eggs whites
1 cup sugar	1 cup water
½ cup cocoa	½ cup light corn syrup
½ teaspoon baking soda	

Combine first 6 ingredients. Beat egg whites, water, and corn syrup with a mixer. Slowly add dry ingredients. Mix well. Put in a 9-inch pan that has been sprayed with non-stick vegetable spray. Bake at 350° for 30 minutes, or until cake springs back when lightly touched. Cool before cutting into squares. **Yield**: 9 servings

Hint: *Serve topped with warm Low-Fat Fudge Sauce (recipe below). Serve plain, iced, or sprinkled with powdered sugar, or with yogurt or berries.*

LOW-FAT FUDGE SAUCE

⅓ cup powdered sugar	4 tablespoons evaporated
⅓ cup light corn syrup	skim milk
⅔ cup cocoa	1 teaspoon vanilla
Dash of salt	2 teaspoons light margarine

Mix first 5 ingredients in top of double boiler. Cook over steaming water for 30 minutes. Do not stir. Remove from heat, and add vanilla and margarine. Store in covered container in refrigerator. **Yield**: 1 cup

Note: *Easy to double, and can be reheated in microwave.*

Hint: *Use as hot fudge topping on frozen yogurt, a dip for fresh fruit, or drizzle over angel food cake.*

Carolyn Grigsby Feather '54
Wife of Baylor Vice-President Robert O. Feather

CHOCOLATE ZUCCHINI CAKE

½ cup margarine, softened
½ cup vegetable oil
1¾ cups sugar
2 eggs or egg substitute
1 teaspoon vanilla
½ cup milk
½ teaspoon baking powder

1 teaspoon baking soda
2½ cups flour
4 tablespoons cocoa
½ teaspoon cinnamon
2½ cups finely-chopped
  zucchini
½ cup chocolate chips

Cream margarine, oil, and sugar. Add eggs and beat well. Add vanilla and milk. Mix together next 5 ingredients; add to creamed mixture and beat well. Stir in zucchini. Pour in a greased and floured 9x13-inch baking pan. Sprinkle chocolate chips over batter. Bake at 350° for 45 minutes or until cake tester comes out clean. **Yield**: 12 servings

Hint: *Frost with a chocolate or butter cream frosting if you want.*

Terry A. Becker
Wife of David S. Becker '77

BANANA CHOCOLATE CHIP CAKE

½ cup shortening
1¾ cups sugar
2 eggs, slightly beaten
1 teaspoon baking soda
1 teaspoon baking powder
2½ cups flour

1 cup sour milk
½ cup chopped nuts
1 cup mashed ripe bananas
1 (6-ounce) package semi-
  sweet chocolate chips

Cream shortening and sugar. Add eggs, and blend thoroughly. Mix dry ingredients together. Add to creamed mixture, alternately with milk. Fold in nuts and bananas. Pour into a greased and floured 9x13-inch baking pan. Sprinkle with chocolate chips. Bake at 350° for 40 to 50 minutes or until cake tester comes out clean. Cut into squares, and serve warm. May be reheated for a few seconds in microwave. **Yield**: 15 to 24 servings

Note: *For sour milk, place 1 tablespoon vinegar or lemon juice in a measuring cup; add milk to make 1 cup. Let stand for 5 to 10 minutes.*

F. Rosalee Hayden Meredith '47

DR PEPPER CAKE

"A Dr Pepper cake for every Baylor Bear"

1 cup margarine
1 cup Dr Pepper
4 tablespoons cocoa
1½ teaspoons cinnamon
3 cups sifted flour
2 cups sugar

½ teaspoon salt
2 eggs, well beaten
½ cup buttermilk
2 teaspoons vanilla
1 teaspoon baking soda
Dr Pepper Frosting

Heat Dr Pepper with margarine, but do not boil. Set aside. Sift together flour, sugar, cinnamon, salt, and cocoa. Beat together eggs, buttermilk, vanilla, and baking soda. Add hot Dr Pepper mixture to dry ingredients. Stir in egg mixture, and blend well. Pour into greased and floured 15x10-inch sheet cake pan. Bake at 350° for 25 minutes. Spread hot cake with Dr Pepper Frosting. **Yield**: 15 to 20 servings

Dr Pepper Frosting:
½ cup Dr Pepper
¼ cup margarine
3 tablespoons cocoa
2½ to 3 cups sifted powdered
    sugar

½ cup chopped pecans
1 teaspoon vanilla

About 5 minutes before cake is done, heat Dr Pepper, margarine, and cocoa. Stir in powdered sugar, pecans, and vanilla.

Sandra Stoesser Wallace '59

LUSCIOUS CARROT CAKE

"Definitely not low fat or sugar, but it is wonderful!"

2 cups flour
2 teaspoons baking soda
2 teaspoons cinnamon
½ teaspoon salt
3 eggs, beaten
¾ cup vegetable oil
¾ cup buttermilk
2 cups sugar
2 teaspoons vanilla

1 (8-ounce) can crushed
  pineapple, drained
2 cups grated carrots
1 (3½-ounce) can flaked
  coconut
1 cup coarsely-chopped nuts
Buttermilk Glaze
Cream Cheese Frosting

Sift flour, baking soda, cinnamon and salt together; set aside. Combine eggs, oil, buttermilk, sugar and vanilla; mix well. Add flour mixture, pineapple, carrots, coconut and nuts. Stir well. Pour into 2 well-greased and floured 9-inch cake pans. Bake at 350° for 55 minutes or until cake tester inserted in center comes out clean. Slowly pour Buttermilk Glaze over hot cake layers. Cool in pans until glaze is absorbed, about 15 minutes. Remove from pans; cool completely. Spread Cream Cheese Frosting between layers, on top and side. Refrigerate until frosting is set. Store in refrigerator. **Yield**: 20 to 24 servings

Buttermilk Glaze:
1 cup sugar
½ teaspoon baking soda
½ cup buttermilk
½ cup butter

1 tablespoon light corn
  syrup
1 teaspoon vanilla

While cake is baking, prepare glaze by combining first 5 ingredients in small saucepan. Bring to a boil. Cook 5 minutes, stirring occasionally. Remove from heat and stir in vanilla.

Cream Cheese Frosting:
½ cup butter, softened
1 (8-ounce) package cream
  cheese, softened
1 teaspoon vanilla

2 cups powdered sugar
1 teaspoon orange juice
1 teaspoon grated orange
  peel

Cream butter and cream cheese until fluffy. Add vanilla, powdered sugar, orange juice and orange peel. Mix until smooth.

Sally Appleberry Edmunds '59

MY MOTHER'S BLACKBERRY JAM CAKE

"A holiday cake that keeps well for weeks"

1 cup butter, softened	2 teaspoons ground cloves
2 cups sugar	1 teaspoon baking soda
6 eggs, beaten	1 cup sour cream
3 cups flour	2 cups seedless blackberry
2 teaspoons cinnamon	jam
2 teaspoons allspice	Caramel Filling

Cream butter and sugar well. Beat in eggs. Stir in flour and spices. Dissolve baking soda in sour cream; stir sour cream mixture and jam into batter. Pour into 2 greased and floured 9-inch cake pans. Bake at 350° for 25 to 35 minutes or until done. Cool. Spread Caramel Filling between layers and on top of cake.

Caramel Filling:

2 cups sugar	2 teaspoons vanilla
1 cup butter	1 cup chopped nuts
1½ cups half-and-half	

Combine sugar, butter, and half-and-half in a saucepan; bring to a boil. Boil to soft ball stage (234° on a candy thermometer). Stir in vanilla and nuts; beat until creamy. **Yield**: One 2-layer cake

At a Baylor gathering in El Paso, a man thanked me for giving his sister the recipe for "that wonderful jam cake that she made for the holidays." I couldn't remember having given her a recipe, and we finally realized that she had read it in the first Baylor alumni cookbook. It was my mother's recipe, one that she used to make every Christmas. I had stopped making it, but I was deeply touched to know that someone, somewhere was still making mother's jam cake at Christmas.

Mona Rogers Burchette '58

MANDARIN ORANGE CAKE WITH PINEAPPLE ICING

1 (18½-ounce) box butter
   cake mix
½ cup butter or margarine
¾ cup vegetable or canola oil

4 eggs
1 (11-ounce) can Mandarin
   oranges, undrained
Pineapple Icing

Beat cake mix, butter, oil, and eggs in a large bowl with an electric mixer about 2 minutes. Add oranges with juice. (Or fold oranges and juice by hand into batter to prevent mashing orange sections.) Spoon into 3 greased 8-inch round pans. Bake at 350° for 20 minutes or until center springs back when lightly touched. Cool; fill layers and top with Pineapple Icing. Keep refrigerated. **Yield**: 10 to 12 servings

Pineapple Icing:
1 (20-ounce) can crushed
   pineapple, undrained
1 (3¾-ounce) package vanilla
   instant pudding mix

1 (8-ounce) frozen whipped
   topping, thawed

Mix ingredients together well.

Note: *Can use a 9x13-inch cake pan.*

Marilyn Holland Hines '57

SWEDISH PINEAPPLE CAKE

2 cups sugar
1 (20-ounce) can crushed
  pineapple, undrained
1 teaspoon baking soda

½ teaspoon baking powder
1 teaspoon vanilla
2 cups flour
Icing

Stir ingredients by hand in order given. (Do not use mixer.) Pour into an ungreased 9x13-inch pan. Bake at 350° for 35 to 40 minutes. Spread Icing over cake while it is hot. Can be refrigerated. **Yield**: 12 to 15 servings

Icing:
1 (8-ounce) package cream
  cheese, softened
½ cup margarine, softened

2 cups powdered sugar
1 cup chopped pecans

Beat cream cheese and margarine until smooth. Mix in powdered sugar and pecans.

Hint: *Cake is good hot or cold.*

I took this cake to a friend's house when her mother died, and her father asked for the recipe. It was delicious and so easy to bake that he prepared it often. He would call his daughter to tell her he had been to a funeral and had taken "the cake." We have since dubbed it "The Funeral Cake."

Alma Outlaw Boone '51

CHERRY PUDDING CAKE WITH PRALINE ICING

"With a can of cherries on the shelf, this cake is always ready to be quickly made to take to a sick friend or to a family in bereavement."

2 cups flour	1 (16-ounce) can pitted
2 cups sugar	cherries, undrained
2 teaspoons baking soda	¼ cup melted butter
½ teaspoon salt	1 teaspoon vanilla
2 eggs, beaten	Praline Icing

In a large bowl, combine first 4 ingredients. Add eggs and beat well. Blend in remaining ingredients. Pour batter into a greased and floured 9x13-inch cake pan. Bake at 325° for 25 minutes or until done. Pour Praline Icing over warm cake. **Yield:** 12 to 14 servings

Praline Icing:

2 tablespoons flour	1 cup water
1 cup brown sugar	1 cup chopped pecans

Mix first 3 ingredients in saucepan. Boil over medium-high heat until thick, stirring constantly. Stir in pecans.

Hint: *Brown sugar won't harden if an apple slice is placed in the container.*

Martha Durr Lemon '59

EASY COCONUT CAKE

1 (18½-ounce) butter cake
   mix
3 eggs
½ cup butter

⅔ cup water
Filling
Topping
1 (7-ounce) can coconut

Prepare cake mix as directed on box. Pour into 2 greased and floured 8-inch round cake pans. Bake at 375° for 30 to 35 minutes. Let cool, and divide cake into 4 layers. Spread Filling between layers. Add Topping to final layer, and sprinkle with canned coconut. Keep refrigerated. **Yield**: One 8-inch cake

Filling:
1 (16-ounce) carton sour
   cream

2 cups sugar
1 (14-ounce) package coconut

Mix ingredients together, and refrigerate at least 12 hours. Before using, reserve 1 cup to add to Topping.

Topping:
1 cup Filling, reserved

1 (8-ounce) carton frozen
   whipped topping, thawed

Combine whipped topping with reserved 1 cup of Filling.

Note: *Filling must be prepared the night before. Cake is better the second day.*

Ladye Ruth Burch Casner '54

CHRISTMAS LEMON PECAN CAKE

Rave reviews from the Baylor Alumni Association staff and other testers.

1 (1½-ounce) bottle lemon
  extract
1 quart pecan halves
1 pound butter
3 cups sugar
4 cups flour
1½ teaspoons baking powder

6 eggs
½ pound candied red
  pineapple, cut into bite-
  size pieces
½ pound candied green
  pineapple, cut into bite-
  size pieces

Pour lemon extract over pecan halves in medium bowl; set aside. Grease a tube cake pan heavily with butter. In a large mixing bowl, cream butter and sugar until fluffy. Sift flour and baking powder together. Add eggs one at a time, alternately, with sifted flour mixture. Fold in fruit and pecans. Pour into greased cake pan. Bake at 275° for 2½ to 3 hours or until cake tester comes out clean. Cool and remove carefully from pan. **Yield**: 20 to 24 servings

Note: *Cake is delicious the day it is made, but is even better after 2 or 3 days.*

For forty years, my dad, a '24 graduate, and I, a '53 graduate, have always made this cake the week before Christmas. This family tradition has become a happy memory of the two of us doing something together in preparation for the holiday season.

Betty Clements Scull '53

MOTHER'S SOUR CREAM POUND CAKE

"The classic recipe for a delicious, traditional pound cake."

1 cup margarine
3 cups sugar
6 eggs
3 cups flour
¼ teaspoon baking soda

1 (8-ounce) carton sour cream
1 teaspoon almond or lemon
    extract
1 teaspoon vanilla

Cream margarine with sugar until light and fluffy. Add eggs one at a time, beating well after each addition. Sift flour and baking soda together. Add flour, alternately with sour cream, to creamed mixture. Add flavorings and blend. Pour into greased and floured bundt pan. Bake at 325° for 90 minutes. **Yield**: 12 to 15 servings

Note: *Chewy crust, tender inside.*

Susan Hudson Huey '73

SIX-FLAVOR POUND CAKE

1 cup butter or margarine
½ cup shortening
3 cups sugar
5 eggs
3 cups flour
½ teaspoon baking powder
1 cup milk

1 teaspoon rum extract
1 teaspoon coconut extract
1 teaspoon butter flavoring
1 teaspoon banana extract
1 teaspoon almond extract
1 teaspoon vanilla

Cream butter, shortening, and sugar until light and fluffy. Add eggs, one at a time, beating after each addition. Combine flour and baking powder. Add alternately with milk to creamed mixture. Add flavorings and mix well. Bake in a greased tube pan at 325° for 1 hour and 30 minutes. **Yield**: 15 to 18 servings

Note: *Too much air in the batter will cause this heavy cake to fall after it is baked. Can be "dressed up" for guests by topping each slice with fresh fruit.*

Lana Johnson Rowland '80

POPPY SEED LOAF CAKE
"Orange glaze makes this tasty and moist."

3 cups flour	1½ cups milk
1½ teaspoons salt	1½ teaspoons almond extract
1½ teaspoons baking powder	1½ teaspoons vanilla
2¼ cups sugar	1½ teaspoons butter
1½ tablespoons poppy seeds	flavoring
1⅛ cups oil	Orange Glaze
3 eggs	

In a large mixer bowl, combine first 5 ingredients. Add oil, eggs, milk, and flavorings; beat 2 minutes on medium speed. Pour into 3 well-greased and floured 1-pound coffee cans. (Cake may also be baked in a tube pan.) Bake at 350° for 1 hour or until a crack forms across the top. Pour Orange Glaze over hot cake. Let sit in cans or tube pan until all glaze is absorbed. Freezes well. **Yield:** 12 to 15 servings

Orange Glaze:

½ cup orange juice	½ teaspoon butter flavoring
¾ cup sugar	½ teaspoon almond extract
½ teaspoon vanilla	

Mix all ingredients in a saucepan. Bring to a boil over medium heat, stirring until sugar dissolves. Remove from heat.

Hint: *Rounds of cake are great as a base for ice cream. Give these at Christmas in a clear bag tied with a bow.*

Carol Hunter Wells '69

LEMON CREAM CHEESE CAKE

"Best idea for a cake mix I've seen in years."

1 (18½-ounce) package
   lemon cake mix with
   pudding
½ cup margarine, softened
¾ cup milk
2 eggs

1 (8-ounce) package cream
   cheese, softened
¼ cup sugar
1 tablespoon lemon juice
1 teaspoon grated lemon
   rind
½ cup chopped nuts

Cut margarine into cake mix until mixture is crumbly. Set aside 1 cup of crumbs for topping. Add milk and eggs to remaining crumb mixture. Beat 2 minutes. Pour into a greased 9x13-inch pan; set aside. Combine cream cheese and next 3 ingredients; beat until smooth. Drop by teaspoons onto cake batter. Add nuts to reserved crumb mixture, and sprinkle over batter. Bake at 350° for 35 to 40 minutes. **Yield**: 8 to 12 servings

Hint: *Even better the second day.*

Beth Warren Harris '68

BUTTERMILK SPICE CAKE

1½ cups sugar
1 cup vegetable oil
3 eggs
2 cups flour
1 teaspoon baking soda

1 teaspoon cinnamon
¾ teaspoon nutmeg
1 cup buttermilk
Topping

Blend sugar, oil, and eggs, beating well. Add flour, baking soda, spices, and buttermilk. Bake in greased and floured 9x13-inch pan at 300° for 1 hour. With a kitchen fork, pierce holes in top of hot cake. As cake cools, mix Topping. While Topping is hot, pour over cake. **Yield**: 15 to 20 servings

Topping:
1½ cups sugar
¾ teaspoon baking soda
½ cup butter

¾ cup buttermilk
3 teaspoons vanilla

Mix all together in large saucepan. Cook over low heat, stirring constantly until mixture boils. (It will foam up quickly and boil over with no attention.) Remove from heat.

Gail Jamison Coker
Wife of David Coker, Assistant Director,
Baylor Alumni Association

GRANDMOTHER BRATCHER'S GINGERBREAD

"Nostalgic"

1 cup sugar	1 teaspoon baking soda
¼ cup margarine	½ teaspoon ginger
½ cup molasses	1 cup flour
1 cup boiling water	1 egg

Cream sugar, margarine, and molasses together. Blend in next 4 ingredients; beat in egg. Pour into greased and floured 8-inch square baking dish. Bake at 350° for 30 to 35 minutes. **Yield:** 9 servings

Hint: *Try spreading warm gingerbread generously with butter. Or top a warm square of gingerbread with applesauce and a dollop of whipped cream.*

Mollie Carpenter Bedwell '65

"Had I but one penny in the world, thou shouldst have it for gingerbread."

from *Love's Labours Lost*, William Shakespeare

CREAMY PUMPKIN ROLL

3 eggs
1 cup sugar
⅔ cup pumpkin
1 teaspoon lemon peel spice
¾ cup flour
1 teaspoon baking powder
2 teaspoons cinnamon

1 teaspoon ginger
½ teaspoon nutmeg
½ teaspoon salt
¾ cup chopped pecans,
  optional
Powdered sugar
Filling

In a mixer bowl, beat eggs at high speed for 5 minutes. Mix in next 3 ingredients. In a separate bowl, combine next 6 ingredients. Stir into pumpkin mixture. Pour into a greased and floured 10x15-inch jelly roll pan. Top with chopped pecans if desired. Bake at 350° for 15 minutes or until cake springs back when lightly touched. Loosen sides; immediately turn out on cloth towel that has been sprinkled well with powdered sugar. Roll up in towel and let cool completely, seam side down. When cool, unroll, remove towel, and spread with Filling. Roll back into roll, and wrap in plastic wrap and refrigerate for several hours. When ready to serve, slice and let warm slightly. **Yield**: 8 to 10 servings

Filling:
1 cup powdered sugar
1 teaspoon vanilla

1 (8-ounce) package cream
  cheese, softened
4 tablespoons butter

Mix together until smooth.

Hint: *Freezes nicely.*

Kelly Malone Rummery '83

PINEAPPLE LEMON FILLING FOR A PREPARED CAKE

"This easy dessert looked scrumptious and was!"

2 eggs, beaten	1 teaspoon vanilla
¾ cup sugar	1 to 2 drops of yellow food
2 tablespoons flour	coloring, optional
Pinch of salt	1 cup whipping cream,
1 (8-ounce) can crushed	whipped
pineapple, undrained	1 (10-inch) angel food cake
Juice of 1 lemon	or pound cake

In a large saucepan, mix beaten eggs with sugar, flour, and salt. Add crushed pineapple with juice and lemon juice. Mix well. Cook over medium heat until thick, stirring constantly. Cool; add vanilla and food coloring, if desired. Chill in refrigerator. Fold in whipped cream. Cut cake into 2 layers. Spread filling between layers and on top of cake. Refrigerate overnight or several hours before serving. **Yield**: 10 to 12 servings

Note: *Cake can be frozen and cut as needed; thaws almost immediately. Use thread or dental floss to divide cake layers in preparation for filling.*

Katy Jennings Stokes '47

When our children were young, I made a green cotton autograph tablecloth. The family signed it first, and then I embroidered over our names in brown thread. Through the years students and friends have signed it, and I have embroidered over their names as well. Memories of those who have signed the tablecloth warm our hearts.

Katy Jennings Stokes '47

CHOCOLATE CHIP CHEESECAKE

A favorite of all our testers—impressive, rich, delicious, and easy to make!

1 cup finely-ground
   chocolate wafer crumbs
2 tablespoons unsalted
   butter, softened
3 (8-ounce) package cream
   cheese, softened
1 cup sugar

2 large eggs, room
   temperature
1 cup sour cream, room
   temperature
1 tablespoon vanilla
1½ cups semi-sweet
   chocolate chips
Glaze

Lightly grease a 9-inch springform pan. Blend wafer crumbs and butter; press crumbs into bottom of pan and up the sides about 1½ inches. Set aside. Beat cream cheese for 30 seconds until creamy. Add sugar and eggs one at a time, beating well. On low speed, stir in sour cream and vanilla. Fold in chocolate chips. Pour batter into pan. Bake at 350° for 40 to 45 minutes, or until the cheesecake has puffed up and feels set when gently touched in the center. Turn oven off, open door slightly, and leave cheesecake in oven for at least 1 hour. Remove from oven, and cool. Smooth Glaze on top of cooled cheesecake. Refrigerate to allow glaze to set, at least 4 hours or overnight. Remove sides of pan, and cut into wedges. **Yield**: 15 to 20 servings

Glaze:
½ cup semi-sweet chocolate
   chips

¼ cup whipping cream

Melt chocolate chips in microwave for 1 to 2 minutes. Add whipping cream and whisk until mixed.

Lori Latch Apon '82

RICH ORANGE CHOCOLATE CHEESECAKE

1½ cups crushed cream-filled chocolate cookies, about 16
¼ cup margarine, melted
3 (8-ounce) packages cream cheese, softened
1 (14-ounce) can sweetened condensed milk
3 eggs
1 (12-ounce) package semi-sweet chocolate chips, melted
2 teaspoons vanilla
Orange-Chocolate Topping

Combine cookie crumbs and margarine. Press onto bottom of 9-inch springform pan. Set aside. Combine cream cheese and milk, mixing at medium speed with electric mixer until well-blended. Add eggs, one at a time, mixing well after each addition. Blend in chocolate and vanilla; pour over crust. Bake at 300° for 1 hour 10 minutes. Loosen cake from rim of pan; cool before removing sides of pan. Spread topping over top and sides of cheesecake. Chill. Remove from refrigerator 30 minutes before serving. **Yield**: 10 to 12 servings

Orange-Chocolate Topping:
⅓ cup margarine
½ cup powdered sugar
1 (6-ounce) package semi-sweet chocolate pieces, melted and cooled
2 teaspoons orange extract

Beat margarine and sugar until light and fluffy. Add chocolate and orange extract, mixing until well-blended.

Note: Keeps well in freezer. Cut small slices.

Candyce Rasner Jones '81

DREAMY CREAM CHEESE PIE

2 (8-ounce) packages fat-free
  cream cheese, softened
3 eggs
⅔ cup sugar

¼ teaspoon almond extract
1 cup fat-free sour cream
1 teaspoon vanilla
3 tablespoons sugar

In a medium bowl, beat cream cheese and add eggs 1 at a time, beating well. Add ⅔ cup sugar and almond extract. Beat until smooth. Pour into greased 9- or 10-inch pie plate. Bake at 325° for 25 minutes. Cool 20 minutes.

Mix sour cream, vanilla, and 3 tablespoons sugar. Pour over pie. Return to oven and bake at 325° for 10 minutes. Cool completely. Refrigerate 4 to 8 hours or overnight before serving. Cut into wedges; top with sliced fresh strawberries or a spoonful of canned fruit pie filling. **Yield**: 8 to 10 servings

Hint: *Using egg substitute for the eggs changes the consistency of the pie.*

Patricia Netherton
Wife of Baylor Vice-President, Dr. James Netherton

AUNT GLORIA'S GLORIOUS CHEESECAKE

This is an "I-have-to-have-this!" recipe.

1⅓ cups graham cracker
   crumbs
¾ cup sugar, divided
½ cup butter, melted
2 (8-ounce) packages cream
   cheese, softened

3 eggs, beaten
Topping
Cinnamon
Sliced almonds

Mix graham cracker crumbs and ¼ cup sugar; stir in melted butter. Press into 11-inch square or 9x13-inch baking dish. Bake at 350° for 5 minutes. Set aside.

Beat remaining sugar, cream cheese, and eggs until smooth. Pour into crust and bake at 350° for 20 minutes. Cool for 10 minutes.

Spoon Topping over cooled cheesecake. Sprinkle with cinnamon and sliced almonds. Bake at 350° for 20 minutes. Cool; chill in refrigerator for 12 to 24 hours. Cut into squares. **Yield**: 12 to 20 servings

Topping:
12 ounces sour cream
1 cup sugar

1 teaspoon vanilla

Mix together until smooth.

Paula Price Tanner, MA '82

BLUEBERRY CHEESECAKE

⅓ cup powdered sugar
½ cup margarine, softened
1½ cups graham cracker
   crumbs
1 cup sugar
3 (8-ounce) packages cream
   cheese

4 eggs
1 teaspoon vanilla
2 cups sour cream
1 (21-ounce) can blueberry
   pie filling

Mix powdered sugar, margarine, and graham cracker crumbs. Line bottom of 9-inch springform pan, packing firmly. In large bowl, mix sugar, cream cheese, eggs, and vanilla; beat well. Pour into springform pan over unbaked graham cracker crust. Bake at 350° for approximately 1 hour, or until the center is rounded and golden brown. (Do not turn oven off.) Remove cheesecake and top with sour cream. Return to oven for 5 minutes. Remove cheesecake and allow to cool. Top with pie filling. Chill overnight. Remove sides of pan, and cut into wedges. **Yield**: 12 to 15 servings

Joyce Cline
Wife of B. Joe Cline '57

DREAM CHEESE CAKES

"Very festive for Christmas parties, and so simple"

3 (8-ounce) packages cream
   cheese, softened
2½ teaspoons vanilla extract,
   divided
1¼ cups sugar, divided

5 eggs
2 cups sour cream
Red and green candied
   cherries

Line 1½-inch muffin tins with fluted paper cups. Set aside. Mix cream cheese with 1½ teaspoons vanilla. Add 1 cup sugar and eggs; beat well. Spoon 1 tablespoon mixture into each paper cup. Bake at 350° about 20 minutes or until top cracks slightly. For topping, combine sour cream, remaining ¼ cup sugar, and remaining 1 teaspoon vanilla; mix well. Spoon small amount of topping onto each cooked cheese cake. Return to oven, and bake 5 minutes. Cool on racks. Decorate with cherries. Refrigerate until ready to serve. **Yield**: 2 dozen cakes

Diane Sanderson '87

🕐 CHOCOLATE PECAN PIE

"Every bit as good as the pie at Stagecoach Inn."

¾ cups firmly-packed light brown sugar	⅛ teaspoon salt
¼ cup butter	1 cup light corn syrup
3 eggs	1 teaspoon vanilla
2 (1-ounce) squares unsweetened chocolate, melted	1 cup chopped nuts
	1 unbaked (9-inch) pie shell

Cream sugar and butter. Add eggs one at a time, beating well after each addition. Beat in next 4 ingredients; stir in nuts. Pour into pie shell. Bake at 350° for 45 to 55 minutes. Cool before cutting. **Yield**: 6 to 8 servings

Hint: *Before measuring syrup or honey, oil the cup with cooking oil and rinse in hot water. All of the syrup will come out of the cup.*

Bernice Leazar Autrey '59

BUMBLEBERRY PIE

"Just the right amount of tartness and sweetness"

2 cups apples, peeled and sliced (about 3 apples)	1 tablespoon lemon juice
1 cup rhubarb, cut into 1 inch pieces	¾ to 1 cup sugar
1 cup raspberries, fresh or frozen, without added sugar	¼ cup flour
	½ to 1 teaspoon cinnamon
	1 tablespoon butter
	1 unbaked (9-inch) double-crust pie shell

Combine apple slices, rhubarb, raspberries, and lemon juice, mixing gently. Fold sugar, flour, and cinnamon into fruit mixture. Pour fruit into pie shell, and dot with butter. Cover with second crust, seal edges, and cut slits in top crust. Bake at 425° for 10 minutes; turn oven to 350° and continue baking for 45 minutes. **Yield**: 6 to 8 slices

Hint: *Use frozen rhubarb if fresh is unavailable. Vanilla ice cream along side a slice of this is extra good.*

Jean M. Spencer Jenness '61

FRENCH APPLE PIE

6 to 8 firm, tart cooking
   apples, pared, cored, and
   sliced (about 3 cups)
¼ cup firmly-packed light
   brown sugar
¼ cup sugar
2 tablespoons flour
¼ teaspoon salt
½ teaspoon cinnamon

¼ teaspoon nutmeg
2 teaspoons lemon juice
¼ cup seedless raisins
¼ cup coarsely chopped
   pecans or walnuts
1 unbaked (9-inch) pie shell
2 tablespoons butter
Topping

In a large bowl, combine first 10 ingredients. Turn apples into pie shell, piling slightly higher in the center. Dot with butter. Sprinkle Topping over pie. Bake at 425° for 40 to 45 minutes. (If oven browns pie too much at this temperature, bake at 450° for 10 minutes; reduce heat to 375° until pie is done and crust is golden.) **Yield**: 6 to 8 servings

Topping:
6 tablespoons butter
5 tablespoons brown sugar

1 cup flour

Cream butter and sugar. Cut in flour with a pastry blender until crumbly.

Ray Burchette, Jr. '57, Executive Vice President,
Baylor Alumni Association

⏱ APRICOT PIE

1 to 2 (16-ounce) cans apricot halves, drained	¾ to 1 cup sugar
	¼ cup flour
1 unbaked (9- or 10-inch) pie shell	1 cup whipping cream

Arrange drained apricots evenly in pie shell. Mix sugar and flour, and sprinkle over apricots. Pour unwhipped cream over pie. Bake at 325° for 1½ hours using a cookie sheet under pie to catch possible spillovers. **Yield**: 6 to 8 servings

Hint: *For easier slicing, cut apricot halves into smaller pieces.*

Marjory Cretien
Wife of Dr. Paul Cretien,
Baylor Professor of Banking and Finance

AUNTIE'S DOUBLE-CRUST LEMON PIE
"An older recipe that is most unusual"

3 eggs	2 teaspoons grated lemon rind
1¼ cup sugar	
1 tablespoon corn starch	3 tablespoons water
2 tablespoons melted butter or margarine	1 unbaked (8-inch) double-crust pie shell
⅓ cup lemon juice	

Beat eggs until lemon-colored, and add sugar and corn starch, beating well. Stir in melted butter, lemon juice, rind, and water. Pour into pie shell; top with second crust. Do not vent top crust. Bake at 400° for 35 to 40 minutes. **Yield**: One 8-inch pie

Judy Lindsey Oberkrom '66

MAMA'S LEMON CHESS PIE

"My only grandchild, a '79 graduate of Baylor, loved this pie so much that as a child she asked for it for her 'birthday cake.'"

2 cups sugar
⅓ cup butter or margarine
4 eggs
1 tablespoon flour
1 tablespoon cornmeal

¼ cup lemon juice
2 teaspoons lemon rind
¼ cup milk
1 unbaked (8-inch) pie shell

Cream sugar and butter. Beat in eggs until mixture is a light yellow. Add flour and cornmeal. Mix lemon juice, lemon rind, and milk together; add and mix thoroughly. Pour into unbaked pie shell. Bake at 350° for 1 hour, or until knife inserted in center comes out clean. **Yield**: One 8-inch pie

Grace Miles Wilson '30

CHESS PIE

"Tastes like the Hot Chess Pie served by the Hickory Stick in Waco in the '70s—rich, warm, and sweet"

2 cups sugar
8 teaspoons cornmeal
4 eggs, slightly beaten
½ cup milk

½ cup butter, melted
1 teaspoon vanilla
1 unbaked (9-inch) pie shell

Mix sugar and cornmeal. Add eggs, and beat lightly. Stir in milk, melted butter, and vanilla. Pour into unbaked pie shell. Bake at 325° for about 1 hour, or until knife inserted in center comes out clean. Serve warm. **Yield**: One 9-inch pie

Note: *May be made ahead and reheated in the microwave.*

Glenajo Beard Shambeck '80

PEANUT BUTTER CRUMBLES CUSTARD PIE

"A regional favorite of Florida—definitely for peanut butter lovers"

¾ cup sifted powdered sugar
⅓ cup crunchy peanut butter
3 eggs, separated
1 cup sugar, divided
½ teaspoon salt
1 tablespoon flour
¼ cup cornstarch

3 cups milk
2 tablespoons butter, melted
1 teaspoon vanilla
1 baked (9-inch) pie shell, cooled
¼ teaspoon cream of tartar

Blend together powdered sugar and peanut butter until it is coarse and crumbly; set aside. Beat egg yolks and set aside. In top of a double boiler, combine ⅔ cup sugar, salt, flour and cornstarch. Add milk. Cook over boiling water until mixture begins to thicken, stirring constantly. Add a little of hot milk mixture to beaten egg yolks to warm them. Then stir egg yolks back into milk in double boiler. Continue to cook, stirring constantly until thick. Add melted butter and vanilla.

Cover bottom of pie shell with 1 cup of peanut butter crumbles. Pour in hot custard. Beat egg whites and cream of tartar until soft peaks form. At medium speed, add remaining sugar, one tablespoon at a time, scraping sugar from sides of bowl. At high speed, finish beating egg whites until stiff.

Mound meringue on top of filling, spreading to edge of crust to seal. Sprinkle remaining peanut butter crumbles over top of pie. Bake at 350° for 12 to 15 minutes until meringue is golden. **Yield**: 6 to 8 servings

Hint: *A meringue pie will cut cleanly if the knife is buttered before slicing.*

Harriet Briscoe Harral '66

PUMPKIN CHIFFON PIE

1 envelope gelatin
¼ cup cold water
3 eggs, separated
1 cup sugar, divided
1 can pumpkin
½ cup milk
½ teaspoon ginger
½ teaspoon nutmeg

½ teaspoon cinnamon
½ teaspoon salt
1 baked (9-inch) pie shell
Whipped cream
Dash of nutmeg
1 tablespoon walnuts,
    chopped

Soak gelatin in cold water, and set aside. Beat egg yolks in top of double boiler. Add ½ cup sugar. Mix in next 6 ingredients. Cook in double boiler over hot water for 20 minutes, stirring very often. Add gelatin, and cool. In separate bowl, beat egg whites until foamy. Gradually beat in remaining ½ cup sugar. Beat until stiff. Fold into custard. Cool in refrigerator. Just before serving, pour custard into baked pie shell and top with whipped cream, a sprinkle of nutmeg, and chopped walnuts. **Yield**: 6 to 8 servings

Margaret McGee Saunders '58

Calories
Methuselah ate what he found on his plate,
And never, as people do now,
Did he note the amount of the calorie count;
He ate it because it was chow.
He wasn't disturbed as at dinner he sat,
Devouring a roast or a pie,
To think it was lacking in granular fat
Or a couple of vitamins shy.
He cheerfully chewed each species of food,
Unmindful of troubles or fears
Lest his health might be hurt
By some fancy dessert;
And he lived over nine hundred years.

Author unknown

SAM COATES' BLACK-BOTTOM PIE

½ cup flour
¾ cup sugar
½ teaspoon salt
2½ cups milk
3 egg yolks
1 tablespoon margarine or
   butter

1 tablespoon rum extract
1½ squares bittersweet
   chocolate, melted
1 baked (9-inch) pie shell
Topping

Combine flour, sugar, salt, and milk in large saucepan; cook over medium heat, stirring constantly until thickened. Beat egg yolks in small bowl. Gradually stir a few spoonfuls of hot mixture into egg yolks to warm, then add yolks back into hot mixture. Cook until very thick, stirring constantly. Remove from heat; stir in margarine and rum extract. Divide custard in half. To one half, add melted chocolate. Pour chocolate custard into pie shell; add plain custard as second layer. Spread pie with Topping, and decorate with shavings of chocolate. Refrigerate until serving time.
Yield: 8 servings

Topping:
1 cup whipping cream,
   whipped

2 tablespoons sugar
2 teaspoons rum extract

Add sugar and extract to whipped cream.

Perhaps the recipe taste-tested by more Baylor alumni than any other recipe is Black-Bottom Pie, a mainstay on the menu at Sam Coates' Restaurant. Because our dad, E. C. (Kirk) Kirkpatrick, was the head cook for Sam Coates for many years, we are very familiar with this mouth-watering pie.

Jewel Kirkpatrick Lockridge '70
and Winona Jean Kirkpatrick '91

BUTTERSCOTCH CREAM PIE

"Try this in the Pecan Pie Crust"

2 cups milk
1 cup brown sugar
2 tablespoons butter
¼ cup cornstarch

2 eggs, slightly beaten
1 teaspoon vanilla
1 (9-inch) pie shell

Heat milk in saucepan to scalding point. Meanwhile, combine brown sugar, butter, and cornstarch; stir into milk. Continue to cook mixture over medium heat, stirring frequently, until custard begins to thicken. Add 2 or 3 tablespoons of the hot custard to beaten eggs; stir in well. Pour egg mixture into hot custard mixture. Continue cooking until thick enough for pie filling. (Remember that it will burn easily.) Remove from heat. Add vanilla. Pour into prepared graham cracker crust or a baked 9-inch pie shell. Top with whipped cream if desired. **Yield**: 6 to 8 servings

When Conrad Walch '64, my future husband, came to visit my family for the first time, my mother made her famous butterscotch cream pie. Conrad asked her what kind of pie it was. She replied, "It's butterscotch, but it doesn't have much butter!" He went home thinking he had eaten a pie full of scotch at that Baptist deacon's house!

Pam Gilliam Walch '65

PECAN PIE CRUST

½ cup margarine
1 cup flour

1 cup finely-chopped pecans

Mix ingredients well and press into 9-inch pie pan. Bake at 350° for 20 minutes. Cool thoroughly before filling. **Yield**: One 9-inch pie shell

Michelle Derrick '88

TOASTED COCONUT PIE

"A family favorite at Thanksgiving"

3 eggs
2½ cups sugar
½ cup flour
½ cup melted butter
1½ cups milk

2 teaspoons vanilla
2 cups flaked coconut
2 unbaked (9-inch) deep-
   dish pie shells

Beat eggs with electric mixer until lemon-colored. Stir in sugar and flour. Blend in butter, milk, and vanilla. Add coconut last. Pour into unbaked pie shells. Bake at 325° for 50 to 60 minutes, or until knife inserted in center comes out clean. **Yield**: Two 9-inch pies

Diane Sanderson '87

RICH IN CHIPS PIE

2 eggs
½ cup flour
½ cup sugar
½ cup firmly-packed light
   brown sugar

¾ cup butter, softened
1 cup chopped nuts, optional
1 (6-ounce) package semi-
   sweet chocolate chips
1 unbaked (9-inch) pie shell

In large mixer bowl, beat eggs at high speed until foamy, about 3 minutes. Beat in flour, sugar, and brown sugar until well blended. Beat in softened butter. Stir in nuts and chocolate chips, and pour into pie shell. Bake at 325° for 55 to 60 minutes, or until knife inserted in middle comes out clean and top is golden. Cool on wire rack. Serve with whipped cream or ice cream, if desired. **Yield**: One 9-inch pie

Hint: Serve warm. For a special treat, top the ice cream with warm fudge sauce!

Candyce Rasner Jones '81

PUMPKIN-MALLOW PIE

1 cup cooked pumpkin
2 (10-ounce) packages
　regular-size
　marshmallows
1 teaspoon cinnamon

¼ teaspoon salt
1 cup whipping cream,
　whipped
1 baked (8-inch) pie shell or
　ginger cookie crust (recipe
　follows)

In a heavy saucepan, stir first 4 ingredients over very low heat until marshmallows are melted. Chill thoroughly. Beat mixture until fluffy; fold into whipped cream. Turn into pie shell, and chill in refrigerator until set. **Yield**: 6 to 8 servings

Peggy Wilson Dobbins '54

GINGER COOKIE CRUST

35 ginger cookies
½ cup butter, melted

1 tablespoon powdered
　sugar

Process cookies in food processor or blender to make fine crumbs. Add butter and powdered sugar, and mix well. Press firmly into an 8-inch pie plate. Bake at 300° for 5 minutes. **Yield**: One 8-inch pie crust

The Cookbook Committee

PEACH PRIDE COBBLER

¾ cup flour
⅛ teaspoon salt
2 teaspoons baking powder
2 cups sugar, divided
¾ cup milk
½ cup butter

2 cups fresh sliced peaches,
    or 1 (29-ounce) can sliced
    peaches, drained
2 teaspoons lemon juice
1 teaspoon cinnamon
Brown Sugar Topping
Sweetened whipped cream

Sift flour, salt, and baking powder; mix with 1 cup sugar. Slowly stir in milk to make a batter. Melt butter until slightly brown in an 8-inch square pan. Carefully pour batter over melted butter. Do not stir. Mix peaches with remaining cup of sugar, lemon juice, and cinnamon. Pour fruit over batter. Bake at 350° for 1 hour. Sprinkle Brown Sugar Topping over hot cobbler. Broil 2 to 3 minutes under direct heat until browned. (Watch carefully.) Serve warm with whipped cream. **Yield**: 10 servings

Brown Sugar Topping:
¼ cup brown sugar
3 tablespoons flour

2 tablespoons butter
½ cup chopped pecans

Mix topping ingredients in small bowl.

Mary Margaret Duckworth Norman '48

⊙ STRAWBERRY PIE-IN-A-HURRY

1 (14-ounce) can sweetened
    condensed milk
1 (10-ounce) package frozen
    strawberries, thawed
3 tablespoons lemon juice

2 bananas, sliced or diced
1 (12-ounce) carton frozen
    whipped topping, thawed
2 baked (9-inch) pie shells

Mix first 5 ingredients together and pour into baked and cooled pie shells. Refrigerate for 3 hours before serving. **Yield**: Two 9-inch pies

Note: *Graham cracker crusts work very well. Also consider freezing these pies for a different texture.*

Lola (Corky) Ball Altenburg '52

CRUSTY PEACH PINWHEELS

1½ cups sugar
2 cups peach nectar or water
½ cup margarine
1½ cups flour
1 teaspoon baking powder

Dash of salt
½ cup shortening
½ cup milk
2 cups peeled and sliced
    fresh peaches

Dissolve sugar in nectar. Set aside. Melt margarine in 9x13-inch pan. Set aside. In a medium bowl, combine flour, baking powder, and salt. Cut in shortening. Add milk, stirring with fork to make a soft dough. Turn dough onto a lightly-floured surface. Roll into a rectangle, about ¼-inch thick. Arrange peaches over dough. Roll dough, with fruit inside, like a jelly roll. Cut roll into 1-inch thick slices like pinwheels. Place pinwheels in pan in melted margarine. Pour sugar-nectar mixture over pinwheels. Bake at 400° for 40 to 45 minutes, or until brown and bubbly. (Pinwheels will be brown and crusty.) **Yield**: About 8 servings

Hint: *Especially good if made with homegrown peaches.*

David Vance Herin '69

VERY CHERRY COBBLER

⅔ cup sugar
2 tablespoons flour
1 (16-ounce) can pitted sour
    red cherries
1 teaspoon vanilla
½ teaspoon almond extract

1 cup flour
1½ teaspoons baking powder
⅛ teaspoon salt
3 tablespoons shortening
⅓ cup milk

Mix sugar, 2 tablespoons flour, cherries, and flavorings. Place in greased 8-inch square pan.

Sift together 1 cup flour, baking powder, and salt. Cut in shortening with 2 knives or pastry blender. Add milk to make soft dough. Roll out on a lightly-floured surface to an 8-inch square. Place over cherries in pan. Cut slits in dough to allow steam to escape. Bake at 400° for 30 minutes. **Yield**: 6 servings

Note: *Serve hot with a scoop of vanilla ice cream.*

Daphne Norred Herring '65

COFFEE ICE CREAM MUD PIE

"Check out this great chocolate sauce!"

18 to 24 chocolate sandwich
cookies, ground in
processor or blender
⅓ cup melted margarine
1 teaspoon instant coffee
powder

½ gallon coffee ice cream,
softened
3 (1.5-ounce) milk chocolate
with butter toffee candy
bars, crumbled
Chocolate Sauce

Mix ground cookies, margarine, and coffee powder. Press on bottom and up sides of 9-inch pie pan. Chill. When crust has chilled, stir ice cream and candy bars together. Fill pie crust, and freeze until firm. Remove from freezer, and cover with plastic wrap or foil. Return to freezer for at least 6 hours or overnight.

Before serving, remove pie from freezer for 15 to 20 minutes. Cut into wedges and spoon warm chocolate sauce over each serving. Refrigerate leftover sauce. **Yield**: One 9-inch pie

Chocolate Sauce:
1 cup chocolate chips
½ cup sugar
1 cup evaporated milk

Pinch of salt
1 teaspoon vanilla

Mix ingredients in a microwave-safe dish. Microwave on high for 2 minute intervals, beating with a whisk between intervals. Continue to cook sauce for 4 to 5 minutes. It will continue to thicken as it cools.

Hint: *Serve the chocolate sauce over vanilla ice cream, too.*

Claudia Burton Johnson, a Baylor mom

MOTHER'S FROZEN LEMON PIE

"Tangy with fresh lemon flavor"

3 eggs, separated
⅓ cup fresh lemon juice
Grated lemon rind from ½
   lemon
⅛ teaspoon salt
½ cup sugar

1 cup whipping cream,
   whipped
1 teaspoon sugar
1 cup crushed vanilla wafers,
   divided

Beat egg yolks until foamy. Combine beaten yolks, juice, rind, salt, and ½ cup sugar in top of double boiler. Cook over boiling water until consistency of custard. Cool.

Beat egg whites until they hold a soft peak. Add 1 teaspoon sugar, and beat until stiff. Fold in whipped cream. Line a 9-inch square pan or 9-inch pie pan with ¾ cup of wafer crumbs. Pour lemon mixture over crumbs. Top with remaining wafers. Freeze. When ready to serve, slice into squares or wedges. **Yield**: 6 to 9 servings

Hint: *Dessert can be put into individual custard cups.*

Edna Holcomb SoRelle White '55, MS '61

FROZEN STRAWBERRY YOGURT PIE

"This low-in-fat dessert tastes light and luscious."

1 (9-inch) graham cracker
   crust
1 quart fat-free or low-fat
   frozen strawberry yogurt,
   softened

1 (12-ounce) carton frozen
   "light" whipped topping,
   thawed
1 pint fresh strawberries
Artificial sweetener, to taste

Using an electric mixer on low speed, stir yogurt and whipped topping together until blended. Spoon into graham cracker crust. Freeze. Before serving, top with crushed strawberries combined with artificial sweetener. **Yield**: One 9-inch pie

Hint: *Use a cholesterol-free graham cracker crust if it is available to you.*

June Page Johnson '45

CRISP SUGAR COOKIES
"A good basic cookie"

1 cup shortening
2 cups sugar
2 eggs
1 teaspoon vanilla
1 tablespoon water

3 cups flour
¼ teaspoon baking soda
½ teaspoon salt
2 teaspoons baking powder

Cream shortening and sugar. Add eggs one at a time. Beat well. Add vanilla and water. Sift flour, baking soda, salt, and baking powder. Add to creamed mixture, and mix well. Roll in small balls, about the size of marbles. Place on ungreased cookie sheet, 1 inch apart, and flatten with fork. Bake at 350° for 10 to 15 minutes. **Yield**: 7 dozen small cookies

Hint: *Colored sugar may be sprinkled on the tops of flattened cookies before baking.*

Ellen Dawne Cleveland '92

DELICATE TEA CAKES
"Reminds me of my grandmother's tea cakes."

½ cup butter
½ cup shortening
2 cups sugar
3 eggs
1 teaspoon vanilla

2 tablespoons milk
5 cups flour
1 teaspoon baking soda
Pinch of salt

Cream butter, shortening, and sugar. Add eggs; beat until fluffy. Add vanilla and milk. Mix thoroughly. Combine flour, baking soda, and salt in a separate bowl. Add to creamed mixture gradually. Chill dough. Roll out small amount of chilled dough on floured surface to ¼-inch thickness. Cut with round cookie cutter. Place on ungreased cookie sheets. Bake at 350° for 8 to 10 minutes. Do not brown cookies. Bake just until set. **Yield**: About 4 to 5 dozen

Note: *Margarine will alter the taste of the cookie. For ease in mixing flour into the dough, use a food processor fitted with the knife blade.*

Nancy Hudson Fields '73

MY NEIGHBOR'S SUGAR COOKIES
"Perfect for Valentine's"

1 cup butter, softened	2 teaspoons cream of tartar
2 cups sugar	1 teaspoon vanilla
4 eggs, well beaten	4 cups flour
1 teaspoon baking soda	Frosting, optional

Cream butter and sugar. Add eggs, and beat well. Stir in baking soda, cream of tartar, and vanilla. Stir in flour to make a very soft dough. Refrigerate for approximately 2 hours to firm dough. Roll out on a heavily-floured surface to ⅛-inch thick. (Work with a small amount of dough at a time, keeping the rest refrigerated.) Cut out cookies with a heart-shape cookie cutter. Place on greased cookie sheet. Sprinkle with sugar or colored sprinkles (or spread Frosting on baked, cooled cookies). Bake at 350° for 10 to 12 minutes. **Yield**: 6 or 7 dozen

Frosting:

2 tablespoons margarine, softened	3 to 4 tablespoons milk
	2 cups powdered sugar
1 teaspoon vanilla	Red food coloring, optional

Beat margarine and vanilla in a small mixing bowl. Add milk a little at a time, alternately with sugar, until frosting is of spreading consistency. Stir in food coloring, if desired.

Donell Teaff
Wife of Grant Teaff, former Baylor head football coach
and athletic director

"During the years that I lived next door to Donell Teaff, I watched her do a lot of cooking. She's one of the best 'clutch' cooks I know. In a jam, she could always put something together in the kitchen. Whether it was for spur-of-the-moment entertaining or for something to take to a friend, Donell's food is always enjoyed."

Frances Durham Prather '44

BON-BONS

1 cup butter	2½ cups flour
1½ cups powdered sugar	1 teaspoon baking soda
1 egg, beaten	1 teaspoon cream of tartar
½ teaspoon vanilla	Almonds or pecan halves
½ teaspoon almond extract	

Thoroughly cream butter and powdered sugar. Add egg, vanilla, and almond extract. Beat well. Sift flour with baking soda and cream of tartar. Add and beat thoroughly. Chill 1 hour. Roll into small balls. Place on greased cookie sheet; flatten slightly, and center each with a blanched almond or small pecan half. Bake at 375° for 10 to 12 minutes. **Yield**: 5 dozen small cookies

Mary Wilson Russell McCall, '40, MSEd '67
Wife of Baylor President Emeritus, Dr. Abner McCall

CARAWAY RYE WAFERS

½ cup butter or margarine	¼ teaspoon salt
⅓ cup sugar	1 teaspoon grated orange
¾ cup unsifted flour	rind
½ cup unsifted medium rye	2 teaspoons caraway seeds,
flour	divided
¼ cup unsifted whole wheat	2 tablespoons cold water
flour	1 tablespoon milk
¼ teaspoon baking powder	

Cream butter and sugar. Gradually add next 5 ingredients. Stir in orange peel and 1 teaspoon of caraway seed. Gradually add water, mixing until moistened. Divide dough in half. On floured surface, working with ½ of dough, roll out to ⅛-inch thickness. Use a 2-inch round biscuit cutter to cut. Place on lightly-greased cookie sheets. Brush with milk and sprinkle with remaining caraway seeds. Roll out last ½ of dough. Bake at 375° for 8 to 10 minutes until lightly browned around edges. **Yield**: 4 dozen

Note: *Freezes well up to 3 months. This is not a sweet cookie.*

Mona Rogers Burchette '58

ALL-AMERICAN ICE BOX COOKIES

"Still an all-time favorite! This wonderful cookie goes back to the days of kitchen 'ice boxes' prior to electric refrigerators."

1 cup brown sugar
1 cup white sugar
1½ cups shortening
2 eggs, well beaten
Pinch of salt
2 teaspoons warm water

1 teaspoon baking soda
1 teaspoon vanilla
1 cup finely-chopped nuts
¼ teaspoon cinnamon
4 cups sifted flour

Cream sugars and shortening. Beat in eggs and salt. Dissolve baking soda in warm water, and stir in. Add vanilla, nuts, and cinnamon. Stir in as much flour as possible, kneading in the rest. Shape into rolls, and wrap in wax paper. Refrigerate overnight. Slice thin (about ¼-inch) using a sharp knife, and bake at 350° for 10 to 12 minutes. **Yield**: About 8 dozen

My parents, Nigle C. Outlaw, LLB '25, and Mildred Pate Outlaw, BA '25, used this recipe as a parental guidance tool. When I was a freshman, living in Alexander Hall, I received a call from my father. In his impressive attorney's voice, he said, "We have not received your expected weekly written communication and are desirous to know the reason." I responded that I was out of stamps. A few days later, a package arrived which contained a batch of ice box cookies and just enough stamps for the rest of the year! I got the message!

Alma Outlaw Boone '51

GINGER BUNNIES

½ cup shortening
½ cup sugar
½ cup light molasses
¼ cup water
2½ cups flour

¼ teaspoon nutmeg
½ teaspoon baking soda
¾ teaspoon salt
¾ teaspoon ginger
⅛ teaspoon allspice

Cream shortening and sugar. Blend in molasses and water. Combine flour and remaining 5 ingredients. Mix into creamed mixture. Cover and chill for 2 to 3 hours. Roll out dough ¼-inch thick on lightly-floured surface. Cut into desired shapes. Place on ungreased cookie sheets. Bake at 375° for 8 to 10 minutes. **Yield**: 2 to 2½ dozen

Note: *Decorate as desired with raisins, colored beads, icing, or sprinkles.*

Because inclement weather each year kept my friend's family from gathering at Christmas, they instead got together with the larger family at Easter. The grandmother, missing the Christmas experience of making gingerbread boys for her grandchildren, made these cut-out cookies in decorative bunny shapes. Hence, the name Ginger Bunnies.

Cynthia Duran Herin '69

OATMEAL COOKIES

"A favorite for Homecoming or for the Vacation Bible School crowd"

1 cup shortening	1½ cups flour
1 cup sugar	1 teaspoon baking soda
½ cup brown sugar	1 teaspoon cinnamon
1 egg	1½ cups rolled oats
2 tablespoons water	¾ cup chopped pecans
1 teaspoon vanilla	

Cream shortening, sugar and brown sugar. Add egg, water, and vanilla, stirring well. Stir in remaining ingredients. Roll into 1-inch balls. Butter bottom of a small, flat glass and dip in sugar. Flatten oatmeal balls. Bake at 350° for 10 minutes. **Yield**: 4 dozen

Louise Shepperd Graves '35

HEART HEALTHY OATMEAL COOKIES

1 cup sugar	2 teaspoons baking soda
¾ cup canola oil	¼ teaspoon salt
¼ cup egg substitute, or egg whites	1½ teaspoon cinnamon
¼ cup molasses	2 cups oatmeal with oatbran added
1½ cup flour	1 cup raisins
	Sugar for coating

In a mixer, combine sugar, oil, egg, and molasses. Mix flour, baking soda, salt, and cinnamon. Stir into creamed mixture. Add oatmeal slowly and work in. Add raisins. Chill. Roll into 1-inch balls. Roll in sugar to coat, and place on a non-stick cookie sheet. Bake at 375° for 10 minutes or until brown and crinkled. Cool 1 minute before removing to a wire rack. **Yield**: 5 dozen

Carolyn Grigsby Feather '54
Wife of Baylor Vice-President Robert O. Feather

GINGER-SPICE COOKIES

Editor's note: This soft, spicy cookie—made for many years by "The Voice of Baylor University"—has been enjoyed by countless alumni.

¾ cup shortening
1 cup sugar
1 egg, well beaten
⅓ cup molasses
2 cups flour
2 teaspoons baking soda

⅓ teaspoon salt
¾ teaspoon ginger
¾ teaspoon allspice
½ teaspoon nutmeg
½ teaspoon cloves
½ teaspoon cinnamon

Beat shortening, sugar, egg, and molasses. Sift dry ingredients together, and mix into creamed mixture. Chill for 1 hour or longer. Roll dough into 1-inch balls. Roll in sugar to cover. Place on lightly greased cookie sheets. Bake at 350° for 10 to 12 minutes. Do not overbake. **Yield**: 4 to 5 dozen

I like to take these Ginger-Spice Cookies to "The Land" for picnics, family reunions, or for Sunday school class meetings. They have a bright taste which warms any group. In fact, I always double this recipe and put the extra dough in the refrigerator. We can have something to serve in 15 minutes. I began making these cookies for Kappa Theta pledge meetings many years ago.

**George M. Stokes '47, retired professor,
Baylor Department of Communication Studies**

GEROME'S GRAHAM STACK-UPS

Whole graham crackers
¾ cup margarine
1 cup sugar
1 egg
½ cup evaporated milk

1 cup chopped pecans
2 cups coconut, divided
1 cup crushed graham
    crackers
Icing

Line a 9x13-inch pan with whole graham crackers. Melt margarine with sugar. Add egg and evaporated milk. Bring to a boil, stirring constantly, and boil for 1 minute. Add pecans, 1 cup coconut, and crushed graham crackers. Mix together and pour over whole graham crackers. Place second layer of whole graham crackers over top. Spread Icing over graham crackers. Sprinkle with remaining coconut. When cool, cut into small bars. Flavor is better the second day. **Yield**: 30 bars

Icing:

¼ cup margarine, melted
2 cups powdered sugar

3 tablespoons evaporated
    milk
1 teaspoon vanilla

Mix all ingredients together.

Betty Gilbreath Price '59

WHITE CHOCOLATE CHUNK COOKIES

9 ounces imported white chocolate	¼ cup sugar
7 tablespoons butter, softened	1 large egg
	1½ teaspoons vanilla
½ cup firmly-packed dark brown sugar	1¼ cups flour
	½ teaspoon baking soda
	Dash of salt

Cut chocolate into squares along markings. Break each square in half or quarters. Set aside. Place butter and both sugars in food processor with metal blade, and process until well blended. Scrape down sides and process again. Add egg and vanilla. Process until mixed. Add flour, baking soda, and salt, and pulse until incorporated. Pour mixture into a mixing bowl, and stir in chocolate. Drop batter by heaping tablespoons about 1½-inch apart onto ungreased cookie sheet. Bake at 350° for 10 to 12 minutes, checking after 8 minutes, until tops are just beginning to brown. Cookies will appear underdone; they will firm as they cool. Allow to set for 2 minutes; remove from cookie sheets to cooling racks. **Yield**: About 3 dozen.

Kay Nethery Elliott '64

SWEET ANGELS
"Must be made 2 days ahead."

1 (6-ounce) package semi-sweet chocolate chips	1 cup powdered sugar
	1 cup chopped walnuts
2 tablespoons butter or margarine	2 cups miniature marshmallows
1 egg	½ cup flaked coconut

Melt chips and butter over low heat. Remove from heat, and beat in egg. Blend in sugar, nuts, and marshmallows. With buttered hands, shape dough into 1-inch balls, including 2 marshmallows in each ball. As hands get sticky, rinse hands in cold water, butter them again, and continue. Roll in coconut. Chill for 48 hours, uncovered. **Yield**: About 4 dozen

Becky A. Dyer '69

CHOCOLATE CARAMEL COOKIES

2½ cups flour
¾ cup cocoa
1 teaspoon baking soda
1 cup sugar
1 cup firmly-packed brown
  sugar
1 cup margarine

2 teaspoons vanilla
2 eggs
48 milk chocolate-covered
  caramels
4 ounces vanilla-flavored
  candy coating

In small bowl, combine flour, cocoa, and baking soda, and mix well. In a large bowl, beat sugar, brown sugar, and margarine until light and fluffy. Add vanilla and eggs; beat well. Add flour mixture and blend. Chill dough briefly. Shape about 1 tablespoon of dough around each caramel, covering completely. (Flour hands to make shaping easier.) On lightly-greased cookie sheet, bake at 375° for 7 to 10 minutes, or until set and slightly cracked. Cool 2 minutes, and remove from cookie sheets. Cool completely on wire racks. Melt candy coating and drizzle over cookies. **Yield**: 3 to 4 dozen

Donna Beck Lewis '75

TRI DELTA TREASURES

The Waco alumnae of Delta Delta Delta traditionally serve this dessert to the graduating seniors of the Baylor chapter after the ceremony welcoming them into alumnae status.

1 (12-ounce) package of
  semi-sweet chocolate
  chips
1 (14-ounce) can sweetened
  condensed milk

¼ cup butter, not margarine
1 teaspoon vanilla
1 cup flour
2 cups pecans, coarsely
  chopped

Place chocolate chips, milk, and butter in microwave-safe bowl. Microwave on medium high heat, stirring occasionally until chips and butter are melted. Do not allow to boil. Stir in vanilla. Add flour, and stir by hand until blended. (Do not use mixer.) Fold in pecans. Drop by teaspoonfuls onto greased baking sheet. Bake at 350° for about 8 minutes. **Yield**: 4 to 5 dozen

Note: *Freezes well.*

Kathy Robinson Hillman '73

BAYLOR BEAR BROWNIES

A favorite from our first cookbook, Flavor Favorites

2 cups sugar
5 tablespoons cocoa
1 cup butter, softened
4 eggs

1½ cups flour
1 teaspoon vanilla
1 cup coarsely-chopped
    pecans

Cream sugar, cocoa, and butter. Add eggs, beating thoroughly. Stir in flour, vanilla and pecans. Pour into a greased 14x9-inch baking pan. Bake at 350° for 30 to 40 minutes. Cut into squares. **Yield**: About 2 dozen

Through the years, Hugh and I have had such pleasure inviting students into our home. Not long ago, we received a long-distance call from a man we hadn't heard from for years. He wanted to thank us again, and he told us he remembered every dish we served him, every time he ate with us. That was almost thirty years ago.

Rinky Chivers Sanders '60

MINT BROWNIES

"Rich and delicious with a taste surprise"

1 cup margarine, softened
    and divided
1 cup sugar
4 eggs
1 (16-ounce) can chocolate
    syrup
1 cup flour

2 cups powdered sugar
2 tablespoons milk
1 teaspoon mint extract
3 drops green coloring
1 (6-ounce) package semi-
    sweet chocolate chips

Cream ½ cup margarine with sugar. Add eggs and beat well. Stir in chocolate syrup. Add flour, and blend. Pour batter into a greased 11x15-inch jelly roll pan. Bake at 350° for 20-25 minutes. Let cool.

    Mix powdered sugar and ¼ cup margarine together. Add milk, mint extract and food coloring. Spread over cooled brownies. Melt chocolate chips and remaining ¼ cup margarine. Swirl over top of mint layer. Chill. Cut into squares to serve. **Yield**: About 3 to 4 dozen.

Kay DeLoach '63

ICED BROWNIE BARS

2 cups sugar
1 cup margarine, softened
4 eggs
2 teaspoons vanilla

¾ cup cocoa
1 cup flour
1 teaspoon baking powder
Icing

Cream together sugar and margarine. Add eggs and beat well. Add vanilla; then stir in remaining ingredients. Spread in a greased 9x13-inch pan. Bake at 350° for 30 minutes. Cool. Spread Icing on cooled brownies. Cut into bars. **Yield**: 2 dozen

Icing:
1 cup brown or white sugar
3 tablespoons cocoa
3½ tablespoons margarine
¼ teaspoon salt

¼ cup milk
1½ cups sifted powdered
   sugar
1 teaspoon vanilla

Mix first 5 ingredients in a medium saucepan, stirring often. Cool. Add powdered sugar and vanilla.

Pam Regan Drumm '79

CHOCOLATE FUDGE MUFFINS
"These went to many a 'Sic'em Bears' tailgate party each fall"

1 cup margarine
4 (1-ounce) squares semi-
   sweet chocolate
1¾ cups sugar

4 eggs
1 cup flour
1 teaspoon vanilla
½ cup chopped pecans

Melt margarine and chocolate together in a saucepan. Add sugar and mix well. Add eggs and beat thorougly. Stir in flour, vanilla and pecans. Spoon into muffin tins that are lined with paper baking cups. Bake at 300°for 30 to 40 minutes. **Yield**: 1½ dozen

Donell Teaff
Wife of Grant Teaff, former Baylor head football coach
and athletic director

APRICOT BARS

"Reminds me of my grandmother's fried apricot pies."

2 cups flour
1 cup sugar
½ teaspoon salt
½ teaspoon baking soda
¾ cup butter or margarine

¾ cup chopped pecans
1 cup flaked coconut
1 (16-ounce) jar apricot jam
  or preserves

Cut first 4 ingredients into butter or margarine until crumbly. Mix in chopped pecans and coconut. Press ½ of crumb mixture into bottom of lightly-greased 9x13-inch pan. Spread mixture with apricot jam or preserves. Cover with remaining crumb mixture, and press down firmly. Bake at 350° for approximately 30 minutes or until set and slightly browned. Cut into bars when cooled. **Yield**: 2 dozen

Ann McDonald Hirschfelt '59

BROWN SUGAR BROWNIES

From the Texas Governor's Mansion to your kitchen

½ cup + 2 tablespoons butter
2 cups brown sugar
1 teaspoon vanilla
2 eggs

1 cup flour
2 teaspoons baking powder
½ teaspoon salt
1 cup nuts, chopped

Melt butter in medium saucepan. Remove from heat, and add brown sugar. Blend thoroughly, and stir in vanilla and eggs. Add dry ingredients, and stir until moistened. Stir in chopped nuts. Pour batter in greased and floured 9-inch square baking pan. Bake at 350° for 30 to 35 minutes, or until edges pull away from pan. Cool and cut into squares. **Yield**: 16 squares

The Honorable Ann Willis Richards '54
Governor, State of Texas

FROSTED APPLE BROWNIES

½ cup shortening
1½ cups sugar
3 eggs
2 cups flour
½ teaspoon salt
1 teaspoon baking soda
1 teaspoon cinnamon

1 cup finely-chopped peeled
  apple
½ cup chopped pecans
1 tablespoon water or milk,
  optional
Cream Cheese Frosting

Cream shortening and sugar, beating well. Add eggs, one at a time, beating after each addition. Combine flour, salt, baking soda, and cinnamon; gradually add to creamed mixture. Fold in apples and pecans. Pour batter into a greased 15x10-inch jelly roll pan. (Add water or milk if dough is too stiff to spread.) Bake at 350° for 30 minutes. Remove from oven, and spread top with Cream Cheese Frosting while slightly warm. Cool completely, and cut into squares. **Yield**: 4 dozen

Cream Cheese Frosting
½ cup butter or margarine,
  softened
2 (3-ounce) packages cream
  cheese, softened

3 cups sifted powdered
  sugar
2 teaspoons vanilla
¾ cup chopped pecans

Mix butter and cream cheese. Blend in remaining ingredients.

Gloria Turner DuBose '62

FROSTED CARROT BARS
"Light and moist—good even without the icing"

2 cups sugar
1¼ cups oil
4 eggs
2 cups flour
2 teaspoons baking soda
1½ teaspoons cinnamon
⅛ teaspoon cloves
½ teaspoon salt
2 (6-ounce) jars baby food
   carrots
Frosting

Beat first 3 ingredients together until well blended. Stir in dry ingredients. Mix in carrots. Pour into an ungreased 11x17-inch jelly roll pan. Bake at 350° for 30 minutes. Cool completely; spread with Frosting, or dust with powdered sugar. Cut into bars. **Yield:** 6 to 7 dozen bars

Frosting:
1 (8-ounce) package cream
   cheese, softened
½ cup margarine, softened
2 cups powdered sugar
2 teaspoons vanilla

Beat cream cheese and margarine together. Stir in powdered sugar and vanilla.

Susan Bedwell Amos '91

COCONUT PECAN BARS
"Flavorful, chewy, and good!"

2 cups flour
1 teaspoon baking powder
½ teaspoon salt
1 cup butter
2 cups firmly-packed brown
   sugar
2 eggs
2 teaspoons vanilla
1 cup coconut
1 cup chopped pecans
Powdered sugar

Sift flour, baking powder, and salt together; set aside. Cream butter and sugar. Add eggs and vanilla, and beat until creamy. Add flour mixture, and mix well. Stir in coconut and pecans. Spread into a greased 10x15-inch jelly roll pan. Bake at 350° for 30 minutes. Cool. Sprinkle with powdered sugar and cut into bars. **Yield:** 4 dozen medium bars

Mary Frances Markley '79

GOODIE BARS

"Very similar to the traditional lemon bar, but a quicker, newer version."

1 (18¼-ounce) box lemon cake mix
½ cup butter or margarine, melted
3 eggs, divided

1 (8-ounce) package cream cheese, softened
1 teaspoon lemon extract
1 (16-ounce) box powdered sugar
1 cup finely-chopped pecans

Mix together cake mix, butter and 1 egg. Press firmly into bottom of 11x15-inch jelly roll pan. (Dampened hands will make this easier.) Beat cream cheese with mixer. Add remaining 2 eggs and powdered sugar, and mix well. Pour over dough in pan. Cover with chopped pecans. Bake at 350° for 30 minutes. Cool completely, overnight if possible. Cut into squares. **Yield**: 3 dozen

Hint: *Use a spice cake mix and top with chopped walnuts. Or use a fudge cake mix and top with chocolate chips and chopped pecans.*

Donalita Grantham Adkins '41

COCONUT PUMPKIN BARS

"Only takes one mixing bowl, so there isn't a lot of cleaning up to do."

¾ cup flour
¾ cup rolled oats
½ cup chopped walnuts
½ cup melted margarine
1 (3-ounce) box butterscotch pudding mix (not instant)
1 cup coconut

1½ teaspoons pumpkin pie spice
1 (16-ounce) can pumpkin
1 (14-ounce) can sweetened condensed milk
2 eggs, beaten

Mix first 5 ingredients together. Press firmly into a 9x13-inch baking pan. Mix remaining ingredients together, blending well. Pour pumpkin mixture over crust, spreading evenly. Bake at 350°for 35 to 45 minutes, or until knife inserted in center comes out clean. Cool and cut into bars. **Yield**: 2 to 3 dozen

Claudia Burton Johnson, a Baylor mom

SANTA'S WHISKERS
"A third-generation recipe"

1 cup butter
1 cup sugar
2 tablespoons milk
1 teaspoon vanilla
2½ cups flour

¾ cup chopped red and
  green candied cherries
½ cup chopped nuts
2¼ cups canned flaked
  coconut, divided

Cream together butter and sugar. Blend in milk and vanilla. Add flour, chopped candied cherries, chopped nuts, and ¾ cup coconut. Place remaining 1½ cups coconut on wax paper or in a shallow bowl. Drop dough by teaspoons into coconut, and roll to coat on all sides. Place on ungreased baking sheet. Bake at 350° for 15 minutes. **Yield**: 7 dozen

Note: *Coconut must be moist to adhere to cookies when rolling. Use a freshly-opened can. Dough can be refrigerated up to one week. When ready to use, let come to room temperature before rolling in coconut.*

Becky A. Dyer '69

 ## NITETY NITES
"A classic favorite"

2 egg whites
⅔ cup sugar
1 cup semi-sweet chocolate
  chips

1 cup chopped nuts
1 teaspoon vanilla
½ teaspoon almond extract
Pinch of salt

Beat egg whites until frothy. Gradually add sugar, and beat until stiff, until meringue holds a stiff peak. Fold in remaining ingredients. Drop by small spoonfuls onto foil-covered cookie sheet. Preheat oven to 350° and then turn off. Immediately place cookies in oven, and leave overnight or until oven is cold. **Yield**: 4 dozen

Denise Cochran Morton '83

MELT AWAY COOKIES

1 cup margarine, softened
¾ cup cornstarch
⅓ cup powdered sugar

1 cup flour
Icing

Mix all of ingredients except Icing. Drop on ungreased cookie sheet in small balls, and flatten slightly. Bake at 350° for 15 minutes. (They should not brown.) When cool, ice. **Yield**: About 4 dozen

Icing:
1 (3-ounce) package cream
   cheese

1 teaspoon vanilla
1 cup powdered sugar

Blend all ingredients until smooth.

The Cookbook Committee

DEATH BY CHOCOLATE

A beautiful dessert, and rated off the chart by our testers.

1 (9-ounce) box Jello
   Chocolate Mousse mix
2 cups whipping cream,
   whipped
1 teaspoon vanilla

¼ cup sugar
1 pan brownies (homemade
   or bakery purchased)
¼ cup Kahlua liqueur
3 Skor candy bars, crushed

Prepare mousse only from box mix, and refrigerate. (Save the crumb mixture for another use.) Add vanilla and sugar to whipped cream. Soak brownies in Kahlua. Assemble in a glass trifle or fruit bowl. Using ½ of each ingredient at a time, layer in the following order: brownies, mousse, whipped cream, candy bars. Repeat layers. Refrigerate. **Yield**: 10 to 12 servings.

Nancy Colleen Newcomb '92

NANAIMO SQUARES

"Time consuming but worth it."

¾ cup butter, divided
¼ cup sugar
3 tablespoons cocoa
1 egg, slightly beaten
1 teaspoon vanilla
2 cups graham cracker
   crumbs
½ cup chopped nuts

1 cup coconut
2 cups powdered sugar
2 tablespoons instant vanilla
   pudding powder
2 tablespoons hot water
2 (1-ounce) squares semi-
   sweet chocolate
1 tablespoon butter

Cook ½ cup butter, sugar, and cocoa in top of double boiler over hot water until sugar dissolves. Slowly add beaten egg and vanilla; remove from heat, add crumbs, nuts and coconut. Spread in greased 8-inch square pan. Refrigerate until set.

Combine ¼ cup butter, powdered sugar, pudding powder and hot water; mix well. (If the batter is too thick, add more water.) Spread over first layer, and return to refrigerator to chill. Melt chocolate with 1 tablespoon butter, and spread on top. Chill until firm. Cut into 2-inch squares. **Yield**: 16 squares

Rhonda Sewell Kehlbeck '86

TRIPLE CHOCOLATE TREAT

1 (16-ounce) package cream-
   filled chocolate sandwich
   cookies, crushed
2 (3-ounce) plain chocolate
   candy bars, broken in bits
½ cup butter or margarine,
   softened
1 (8-ounce) package cream
   cheese, softened

1 cup powdered sugar
2 (3½-ounce) packages
   instant chocolate pudding
   mix
3 cups milk
1 (8-ounce) carton frozen
   whipped topping, thawed

Mix cookies and bits of chocolate; set aside. Cream together butter, cream cheese and powdered sugar; set aside. Combine pudding mix and milk, and stir until thick. Fold whipped topping
into pudding. Combine pudding and cream cheese mixtures. In
a 9x13-inch pan, layer in the following order: ⅓ of cookie mixture, ½ of pudding mixture, ⅓ of cookies, remaining pudding,
and last ⅓ of cookies. Chill until serving time. **Yield**: 10 to 12
servings

Note: *Some people enjoy serving this in new, foil-lined clay flower
pots, complete with fresh flowers (inserted through pieces of plastic
drinking straw.)*

Joanne Briscoe Jones '70

AUTUMN APPLE-CRANBERRY DESSERT

3 cups chopped fresh apples
2 cups fresh cranberries
1 cup sugar
1 cup chopped nuts

1½ cups oats, uncooked
½ cup melted margarine
⅓ cup flour
½ cup brown sugar

Mix all ingredients together. Pour into a buttered 9x13-inch baking dish. Bake at 325° for 1 hour. Serve warm. **Yield**: 8 to 10 servings

Hint: *Serve warm with ice cream on top. Even better the next day.*

The Cookbook Committee

🕐 LAYERED ECLAIR SQUARES

2 (3-ounce) packages French
   vanilla instant pudding
   mix
3 cups milk
1 (8-ounce) carton frozen
   whipped topping, thawed

1 (16-ounce) box graham
   crackers
1 (16-ounce) container
   prepared chocolate
   frosting

Prepare pudding with milk, following directions on package.
Blend in whipped topping. Line a 9x13-inch pan with a layer of
graham crackers. Top with ½ of pudding mixture, another layer
of crackers, and remaining pudding mixture. Add last layer of
crackers. Heat frosting for 2 or 3 minutes in the microwave to
make it easier to spread.

Spread chocolate frosting on top. Refrigerate for at least 6 hours
or overnight before serving. **Yield**: 10 to 15 servings

Diane Waters Davis '66

MAGNOLIA PECAN SQUARES

3 whole eggs
2 cups firmly-packed brown
   sugar
2¼ teaspoons baking powder
¼ cup flour
¼ cup butter

1 cup cake crumbs (bakery
   or frozen pound cake is
   easy)
2 cups chopped pecans or
   walnuts
1 teaspoon vanilla
3 egg whites
Whipped cream

In large bowl of electric mixer, beat whole eggs; add next 4 ingredients and blend. Stir in cake crumbs, nuts, and vanilla. In separate bowl, beat egg whites till stiff and dry; fold into cake mixture. Spoon into well-greased 9x13-inch baking pan. Bake at 350°
about 1 hour or until knife inserted in center comes out clean.
Cool slightly; cut into squares, and top with whipped cream.
Yield: About 1 dozen squares

Hint: *May be cut into bars and rolled in powdered sugar.*

Nancy Derrick Lacy '89

🕐 HOT FRUIT COMPOTE

"A very versatile dish"

1 (16-ounce) can whole
   cranberry sauce
1 (16-ounce) can applesauce
1 (16-ounce) can pears, well
   drained and diced
1 (15½-ounce) can pineapple
   tidbits, well drained

1 (16-ounce) can apricots,
   well drained and diced
1 cup blueberries, frozen
2 bananas, sliced
½ cup brown sugar
¼ cup butter or margarine

Mix cranberry sauce and applesauce together; spread ½ of mixture over bottom of 9x13-inch baking dish. Cover with remaining fruit. Spoon remaining sauce mixture on top; sprinkle with brown sugar and dot with butter or margarine. Bake at 350° for 30 minutes. Serve hot. **Yield**: 12 to 15 servings

Hint: Serve as a side dish with holiday turkey or ham, as a light dessert with brunch, or over vanilla ice cream—any time.

Donalita Grantham Adkins '41

"'How long does getting thin take?' Pooh asked anxiously."

from *Winnie the Pooh* by A. A. Milne

STRAWBERRY DELIGHT
"It's beautiful!"

1 cup flour
¼ cup firmly-packed brown sugar
½ cup chopped pecans
¼ teaspoon cinnamon
½ cup butter or margarine, melted
2 egg whites
1 cup sugar
1 (10-ounce) package frozen strawberries, thawed
1 tablespoon lemon juice
1 (8-ounce) carton frozen whipped topping, thawed
Whole strawberries, optional
Mint sprigs, optional

Combine first 4 ingredients, mixing well. Stir in melted butter until blended. Spread mixture in jelly roll pan. Bake at 350° for 15-20 minutes, stirring often. Mixture should be crumbly and not too brown. Cool. In large bowl of electric mixer, beat egg whites until foamy. Gradually add sugar, beating until very thick. Add undrained strawberries and lemon juice. Beat at high speed at least 10 minutes until mixture is very light and fluffy. Gently fold in whipped topping, blending well. In a buttered 9x13-inch pan or freezer dish evenly distribute ¾ of cooked crumbly mixture. Carefully spoon on strawberry whip, spreading evenly. Sprinkle with remaining crumbs. Cover and freeze overnight. Remove from freezer about 20 minutes before serving. Garnish each serving with a whole strawberry and a mint sprig, if desired. **Yield**: 12 servings.

Claire Hirschfelt Hogg '89

CHERRY BERRIES ON A CLOUD

"A great make-ahead dessert for special occasions"

6 egg whites
½ teaspoon cream of tartar
¼ teaspoon salt
2¾ cups sugar, divided
2 (3-ounce) packages cream
   cheese, softened
1 teaspoon vanilla
1 cup sour cream
1 cup whipping cream,
   whipped

2 cups miniature
   marshmallows
1 (21-ounce) can cherry pie
   filling
1 teaspoon lemon juice
2 cups fresh strawberries,
   sliced or 1 (16-ounce) bag
   frozen strawberries,
   thawed

Beat first 3 ingredients until frothy. Gradually beat in 1¾ cups sugar. Beat until very stiff and glossy, approximately 15 minutes. Spread in a greased 9x13-inch baking pan. Bake at 275° for 1 hour. Turn off oven and leave meringue in oven until cool. Mix cream cheese with remaining sugar and vanilla. Gently fold in sour cream, whipped cream, and marshmallows. Spread over meringue; refrigerate overnight. Mix last 3 ingredients together. Cut dessert into squares, and top with cherry-berry mixture before serving. **Yield**: 12 to15 servings

Note: *Must be prepared the day before and finished just before serving.*

Frances Adkins Cleveland '67

BAKLAVA

"Rich and wonderful—a winner"

3 cups finely-chopped
   walnuts or almonds
¾ cup sugar
2 teaspoons cinnamon
1 teaspoon allspice

1 (16-ounce) box pastry
   sheets (filo)
1 pound butter, melted
Whole cloves
Honey Syrup

Mix walnuts with sugar and spices. Cut filo to fit 9x12-inch baking dish. (Keep filo covered with damp cloth while in use.) Brush dish with butter. Place 6 sheets of filo in bottom of baking dish, brushing each with melted butter. Cover with thin layer of walnut mixture. Cover with 1 filo sheet. Apply melted butter. Repeat until all nuts are used. Then place 6 filo sheets, each brushed with melted butter, on top.

With sharp knife, cut baklava diagonally into strips 1½-inches wide, forming diamond-shape pieces. Stick 1 clove in center of each piece. Heat any remaining butter, and pour into knife slits between strips. Bake at 300° about 1 hour.

When baklava is slightly browned, pour some boiling hot Honey Syrup over it slowly. Increase temperature to 400°, and return to oven for few minutes until syrup has penetrated and top is golden brown. Check in 5 minutes. Remove from oven; pour as much syrup over top as it will absorb. Let stand at least 3 hours before serving. **Yield**: 3 to 4 dozen pieces

Honey Syrup:
1 cup sugar
1 cup water

1½ cups honey
2 teaspoons vanilla

Cook sugar with water about 10 minutes until syrup foams. Add honey and vanilla, and cook 5 more minutes.

Hint: *Best if made 2 or 3 days ahead.*

Dottie Gilleland Mathews '58

APPLE MINT ANGEL SHELLS

3 egg whites
¾ cup sugar
½ teaspoon vanilla
½ teaspoon baking powder
14 round buttery salted
  crackers

¾ cup chopped pecans or
  walnuts
1½ pints vanilla ice cream
Apple Mint Sauce

Beat egg whites very stiff. Gradually add sugar, beating constantly. Add vanilla and baking powder. Break crackers into pieces about the size of a dime; fold into meringue along with chopped nuts. Cover cookie sheet with parchment or heavy paper (not wax paper). Moisten slightly. Spoon out 6 mounds of meringue 3 to 4 inches in diameter. Make a deep well in center of each meringue. Bake at 275° for 50 minutes. Cool and remove meringues from paper. (If meringues stick, wipe the bottom of the paper with a damp cloth). Store immediately in tightly-covered container. Just before serving, place a scoop of ice cream in center of shells and top with Apple Mint Sauce. Serve immediately. **Yield**: 6 servings

Apple Mint Sauce:
2 teaspoons cornstarch
2 cups canned applesauce
⅔ cup sugar

¼ teaspoon peppermint
  extract
6 drops green food coloring

Moisten cornstarch with several drops of cold water; combine with remaining ingredients in saucepan. Cook slowly, stirring until sauce thickens. Chill.

Hint: Mint leaves make a nice garnish. May use chocolate sauce flavored with mint extract in place of Apple Mint Sauce.

**Sadie Jo Black '50, retired professor,
Baylor Department of Home Economics**

HEAVENLY GOO

Someone took a bite and said, "What on earth is this 'heavenly goo'?"

1 cup fine graham cracker
   crumbs (12 to 14 crackers)
½ cup margarine, divided
1¼ cup powdered sugar
2 eggs, separated

1 teaspoon vanilla
1 cup whipping cream,
   whipped
1 cup nuts, broken

Combine graham cracker crumbs and ¼ cup melted margarine. Press ½ of crumb mixture into lightly-greased 9x13-inch dish for crust; reserve other ½ for topping. To remaining ¼ cup margarine, add powdered sugar, egg yolks, and vanilla. Mix well. Beat 2 egg whites until stiff, and fold into creamed mixture. Fold in whipped cream and nuts. Pour into prepared crust, and top with crumbs. Cover with foil, and freeze. Serve frozen; it will not be hard. **Yield**: 15 servings

Barbara Schultz Cunningham '54

SAN ANTONIO TORTILLA TORTE

"Great ending to a Mexican food meal, and it's gorgeous."

1 (12-ounce) package semi-
   sweet chocolate chips
3 cups sour cream, divided
10 7- or 8-inch flour tortillas

¼ cup sifted powdered sugar
Chocolate curls
Fresh strawberries, optional

In medium saucepan, melt chocolate pieces over low heat, stirring occasionally. Stir in 2 cups sour cream. Remove from heat and cool. Place 1 tortilla onto a serving plate. Spread about ⅓ cup chocolate mixture on top. Continue layering with tortillas and chocolate mixture, ending with last tortilla. In a small bowl, stir together remaining 1 cup sour cream and powdered sugar. Spread on top of torte. Cover and chill overnight to soften the tortillas and to make torte easy to slice and serve. Before serving, garnish with chocolate curls and strawberries. **Yield**: 12 servings

Note: *Must be made the night before.*

Phyllis Wyrick Patterson '74

CHOCOLATE TORTE WITH RASPBERRY SAUCE

1 (6-ounce) package semi-
    sweet chocolate chips,
    melted
1 cup unsalted butter,
    softened

1 cup sugar
8 very fresh large eggs,
    separated
Sweetened whipped cream
Raspberry Sauce

In large bowl, combine melted chocolate, butter, and sugar. Cool. Add egg yolks one at a time, beating well after each addition. In separate bowl, beat egg whites until stiff. Fold egg whites gently into chocolate mixture. Butter and flour a 9-inch springform pan. Pour ⅔ of the batter into pan. Bake at 325° for 30 to 40 minutes or until pick inserted in center comes out clean. Cool to room temperature. (The center will fall.) Spread remaining batter over the top. Refrigerate at least 8 hours or overnight. Cut into wedges. Serve with sweetened whipped cream and Raspberry Sauce. **Yield**: 10 to 12 servings

Raspberry Sauce:

2 (10-ounce) packages frozen
    raspberries, thawed and
    well drained, saving ½ of
    juice

¼ cup sugar
3 tablespoons Grand
    Marnier liqueur, optional

Puree raspberries, reserved juice, sugar, and liqueur in food processor. Strain to remove seeds. Chill.

Hint: *Use a hot knife to cut wedges. To determine whether an egg is fresh, immerse it in a pan of cool, salted water. If it sinks, it is fresh. If it rises to the surface, throw it away.*

Betty Harper Phillips '52

RASPBERRY WALNUT TORTE
"Tart, tangy, delicious"

1¼ cups flour, divided
⅓ cup powdered sugar
½ cup butter, softened
1 (10-ounce) package frozen
    raspberries, thawed and
    drained, reserving syrup
¾ cup chopped walnuts

2 eggs
1 cup sugar
½ teaspoon baking powder
½ teaspoon salt
1 teaspoon vanilla
Whipped cream
Raspberry Sauce

In a small mixing bowl, combine 1 cup flour, powdered sugar, and butter; blend well. Press into bottom of ungreased 9-inch square pan. Bake at 350° for 15 minutes. Cool.

Spread drained berries over crust; sprinkle with walnuts. With an electric mixer, combine eggs, sugar, remaining flour, baking powder, salt, and vanilla. Blend well at low speed. Pour over berries and nuts. Bake at 350° for 35 to 40 minutes until golden brown. Cool. Cut into squares, and serve with whipped cream and Raspberry Sauce. **Yield**: 9 servings

Raspberry Sauce:
½ cup sugar
2 tablespoons cornstarch
½ cup water

Reserved raspberry syrup
1 tablespoon lemon juice

In small saucepan, combine first 4 ingredients; cook, stirring constantly, until thick and clear. Stir in lemon juice. Cool.

Ethel Ann de Cordova Porter '58

APPLE NUT TORTE WITH BROWN SUGAR SAUCE

1 cup sugar
¼ cup margarine
1 cup flour
1 teaspoon baking soda
¼ teaspoon nutmeg
½ teapoon cinnamon

½ teaspoon salt
2 cups finely-chopped apple, unpeeled
½ cup pecans or walnuts
Brown Sugar Sauce

Cream sugar and margarine in a large mixing bowl. Mix in dry ingredients, and stir well. Fold in chopped apples and nuts. Pour into an 8-inch square baking pan that has been coated with non-stick vegetable spray. Bake at 350° for 40 minutes. Cool in pan. To serve, cut into squares like large brownies. Top each square with warm Brown Sugar Sauce. **Yield**: 8 to 10 servings

Brown Sugar Sauce:
½ cup brown sugar
½ cup sugar
2 tablespoons flour

¼ cup margarine
½ cup boiling water

Cook until thick, stirring constantly.

Note: *Apples provide the moisture during baking.*

Claudia Burton Johnson, a Baylor mom

LEMON TORTE WITH RASPBERRIES

"Excellent for low cholesterol diets — very easy to prepare"

1 (4-ounce) package low-calorie lemon-flavored gelatin
½ cup boiling water
½ cup frozen lemonade, thawed

1 (12-ounce) can evaporated skim milk
2 cups cubed angel food cake
2 cups fresh raspberries
1 to 2 tablespoons sugar, or to taste

In a large bowl, dissolve gelatin in boiling water. Stir in lemonade and milk. Cover and chill in refrigerator for 1 to 1½ hours or until mixture mounds with spoon.

After chilling, beat mixture with electric mixer on medium to high speed for 5 to 6 minutes or until fluffy.

Spray bottom only of an 8-inch springform pan with non-stick vegetable spray. Arrange cake cubes in bottom of pan. Pour gelatin mixture over cake cubes. Cover and chill in refrigerator for 4 hours or until firm. Stir together raspberries and sugar. Chill 2 hours. Remove sides of springform pan. Cut torte into wedges and serve with raspberries. **Yield**: 12 servings

Note: *Freezes well.*

Karen Davenport Smith '77

During Welcome Week before fall classes begin, faculty members invite groups of freshmen into their homes one evening for dinner. The students enjoy seeing that faculty members are real people who actually live in houses and have meals just as normal people do. On one of these occasions, one freshman — having demolished his dessert — proudly proclaimed, "Mrs. Francis, that dessert was awesome — the best dessert I've ever eaten!"

Of course, it was not the best dessert he'd ever eaten, but to a lonely freshman, away from home for the first time, it was a dessert prepared in a home — a home probably not unlike his own.

Judith Witt Francis '66, MA '71
Baylor Department of English

ELEGANT TOP-OF-STOVE BREAD PUDDING

Editor's note: Our testers and their guests, plus the alumni office staff, said this recipe is 5-star for sure.

½ cup butter
1 cup firmly-packed brown
   sugar
¼ cup raisins, optional
6 to 7 slices quality bread
   (day-old French bread
   with crusts is best)
Butter

2 eggs
1 cup warm milk, scalded
½ cup sugar
Pinch of salt
1 teaspoon vanilla
Whipped cream, optional
Ice cream, optional

Place butter in top of a double boiler, and place brown sugar on top with raisins. Butter bread slices (trim crusts from bread if desired), and cut into cubes. Put on top of brown sugar and butter. Mix next 5 ingredients, and pour over bread cubes. Cover, place over simmering water; steam for 1½ hours. (Do not lift lid; do not stir. Watch water level in bottom of double boiler.) Serve warm in stem glasses. Ladle caramel sauce, which forms under the pudding, over each serving. Dollop with whipped cream or ice cream if desired. **Yield**: 6 servings

Hint: *This requires no attention once it is on the stove.*

Canon George Wesley Monroe '62

BEST BANANA PUDDING

1½ cups sugar, divided
3 cups low-fat milk, divided
⅔ cup flour
½ teaspoon salt
4 egg yolks
3 tablespoons margarine

2 teaspoons vanilla
1 cup whipping cream,
   whipped
Vanilla wafers
6 bananas, sliced

In a small saucepan, combine ¾ cup sugar and 1½ cups milk. Cook over medium high heat, stirring frequently until the mixture steams. In a larger saucepan, combine remaining sugar, flour, and salt. Very gradually stir in remaining 1½ cups milk. Cook over medium heat, stirring constantly. As mixture thickens, add mixture from small saucepan. Boil for 2 minutes, stirring constantly. Beat egg yolks in small bowl. Stir a few spoonfuls of hot mixture into eggs yolks, and then add yolks to saucepan. Boil for 2 more minutes, stirring constantly. Remove from heat, and stir in margarine and vanilla. Cool to room temperature. Gently fold in whipped cream. Line large bowl with ½ of wafers; layer with sliced bananas and pudding. Repeat layers, using more wafers, bananas, and remaining pudding. Stand wafers around edge of dish, and decorate top of pudding with more wafers, if desired.
Yield: 8 to 10 servings

Hint: *Wait until hot pudding has cooled slightly, and then cover saucepan to prevent dryness.*

Lanette Lemons Whitley '70

FRUITED TRIFLE

2 cups milk
4 eggs, separated
½ cup sugar
3 tablespoons cornstarch
¼ teaspoon salt
2 tablespoons butter
1 teaspoon vanilla
½ (16-ounce) pound cake,
   cut into ½-inch slices
¼ to ½ cup raspberry syrup
1 pound strawberries or
   fresh peaches, sliced
2 bananas, peeled and sliced
   (about 2 cups)
1 (11-ounce) can mandarin
   orange sections, drained,
   or 1 pint blueberries
2 kiwi, peeled and sliced
1 cup whipping cream
2 tablespoons powdered
   sugar
Whole strawberries and
   mint sprigs for garnish

Combine milk, egg yolks, sugar, cornstarch and salt in blender or processor and mix well. Pour into medium glass bowl. Cook on high in microwave until thick, about 6 to 7 minutes, stirring halfway through cooking time. Whisk in butter and vanilla. Cover custard, and refrigerate until cool and softly set. Brush cake slices generously with syrup. Arrange ½ of slices in single layer in trifle or other deep bowl. Layer with ½ of strawberries (or peaches), bananas, orange sections (or blueberries) and kiwi. Spoon ½ of custard over fruit. Repeat layering with remaining ingredients. Whip cream in medium bowl until soft peaks form. Add powdered sugar, and continue beating until stiff. Spoon cream over top of trifle. Garnish with strawberries and mint sprigs. Chill until ready to serve. **Yield**: 10 to 12 servings

Anne Rike Winstead '52

CAKE IN A PUNCH BOWL

1 (18½-ounce) box yellow
  cake mix
2 (3-ounce) boxes of French
  vanilla instant pudding
  mix
4 bananas, sliced
1 (21-ounce) can cherry pie
  filling

1 (20-ounce) can crushed
  pineapple, drained
1 (12-ounce) carton frozen
  whipped topping, thawed
Coconut, maraschino
  cherries, toasted almonds
  for garnish

Bake cake in 2 layers as directed on box . Cool completely. Crumble 1 layer of cake into punch bowl. Mix pudding as directed on box. Cover cake crumbs with ½ of pudding. Cover with 2 bananas, ½ of cherry pie filling, ½ of pineapple, and ½ of whipped topping. Repeat layering. Sprinkle top with coconut, cherries, and almonds. Chill well before serving. Fills a punch bowl. **Yield**: 12 to 15 servings

Hint: *Serve in sherbet glasses with a cookie at the side. Also make with available fruit in season.*

Dixie Draper Armstrong '58

TEXAS GOVERNOR'S MANSION CREME BRULEE

8 egg yolks, beaten
2 cups heavy cream
¼ cup sugar

¼ teaspoon vanilla
Pinch of salt
Light brown sugar

Beat egg yolks thoroughly in a large bowl, and set aside. Scald cream, sugar, vanilla and salt in a heavy, non-aluminum saucepan. (Do not boil.) Slowly add hot cream mixture to yolks while mixing, being careful not to beat air into it. Strain mixture through cheesecloth. Pour into ovenproof custard cups (about 4 ounces each). Place custard cups in pan filled with water ⅔ up side of the cup. Bake at 350° for 25 to 40 minutes. Chill. Before serving, spread 1 to 2 teaspoons of light brown sugar on top. Place under broiler until bubbly and toasted. **Yield**: 6 servings

The Honorable Ann Willis Richards '54
Governor, State of Texas

NANA'S BOILED CUSTARD

"The Burleson family knows that this is Nana's cure-all for an ill family member. This is also very good when you're feeling great!"

4 cups milk
8 eggs
½ cup sugar
1 tablespoon vanilla

1 cup whipping cream, whipped
2 tablespoons sugar

In a large double boiler, scald milk over hot water. (Milk is scalded when it 'puckers' on top.) In a large bowl, beat eggs well. Add sugar and beat well. Add to milk and cook, stirring constantly, until mixture coats a metal spoon. Set boiler containing custard into a shallow pan of cold water; add ice to water. Cover boiler; let stand until lukewarm. Add vanilla and whipped cream, which has been sweetened with 2 tablespoons sugar. Pour into a 2-quart container. Keeps in refrigerator for several days. **Yield**: 8 servings

Hint: *Cream will whip faster and better if the cream, bowl, and beaters are chilled first.*

Maurine Couch Burleson '29

GALVAN FLAN

3 tablespoons sugar
¾ cup blanched almonds
1⅓ cups sweetened condensed milk

3 whole eggs
3 egg yolks
¾ cup cream

Measure sugar into 8-inch layer cake pan or a flan pan. Place over heat, stirring constantly until sugar melts and turns a dark color. Let cool. Chop almonds in electric blender. Add remaining ingredients to blender. Stir to mix, then blend at high speed for 8 to 10 seconds. Pour into caramelized pan; set pan in a larger pan containing about ½-inch hot water. Bake at 325° for 45 minutes until set. Cool and refrigerate overnight. Do not remove from pan until the next day. Invert onto a chilled platter; flan will quickly unmold. **Yield**: 8 to 10 servings.

Edythe Galvan Hoeltzel '71

BANANA SPLIT ICE CREAM

4 eggs
1¼ cups sugar
6 cups milk
½ teaspoon salt
1 (14-ounce) can sweetened
  condensed milk
2 cups half-and-half

1 tablespoon vanilla
2 bananas, chopped
1 (10-ounce) jar maraschino
  cherries, drained and
  chopped
¾ cup chopped pecans

Beat eggs with electric mixer at medium speed until frothy. Gradually add sugar, beating until thick. Add 6 cups milk and salt. Mix well. Pour egg mixture into large saucepan. Place over low heat; cook , stirring constantly, until thoroughly heated. Combine egg mixture, sweetened condensed milk, half-and-half, and vanilla. Stir well. Add bananas, cherries, and pecans. Pour mixture into 1-gallon freezer can of an ice cream freezer. Freeze according to manufacturer's instructions. Let ripen at least 1 hour. **Yield**: 1 gallon

Hint: *Top each serving with a small dollop of whipped cream, chocolate syrup, and a whole cherry, like an old-fashioned banana split.*

Martha Lou Chadwick Scott '71
Baylor Dean for Student Life

APRICOT ICE CREAM

2 (12-ounce) cans apricot
  nectar
Juice of 2 oranges
Juice of 2 lemons
1 (14-ounce) can sweetened
  condensed milk

1 (12-ounce) can evaporated
  milk
2 cups sugar
Milk

Combine ingredients in large bowl, stirring thoroughly. Pour into 1-gallon ice cream freezer can. Finish filling can almost to top with milk. Freeze according to manufacturer's instructions, using plenty of rock salt with the ice. **Yield**: 1 gallon

Colleen Ward Hightower '49

CINNA-BANANA ICE CREAM

2 cups sugar
2 tablespoons flour
6 eggs, separated
2 (12-ounce) cans evaporated
   milk

1 cup water
1 tablespoon vanilla
5 very ripe bananas, mashed
2 tablespoons cinnamon
1 quart whole milk

Mix sugar and flour. Beat egg yolks well in large bowl. Add sugar mixture, evaporated milk, water, and vanilla; stir well. In medium bowl, beat egg whites until stiff; fold into milk mixture. Mix in mashed bananas and cinnamon. Pour into 1-gallon freezer can of ice cream freezer. Pour enough milk into can to almost fill. Freeze until firm, following manufacturer's instructions. Remove dasher; replace lid and pack down with more ice to ripen several hours. **Yield**: 1 gallon

Hint: *Always let the children eat the cream from the dasher while waiting!*

Martha Jo Cooke Rutherford '59

STRAWBERRY BIG RED SHERBET

2 (14-ounce) cans sweetened
   condensed milk
2 (10-ounce) packages frozen
   strawberries, thawed and
   chopped
2 cups whipping cream

2 (16-ounce) bottles red
   carbonated soda
2 teaspoons vanilla
Milk sufficient enough to
   fill freezer can

Blend first 5 ingredients well in 1-gallon freezer can. Insert dasher and add enough milk to fill can. Stir again. Freeze according to manufacturer's directions. **Yield**: 1 gallon

Ann Hudson Cook '51

SMOOTH-AS-SILK CHOCOLATE ICE CREAM

1¼ cups sugar, divided
3 tablespoons flour
6 tablespoons cocoa
¼ teaspoon salt
4 cups whole or 2% milk, plus extra to finish filling freezer can

3 eggs, separated
½ (14-ounce) can sweetened condensed milk, about ⅔ cup
1 cup half-and-half
1 tablespoon vanilla

In medium saucepan, mix together 1 cup of the sugar with next 3 ingredients. Stir in milk. Cook over medium heat, stirring constantly. As mixture begins to thicken, remove from heat. Beat egg yolks until lemon-colored. Stir a few spoonfuls of hot mixture into beaten egg yolks until blended, and then add egg yolks back into saucepan. Return to heat, and stir until custard thickens. Set aside to cool.

Add sweetened condensed milk, half-and-half, and vanilla. Whip egg whites with remaining ¼ cup sugar until stiff. Fold in cooled custard. Pour into 1-gallon freezer can, and add enough milk to fill freezer can 4/5 full. Stir until blended. Freeze until very firm. Remove dasher, and place a piece of plastic wrap over the can. Replace lid and pack down with more ice. Let ice cream get very firm. **Yield**: 1 gallon

Note: *Because the base is cooked, leftover ice cream stays smooth in the freezer.*

Frances Newland '83

COOL IT! SLUSH
"A refreshing, slushy dessert"

1½ cups sugar
2 cups boiling water
1 (12-ounce) can frozen
   orange juice, thawed

1 (27-ounce) can crushed
   pineapple in heavy syrup,
   undrained
6 ripe bananas
1 (10-ounce) box frozen
   strawberries, thawed

Dissolve sugar in boiling water. Add orange juice with required water as directed on can. Stir in crushed pineapple and syrup. Mash bananas and strawberries, and add to mixture. Freeze. Stir several times over 24-hour period. Set out of freezer at least 30 minutes before serving (or microwave a few seconds.) **Yield**: 20 servings

Hint: *A great cool dessert served in parfait glasses for hot Texas summers. Or as a different appetizer served from a small punch bowl.*

Peggy Reynolds Reidland '46

EASY FUDGE GRAHAM PRALINES
A quick and easy dessert that received rave reviews from our testers

Graham Crackers
1 cup butter or margarine
1 cup light brown sugar

1 cup chopped nuts
6 (1½-ounce) plain chocolate
   bars

Line a 9-inch square pan with graham crackers. In a medium saucepan, melt butter and add brown sugar and nuts. Boil until mixture bubbles, about 3 minutes. Pour over graham crackers. Bake at 350° for 8 minutes. Remove from oven. Immediately arrange chocolate bars on top, and spread with knife when softened. Chill until chocolate hardens. Cut into bars with sharp knife. **Yield**: 20 bars

Jo McDonald Cranford '46

MILLION DOLLAR FUDGE

"Smooth and wonderful and lots of it"

4½ cups sugar
1 (12-ounce) can evaporated
   milk
2 cups marshmallow creme
3 (4½-ounce) plain chocolate
   candy bars

2 (6-ounce) packages semi-
   sweet chocolate chips
1 teaspoon vanilla
1 tablespoon butter
1 pound pecans

Mix sugar and milk in a heavy 6 to 8-quart saucepan. Bring to a boil. Reduce heat to low, and cook 6 minutes, stirring constantly. Fold in marshmallow creme, stirring until melted. Mix in chocolate candy bars, chips, vanilla, and butter. Melt, stirring constantly. Fold in nuts. Spread into greased 11x15-inch jelly roll pan, or drop candy from a spoon onto wax paper. Let stand 4 to 6 hours (it will be slow to harden), or until completely cooled before cutting or removing from wax paper. **Yield**: Approximately 6 pounds

Hint: *Use a pizza cutter to cut fudge made in a sheet pan.*

Sally Mebane Dickenson '83

TIGER BUTTER (FOR BEARS)

1 pound white chocolate
½ cup creamy peanut butter

1 (6-ounce) package semi-
   sweet chocolate chips

Melt white chocolate and peanut butter together in a glass baking dish in microwave on medium, stirring several times. Melt chocolate chips in the same manner. While chocolate chips are melting, spread peanut butter mixture on a foil-lined 11x15-inch cookie sheet. Drizzle melted chocolate chips over peanut butter mixture, and swirl together to create a marble effect. Chill thoroughly, and break into pieces. For a nutty taste, use crunchy peanut butter. For best results, keep candy refrigerated. **Yield**: Approximately 1½ pounds of candy

Hint: *To make softer candy, add as much as 1 cup peanut butter.*

Frances Reagan Wheat '59

CHRISTMAS CANDY

"This is also called Martha Washington Candy, but I guarantee I have used the recipe more than she did!" **B.L.**
Editor's note: Starting each Thanksgiving, Judge Logue begins making as many as 75 batches of this candy for holiday gifts, and each piece is eagerly awaited by his friends.

3 cups chopped pecans
1 (7-ounce) can flaked
  coconut
½ cup margarine, softened
1 (14-ounce) can sweetened
  condensed milk

2 (16-ounce) boxes powdered
  sugar
¼ pound paraffin, cut into
  pieces
1 (12-ounce) package semi-
  sweet chocolate morsels

Combine pecans and coconut in a large bowl. Mix in margarine with fingers. Stir in condensed milk. Add powdered sugar, and mix well by hand. Shape into small balls; place on wax paper.

Combine paraffin with chocolate in a double boiler. Cook and stir until melted and blended. Pierce each ball with a wooden pick to use as a "handle." Dip in chocolate, and place on wax paper to set. **Yield**: About 5 dozen balls

Note: *Any extra coating can be refrigerated and used again.*

Judge Bill Logue '47, JD '49

TEMPT-ME TRUFFLES

4 cups powdered sugar
1 (8-ounce) package cream
  cheese, softened
5 (1-ounce) squares
  unsweetened chocolate,
  melted

1 teaspoon vanilla
Chopped toasted almonds
Cocoa

Gradually add powdered sugar to cream cheese, mixing well after each addition. Stir in chocolate and vanilla; mix well. Chill several hours. Shape into 1-inch balls; roll in almonds, cocoa, or additional powdered sugar. Chill. **Yield**: 4 dozen

Phyllis Wyrick Patterson '74

COCO-NUTTY CANDY CLUSTERS

1 (12-ounce) package semi-
   sweet chocolate chips
1 (12-ounce) package milk
   chocolate chips

1 (12-ounce) can peanuts,
   roasted

In top of a double boiler, melt chips over simmering water (or use microwave on medium, stirring several times, until melted.) Remove from heat, and add peanuts. Drop by teaspoons onto wax paper. Let harden and then refrigerate. **Yield**: 4 to 5 dozen

Hint: *Try peanut butter chips and chocolate chips.*

Judy Lynn Pitman '71

PRALINES
"These are super excellent."

2 cups white sugar
1 cup light brown sugar
½ cup milk
½ cup sweetened condensed
   milk

¼ cup butter or margarine
¼ teaspoon salt
3 cups broken pecans, or
   halves

In 3-quart saucepan, combine all ingredients except pecans; bring to a rolling boil over medium heat. Stir occasionally to scrape sugar off sides of pan. Add pecans and continue boiling until candy reaches soft-ball stage when tested in cold water (234° on a candy thermometer). Remove from heat, and stir until candy is creamy and starts to thicken. Drop by tablespooons onto wax paper or buttered cookie sheets. **Yield**: 30 large pralines

Holly Zumwalt Taylor '90

FRENCH PRALINES
"When they're warm, they melt in your mouth."

Peel of 1 orange, cut into
   very thin strips
1½ cup water, divided
1 cup sugar

½ stick butter or margarine
½ teaspoon vanilla
2 cups pecans

Bring orange peel to a boil in 1 cup of the water. Drain. In a heavy saucepan, combine drained orange peel with remaining ½ cup water, sugar, and margarine. Bring to a slow boil, and simmer to soft ball stage (234° on a candy thermometer). Remove from heat; add vanilla and pecans, and toss until sugary. Pour onto wax paper, and break apart when cool. **Yield**: Approximately 1½ dozen pieces

The late Martha Leuschner, '21
Contributed by Katy Jennings Stokes '47

Martha lived at 1313 S. 7th (right across from Pat Neff Hall before there was even an idea of that building) from 1917—when her family moved to Waco from Otto, Texas—and she became a student at Baylor. Mart lived there until her death in 1988. The big youth revival movement of the '40s gained impetus around her large kitchen table where she fed all the movers of that unusual event—Howard Butt, Jess Moody, Jackie Robinson, Charles Wellborn.

Katy Jennings Stokes '47

Index

ACKNOWLEDGEMENTS

Whether you submitted recipes or memories, tested recipes, or did all of these and more, please accept our thanks. We hope you will be pleased with the book you helped produce.

Sondra Blalock Adair
Cozy Story Adams
Karen Wroten Adams
Katie Smith Adcox
Donalita Grantham Adkins
Sara Norris Alleman
Lola (Corky) Ball Altenburg
Sharon Amelunke
Susan Bedwell Amos
Lori Latch Apon
Dixie Draper Armstrong
Joan Maples Atwood
Bernice Leazar Autrey
Lavoyce Roper Avery
Anita O'Quinn Baker
Shala Mills Bannister
Phil Barclay
Carol Watson Barclay
Lanelle Andrews Barfield
Corwinna McCharen Barnette
Grace Z. Barnick
Lisa Abercrombie Beach
Kara Beale
Vanessa Wienecke Beard
Dorcas M. Beaver
Judy Trice Beavers
Dodie Williams Beazley
Terry A. Becker
Mollie Carpenter Bedwell
Betty Beniteau Bell
John B. Belvin III
Patricia Erwin Bielamowicz
Sadie Jo Black
Carolyn Dublin Blackburn
Darlene Griffin Blair
Doris Hughes Bloodworth
Lois Wroten Boatwright
Marti Bodine
LaVerne Boles
Diana Lemay Bomback
Alma Outlaw Boone
Delisa Vaughn Boyd
Ernie Boyd
Jeannine Delamater Boyles
T'Dee Lifland Bracken
Becky Bradley

Polley Cawood Brannan
Caroline Franklin Brelsford
Jana Lynn Brewer
Ann Emmett Brian
Eileen Erickson Bright
Barbara Shergold Britton
Ann Bailey Brothers
Betty Rogers Bryant
Judy Bryant
Bob Bullock
Mona Rogers Burchette
Ray Burchette, Jr.
Debra Dobbins Burleson
Maurine Couch Burleson
Ellen Stoesser Byrd
Darlene Bobo Caddell
Kelley Victoria Caldwell
Sarah Wells Calvert
Princess Mike Cameron
Gwen Schutte Campbell
Martha Mitchell Carroll
Tonia Frazier Carpenter
Ken Casner
Ladye Ruth Burch Casner
Don Castello
Sherry Boyd Castello
Thomas P. Chaney
Hilda Chapa
Jean Chapman
Carol Ohlenbusch Chappell
Mary Chavanne
Alice Dawson Cheavens
Marilyn Barron Chrisman
Janette Cinek
Ellen Dawne Cleveland
Frances Adkins Cleveland
David Garrett Cleveland
Joyce Bain Cline
Nancy Ellis Clines
Vivian Saxon Cochran
David Wayne Cochran
David M. Coker
Gail Coker
LaNell Holbrook Coltharp
Amarylis Colvin
Dodie Cook

Mary Leigh Cook
Ann Hudson Cook
Joan Martin Cook
Bill Cooper
Thelma Cooper
Suzanne Ross Copeland
Linda Corbin
Orlin R. Corey
Maurina Wiese Corley
Rachel Corley
Susan McNeely Cothern
Julie Covington
Sandra Cartlidge
   Covington
Elise Britton Crane
Jo McDonald Cranford
Katherine Godsey Craun
Alma Burton Crawley
Marjory Cretien
Porter Crow
Donna Gerlich Culliton
Barbara Schultz
   Cunningham
Karen Thompson Curlee
Regina McKinney Curtis
Sharon Harper Cushman
Diane Wimberly Danner
Catherine Osborne
   Davenport
Mays Davenport
Merle Dielman Davis
Bonnie (Missy) Davis
Diane Waters Davis
Sue Dickson Davis
Diane Gajdica Deily
Kay DeLoach
Eva Dudley DenBesten
Michelle Derrick
Phyllis Derrick
Karla McCain Devin
Kathryn White Devine
Sally Mebane Dickenson
Betty Skinner Dison
Peggy Wilson Dobbins
Phyllis Claunch Draughn
Linda Dreyer

Barbara Byrom Driver
Pam Regan Drumm
Gloria Turner DuBose
Lori Leavelle Dulany
Amy B. Duncan
Becky A. Dyer
Susan Gothard Easley
Patricia Jane Edmonds
Sally Appleberry Edmunds
Kay Nethery Elliott
Marge Clayton Ellis
Lynn Goelzer Engelke
Zora Outlaw Evans
Carolyn Grigsby Feather
Lois Pogue Ferguson
Pat Piper Ferguson
Sandra Fleming Ferguson
Nancy Hudson Fields
Marguerite Shearer Fleener
Susan Reed Fletcher
Brenda Shattles Fohlmeister
Holly Beth Ford
Julie Ford
Elizabeth Knight Fougerat
Judith Witt Francis
Pat Parchman Franklin
Becky Rubarts Freeman
Lynn Freyer
Doris Hollingsworth Gage
Martha Newton Garber
Carla Sue Ferguson Garrett
Greg Garrett
Sherron Nickelson Garrison
Susan Callison Geddie
Kay Deaton Gentsch
Lou Nelle Beall George
Judith Wright Gibbs
Nancy Cox Gibson
Jonathon Edwin Glover
Royce A. Goforth
Mike Gonzales
Tracy Davenport Gonzales
Kathy Casner Goodrich
Linda Hull Goodwin
Darlene Winkelmann Gorham
Roxanne Nemmer Gottlich
Victor G. Granberry
Susan Grast
Judy McConathy Graves
Louise Shepperd Graves
Edna Peacock Gray
Eleanor Green
Julia Elizabeth Gregoris
Ginny Sims Griffith
Jane Renfrow Griggs

Peggy Watson Grimes
Nancy Harrison Guy
Sarah C. Hadley
Janet Riola Hale
Melba Caldwell Hall
Patricia Inman Halsell
Stephanie Carlson Hansen
Harriet Briscoe Harral
Emily Eichelberger Harrell
Becky Wallace Harris
Beth Warren Harris
Kelly Bower Harris
Linda Holt Harrison
Maxine Barton Hart
Patricia Berryhill Hassell
Helen Hargrove Hastings
Johnnie Hughes Hatfield
Carol Pitts Hawks
Debbie Russell Hembree
Mildred Dunlap Henderson
Carolyn Anderson
  Hennessee
Hugh E. Henson, Jr.
Peggy O'Neal Herbert
David Vance Herin
Cynthia Duran Herin
Daphne Norred Herring
Jan Cranford Herrstrom
Marcia Lee Maxey Hicks
Shirley Slagle Hicks
Charles H. (Chuck) Hicks
Denise Moore Hidalgo
Kathy Robinson Hillman
Barbara Hollenbeck Hills
Marilyn Holland Hines
Mary Elizabeth Hines
Amy Fitzpatrick Hinrichs
Ann McDonald Hirschfelt
D'Anne Powell Hobbs
Edythe Galvan Hoeltzel
Claire Hirschfelt Hogg
Margaret Wynn Hollis
Carol Todd Horner
Sharon Elaine Howard
Julie Williams Howerton
Lori Butcher Huckabay
Susan Hudson Huey
John T. Hull
Mary Chambers Hull
Karen Gibson Hunter
Margaret Dahse Hunter
Marilyn Wyrick Ingram
Dorothy Jane Beck Irwin
Melissa Hay Ishio
Jessie Lee Wolfe Janes

Jean M. Spencer Jenness
June McLean Jeter
Betty Johnson
Claudia Burton Johnson
Denna Johnson
Doris Jean Wilkes Johnson
June Page Johnson
Patricia Johnson
Peggy Basden Johnson
Susan White Johnson
Sherilyn Johnston
Barbara Jones
Candyce Rasner Jones
Carolyn Coley Jones
Elizabeth Saxon Jones
Joanne Briscoe Jones
Judy E. Jones
Leah Jones
Leslie Peebles Jones
Madelyn Jones
Marilyn Jeanne Jones
Annette Reid Joseph
Fontina Farr Joyce
Barbara Rhodes Justman
Kathy Justman
Ann Williamson Karaffa
Sandra Bobo Karnes
Carolyn Griffin Keathley
Suzanne Richardson
  Keener
Rhonda Sewell Kehlbeck
Peggy Simmons Kemble
Loraine Khoury
Cherry Clark Kimmy
Ken King
Geneva Prestidge
  Kirkland
Jill Barnett Kirkonis
Winona Jean Kirkpatrick
Nick Klaras
Dorothy Eubank Knox
Lauren Natoli Kopp
Catherine Bedwell
  Kowalewski
Lenora Reid Kreitz
Dorothy Barfield Kronzer
Juliann Krumbholz
Debbie Gibson LaChey
Nancy Derrick Lacy
Deanna Cochran Laird
Robbie Lamkin
Kathi Lancaster
Kaye Leavelle
Wanda May LeMaster
Martha Durr Lemon

Donna Beck Lewis
Diane Busby Livesay
Lisa Dysart Lock
Marsha Mayfield Lockett
Jewel Kirkpatrick Lockridge
Bill Logue
Ethel Logsdon
Ardis Freeman Long
Susan Jay Lorance
Janell King Luce
Virginia Myers Malone
Jean Irvin Mallory
Mary Massar Malone
Debra Bradley Mann
Mary Frances Markley
Pat McCarty Marshall
Dot C. Martin
Karen Kernodle Martin
Dottie Gilleland Mathews
Mary Andrews Mayne
Melissa Morris McBurney
Mary Wilson Russell McCall
Doris McCluskey
Janet McMurtry McConnell
Gretchen McCormack
Joylee Zachary McCoy
Gladys Melton McFadden
Nancy McKinney
Toni Roberson McWilliams
Anne Glasscock Meacham
Lucy Lattimore Mebane
F. Rosalee Hayden Meredith
Susan Marx Middleton
Lisa Davis Miller
Annie Laurie Cunningham
  Miller
Ann Vardaman Miller
Judy Allen Mitchell
Nancy Haley Mohrman
Canon George Wesley
  Monroe
Kay Washington Moore
Wayne H. Morgan
Denise Cochran Morlen
Eleanor Shattles Morris
Mrs. Alan Morrison
Faithanne Johnson Mudd
Roblyn Mui
Betty Moran Mullins
Richelle Nimmer Munn
Katherine Gordon Murphy
Lois Smith Myers
Cheryl Schellinger Nace
Kim LeMaster Neal
Oma Nell Nemmer

Patricia Netherton
Nancy Colleen Newcomb
Frances R. Newland
Dorothy Swift Newsom
Mary Margaret Duckworth
  Norman
Melissa Boykin Norris
Susan Cromwell Norris
Becky Key Norsworthy
Jeanne Price Nowlin
Jeanne Wood Nowlin
Kathleen Day Oates
Mina Jones O'Bannon
Judy Lindsey Oberkrom
Jan Oden
Susan Puckett Oursland
Priscilla Richman Owen
Joyce Hornaday Packard
Marjorie Page
Debbie Wilson Panico
Gloriana Simmons
  Parchman
Carol Hudgins Park
Martha McCullough Park
Vicky Hanson Parkey
Myrna Darden Parsons
Joan Parsons
Phyllis Wyrick Patterson
Mary Ann Ragland
  Patterson
Wynell Gillen Patterson
Jeanette Hutyra Pavelka
Fonda Graves Paxton
Deanna Stephens Payne
Nancy Mitchell Pearce
Carrie Anna Millard Pearce
Jean Irwin Pearson
Betty Sewell Peebles
Patricia Green Pennington
Elna Rae Leazar Peoples
Patsy Ware Phillips
Betty Harper Phillips
Judy Lynn Pitman
Laura Ponder
Ethel de Cordova Porter
Fran Booth Porter
Barbara Powell
Linda Runyan Powell
Mary Fisher Powell
Pat Belew Powell
Buddy Prather
Frances Durham Prather
Judy Henderson Prather
Sarah Jane Harris Prewett
Betty Gilbreath Price

Carolyn Price
Dan Joseph Proctor
Jan Ross Purdy
Katherine Ann Ragan
Leanne Slaughter Ralston
Bocca Sue McKellar Rambo
Brenda Ramey
Lore Canion Ramsey
Angela Rankin
Marcell Reed
Jan Reedy
Annett Reid
Peggy Reynolds Reidland
Eleeza Littlejohn Rex
Joy Copeland Reynolds
Rebecca Bartlett Reynolds
Wanda J. Rice
Ann Willis Richards
D. L. Richardson
Laurie Grusendorf
  Richardson
Betty Stoesser Ritchie
Ann Melbern Robinson
Susie McDonald Robinson
Martha Whiteman Rogers
Anita Ward Rolf
Lana Johnson Rowland
Michele Royal
Kelly Malone Rummery
Linda Rudd
Martha Jo Cooke
  Rutherford
Randall G. Sadler
Lorna Walker Salgado
Jo Sparks Salmon
Judy Washington Salmon
Rinky Chivers Sanders
Diane Sanderson
Evelyn Nelson Sandlin
Celeste Sauls
Margaret McGee Saunders
Paige McCann Savage
Thurman Hugh Saxon
Thomas (Tommy) Wesley
  Saxon
Liz Schmitz
Cindy Waltman Schumann
Ellen Flaten Schuster
Vera Wilcoxson Scirratt
Martha Lou Chadwick
  Scott
Terry Scott
Betty Clements Scull
Ruth Stoesser Seaberg
Denyse Seaman

Marilyn Sebesta
Patty Seegars
Mary Kemendo Sendon
Bob Anne McMullan Senter
Linda Howard Senter
Glenajo Beard Shambeck
Cheryl Blalock Shamburger
Millie Hislop Shankle
Judy Showalter
Clint Showalter
Lois Bowes Shumate
Kyrene Sims
Margaret Fast Skimmyhorn
Margaret Geer Sledge
Sharlande Sledge
Eugenia Gill Smith
Karen Davenport Smith
Kay Niederer Smith
Susan Frick Smith
Beverly Barron Smith
Dixie Cavitt Soong
Marcy Koch Sosnowski
Doris Davis Sosnowski
Kelly Korene Soter
Lynda Miller Southwick
Kathy Sparkman
Mickey Sparkman
Carole (Penny) Nichols
  Spearman
Virginia King Speasmaker
Cynthia Yelderman Squires
Frances Hujar Stacy
Sarah Rutherford Starr
Judi Nance Staton
Virginia Hollifield Stegall
Jennifer Jo Stein
Martha Moody Stephens
Michelle Bodine Stevenson

Katy Jennings Stokes
George M. Stokes
Andrea Stork
Peggy O'Neill Strode
Carol Adams Stutzenbecker
Ann Garner Sullivan
Louise Gonce Taff
Paula Price Tanner
Judith Taylor
Holly Zumwalt Taylor
Donell Teaff
Gretchen Peterson Thomas
Nancy Thomas
Toni Thompson
Aurora Thorsen
Melanie Manske Tidwell
Dotty Gawenka Tompkins
Laurie Castello Tsuchiya
Libby Allred Turner
Elizabeth Roloff Twadell
Alta Faye Lilly Underwood
Mary Underwood-Presley
Robin Wooldridge Vasek
Annette Thornton Villaflor
Lisa Mullins Vines
Pam Gilliam Walch
Gladys Graham Walker
Millie Gholson Walker
Lisa Wallace
Paula Pounds Wallace
Sandra Stoesser Wallace
Sherri Wallace
Lisa Estrada Wallace
Larry Warneke
Kimberly Warren
Jennifer Harmon Webb
Carol Hunter Wells
LaVerne Wellborn Wentworth

Louanna Ruth Werchan
Natalie West
Frances Reagan Wheat
Edna SoRelle White
Julia Teegerstrom White
Linda Gale Thompson
  White
Lanette Lemons Whitley
Lillian Ashorn Wilhelm
Lori Reid Wilkerson
Ruth Collins Wilkerson
Carolyn Logsdon Wilkes
Gary Wilkes
Carla Hawkins Wilkins
Marian Haile Williams
Corinne Rucker Williams
Amy Williamson
Glenda Coward
  Williamson
Linda Key Willingham
Betty Willis
Jennifer Lee Willis
Mrs. M. H. Wills
Andrea Wilkes Willson
Gary Willson
Grace Miles Wilson
Mary Elizabeth Plummer
  Wimpee
Yana Wingate
Hal Wingo
Anne Rike Winstead
Beth Woodridge
Maydell Pickett Wyrick
Karen Koonce Ytterberg
Karen McNeely Zecy
Kerri McPhillips
  Zschappel

We also want to give a special "thank you" to our families for their patience and encouragement. They have been pulled into testing and tasting unfamiliar foods, have been served cold dinners because of "cookbook meetings," and occasionally have been served no dinner at all!